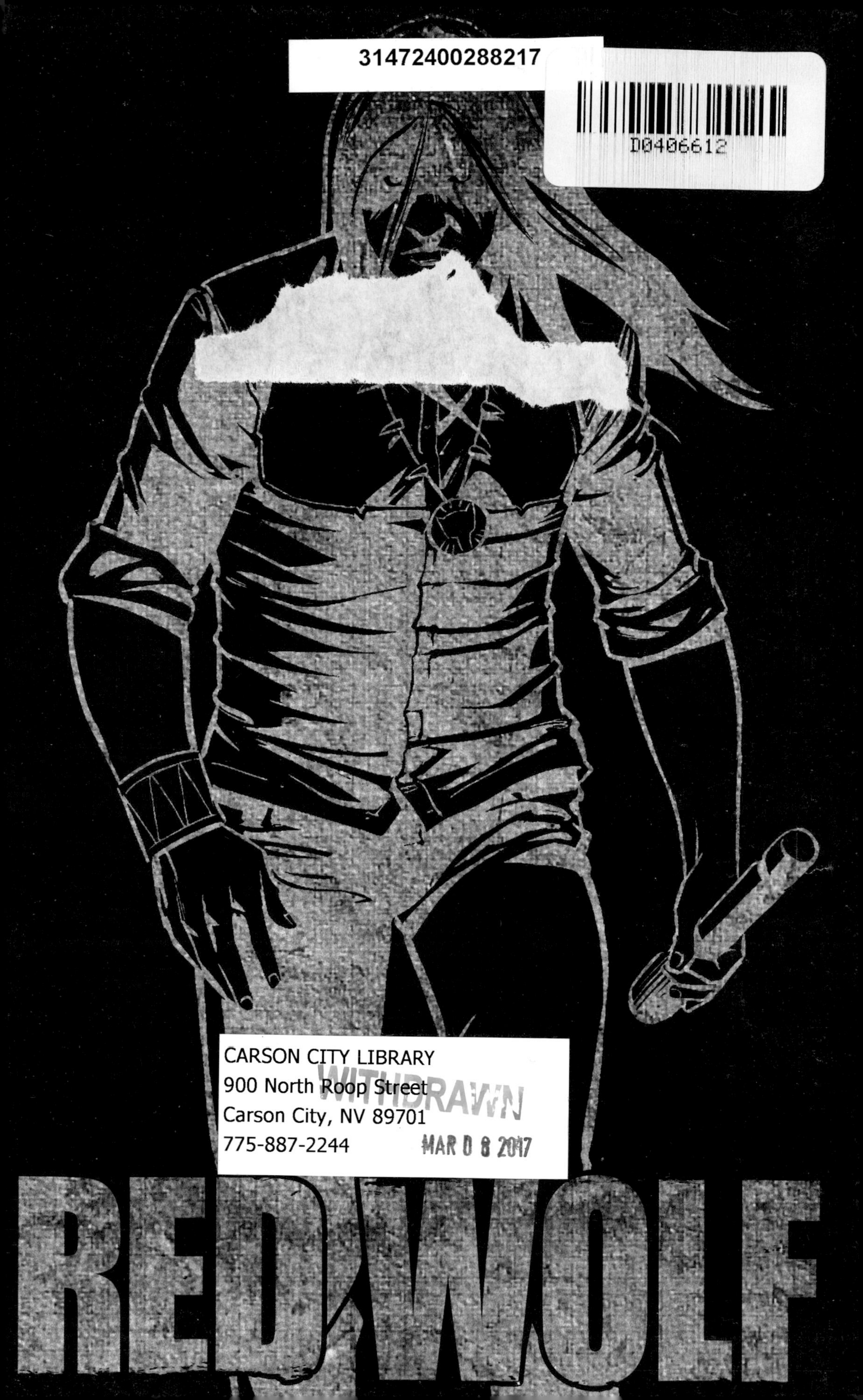
RED WOLF

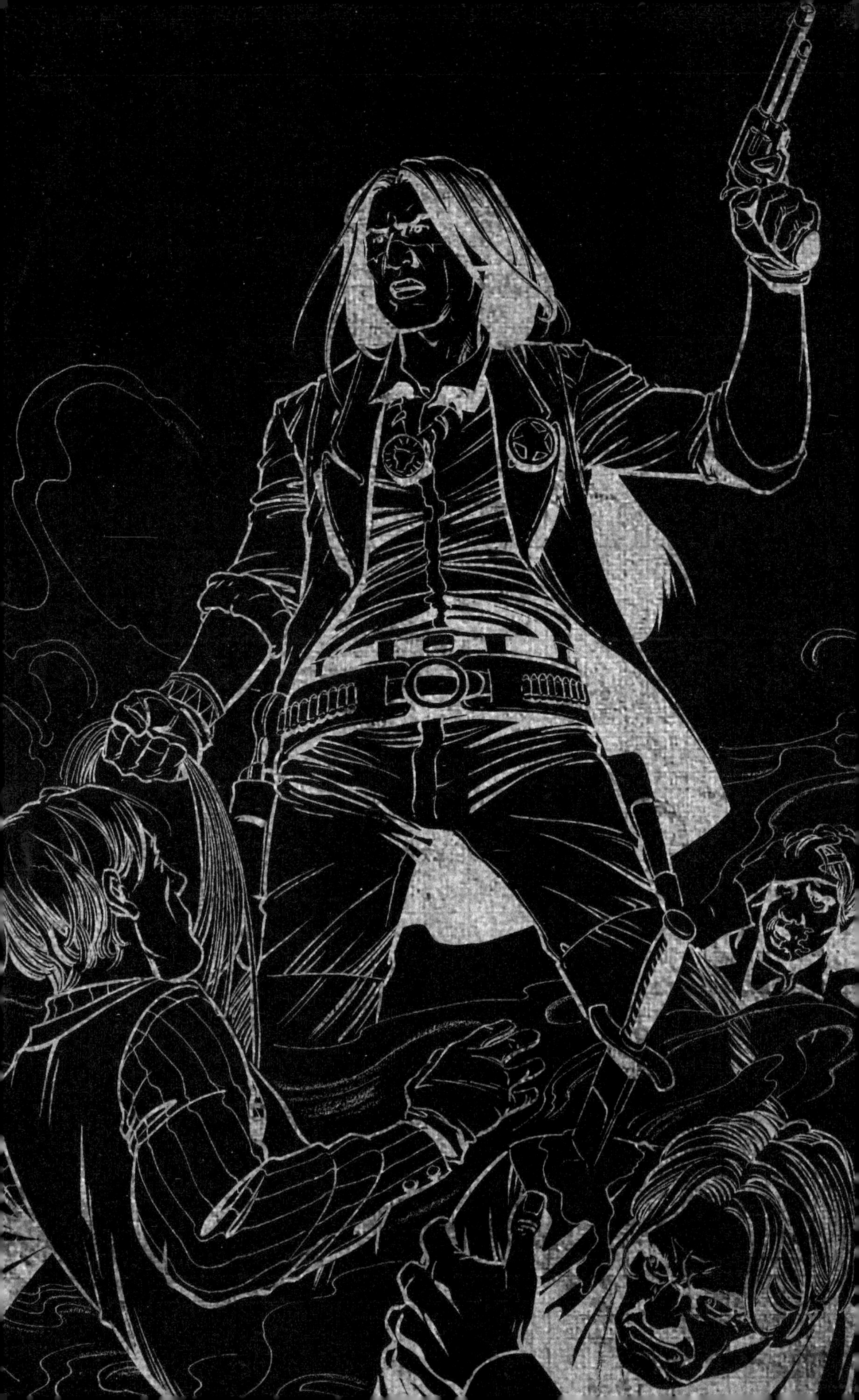

RED WOLF

WRITER
NATHAN EDMONDSON

PENCILER
DALIBOR TALAJIĆ

INKER
JOSÉ MARZAN JR.

COLORIST
MIROSLAV MRVA

LETTERER
VC's CLAYTON COWLES

CONSULTANT & COVER ARTIST
JEFFREY VEREGGE

ASSISTANT EDITOR
KATHLEEN WISNESKI

EDITOR
JAKE THOMAS

COLLECTION EDITOR **ALEX STARBUCK**
ASSOCIATE EDITOR **SARAH BRUNSTAD**
EDITORS, SPECIAL PROJECTS **JENNIFER GRÜNWALD & MARK D. BEAZLEY**
VP, PRODUCTION & SPECIAL PROJECTS **JEFF YOUNGQUIST**
SVP PRINT, SALES & MARKETING **DAVID GABRIEL**
BOOK DESIGNER **ADAM DEL RE**

EDITOR IN CHIEF **AXEL ALONSO**
CHIEF CREATIVE OFFICER **JOE QUESADA**
PUBLISHER **DAN BUCKLEY**
EXECUTIVE PRODUCER **ALAN FINE**

RED WOLF: MAN OUT OF TIME. Contains material originally published in magazine form as RED WOLF #1-6. First printing 2016. ISBN# 978-1-302-90037-3. Published by MARVEL WORLDWIDE, INC., a subsidiary of MARVEL ENTERTAINMENT, LLC. OFFICE OF PUBLICATION: 135 West 50th Street, New York, NY 10020. **Printed in Canada.** ALAN FINE, President, Marvel Entertainment; DAN BUCKLEY, President, TV, Publishing & Brand Management; JOE QUESADA, Chief Creative Officer; TOM BREVOORT, SVP of Publishing; DAVID BOGART, SVP of Business Affairs & Operations, Publishing & Partnership; C.B. CEBULSKI, VP of Brand Management & Development, Asia; DAVID GABRIEL, SVP of Sales & Marketing, Publishing; JEFF YOUNGQUIST, VP of Production & Special Projects; DAN CARR, Executive Director of Publishing Technology; ALEX MORALES, Director of Publishing Operations; SUSAN CRESPI, Production Manager; STAN LEE, Chairman Emeritus. For information regarding advertising in Marvel Comics or on Marvel.com, please contact Vit DeBellis, Integrated Sales Manager, at vdebellis@marvel.com. For Marvel subscription inquiries, please call 888-511-5480. **Manufactured between 4/29/2016 and 6/6/2016 by SOLISCO PRINTERS, SCOTT, QC, CANADA.**

10 9 8 7 6 5 4 3 2 1

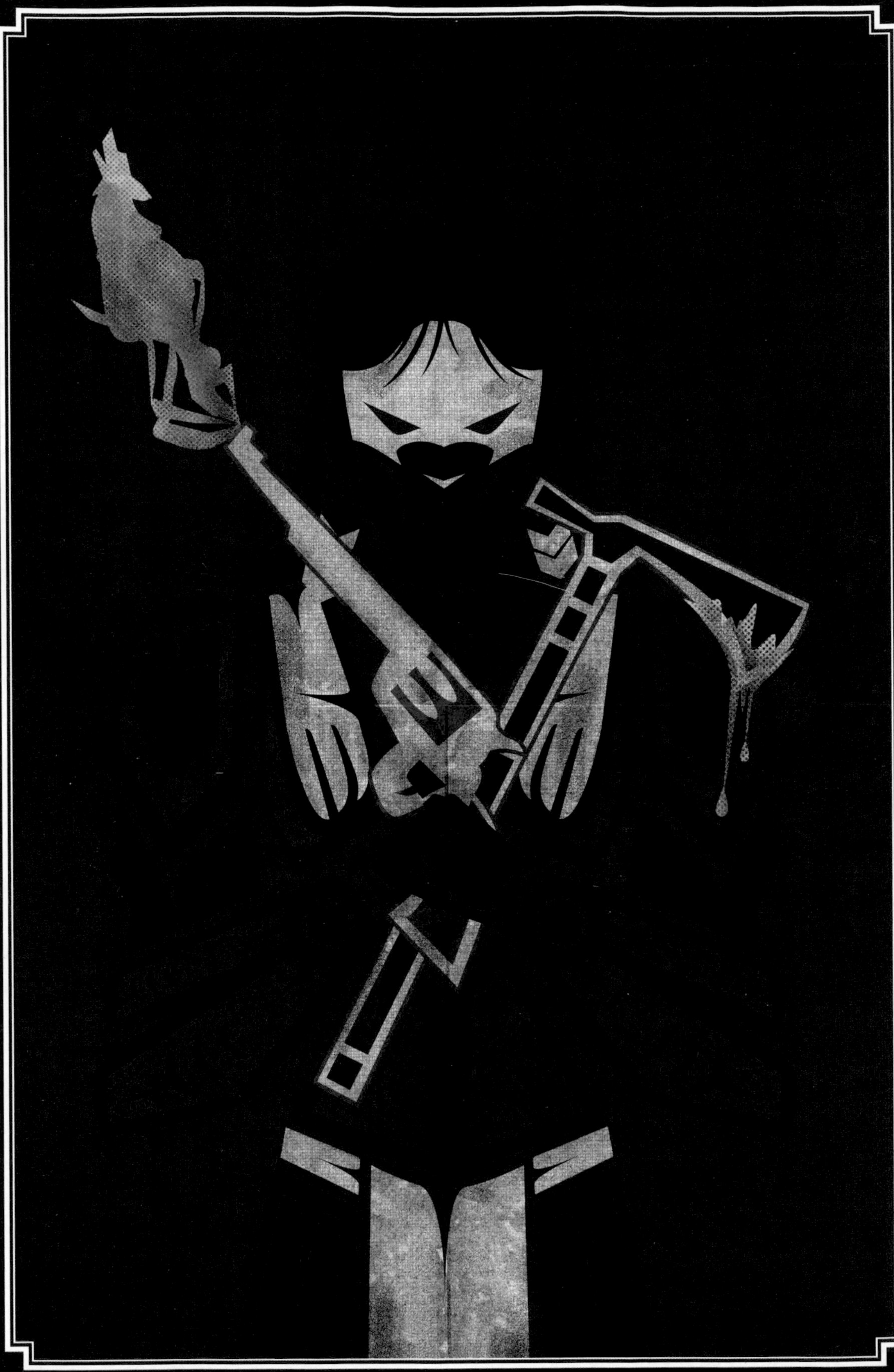

1

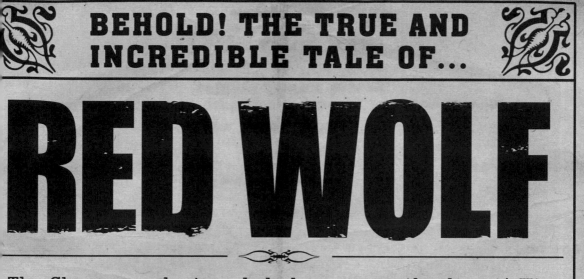

BEHOLD! THE TRUE AND INCREDIBLE TALE OF...

RED WOLF

The Cheyenne who traveled alone across the desert! His destination: the town of **TIMELY**, where the corrupt government had deprived Red Wolf's people of their water. After Timely's Sheriff, Steve Rogers, was **MURDERED** for defending Red Wolf, Red took up the Sheriff's badge and all the responsibility that comes with it.

Red is still a loner, though he fought alongside others to clean up the town. But he is also the only man **RIGHTEOUS** enough to wear the star. Prepare for **THRILLS! DANGER! ACTION!** For anywhere Sheriff Red Wolf goes, adventure follows!

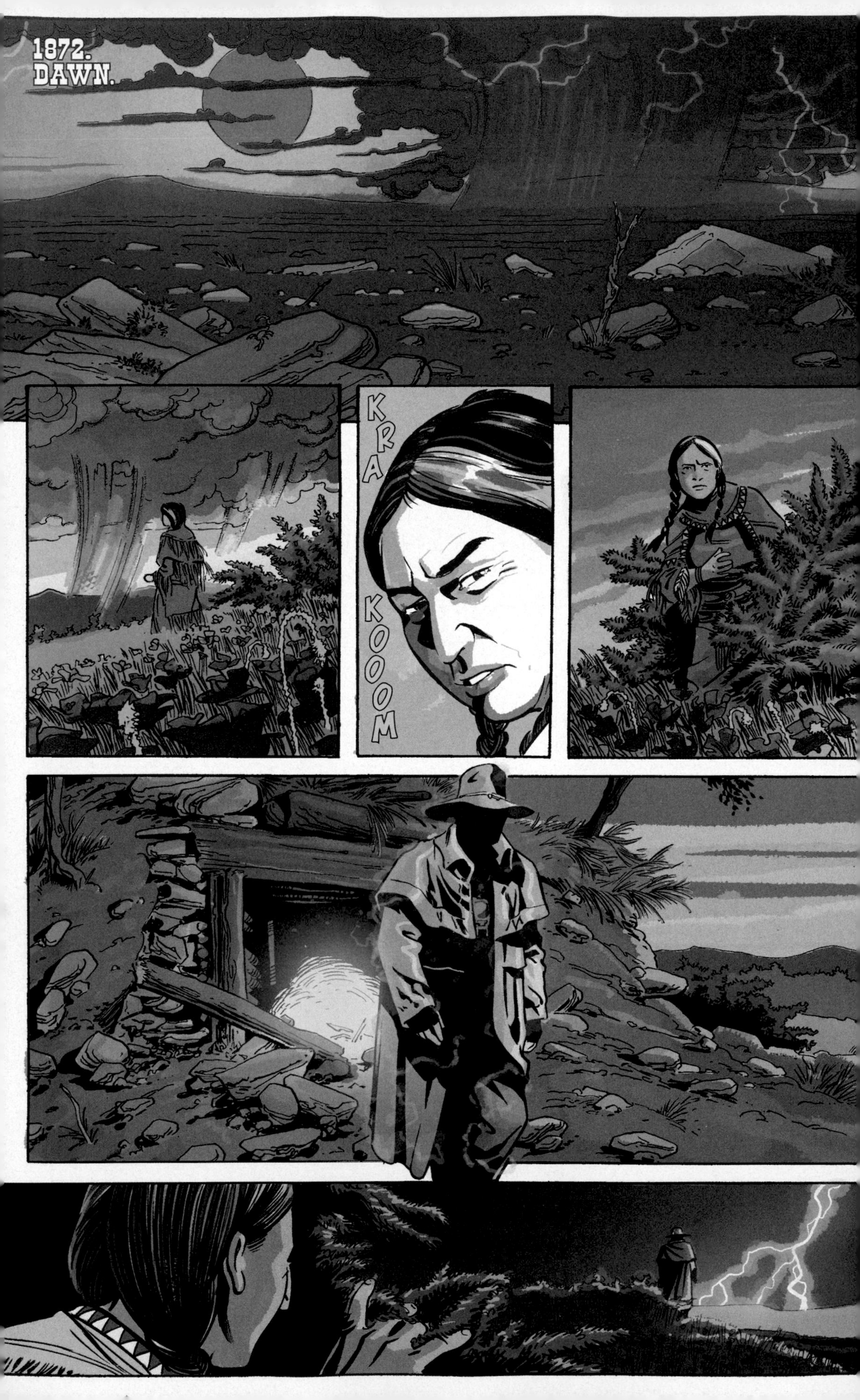
1872.
DAWN.
KRA
KOOOM

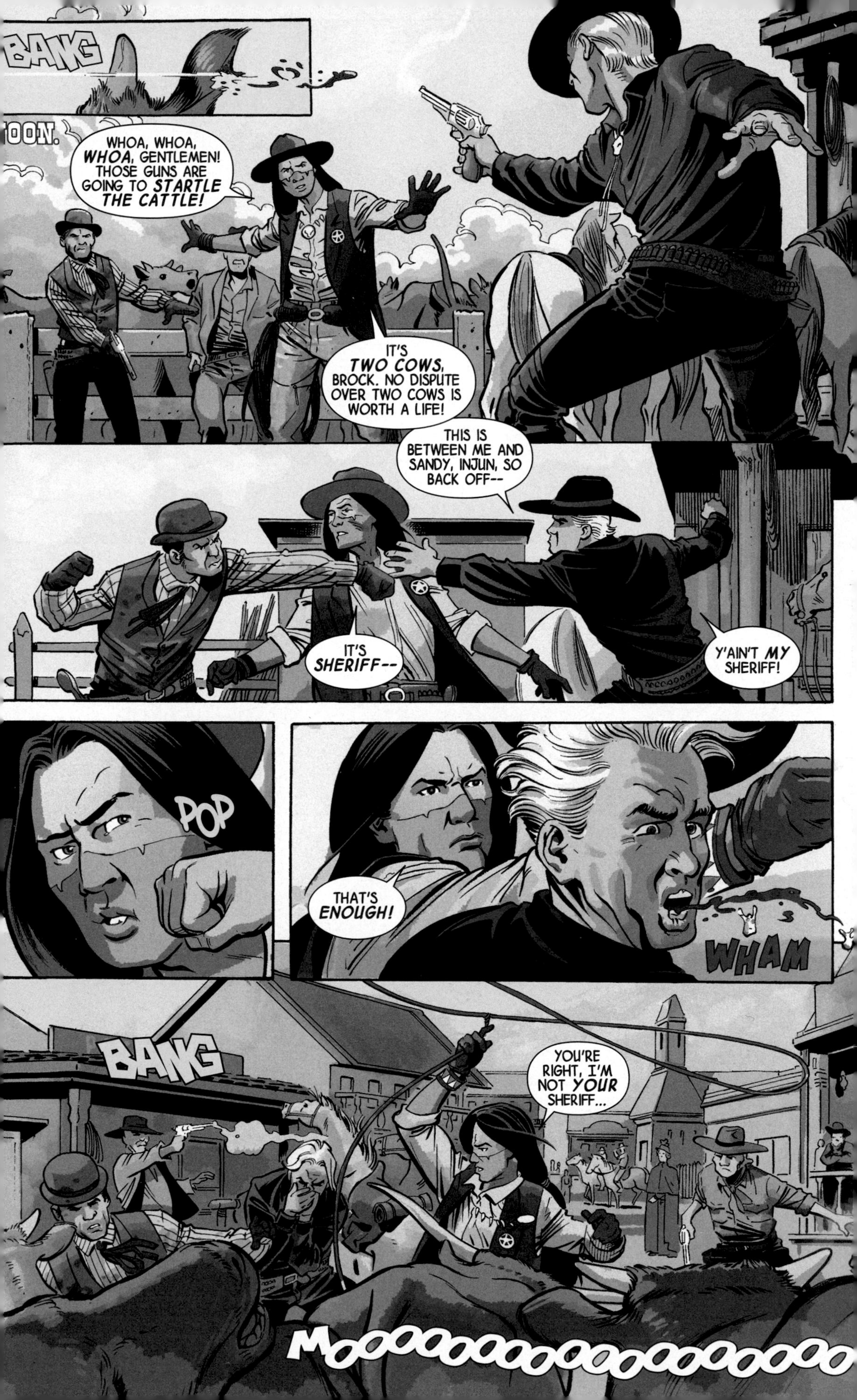
BANG
OON.
WHOA, WHOA, WHOA, GENTLEMEN! THOSE GUNS ARE GOING TO STARTLE THE CATTLE!
IT'S TWO COWS, BROCK. NO DISPUTE OVER TWO COWS IS WORTH A LIFE!
THIS IS BETWEEN ME AND SANDY, INJUN, SO BACK OFF--
IT'S SHERIFF--
Y'AIN'T MY SHERIFF!
POP
THAT'S ENOUGH!
WHAM
BANG
YOU'RE RIGHT, I'M NOT YOUR SHERIFF...
MOOOOOOOOOOOOOOOOOOO

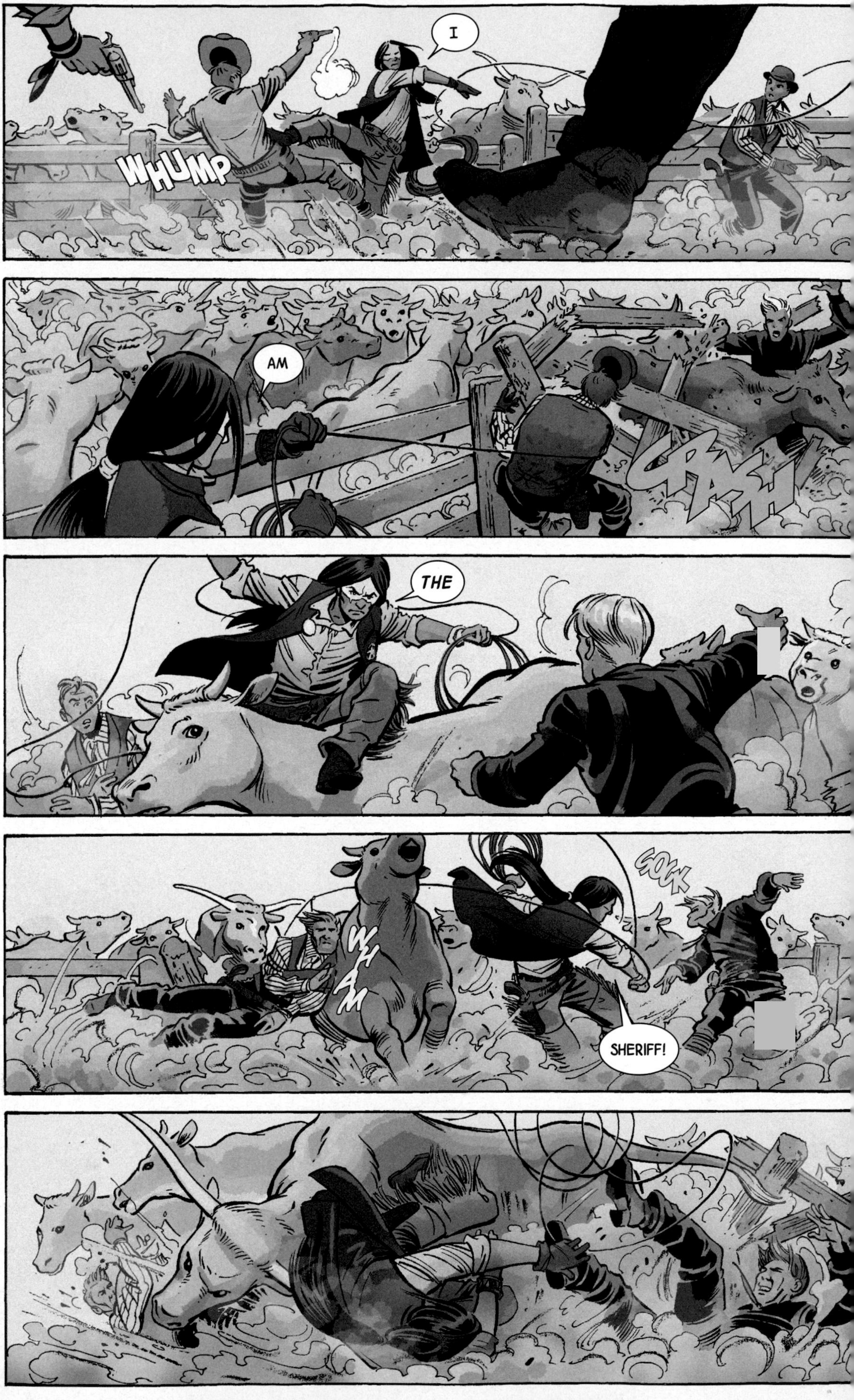
I
WHUMP
AM
CRASH
THE
SOCK
WHAM
SHERIFF!

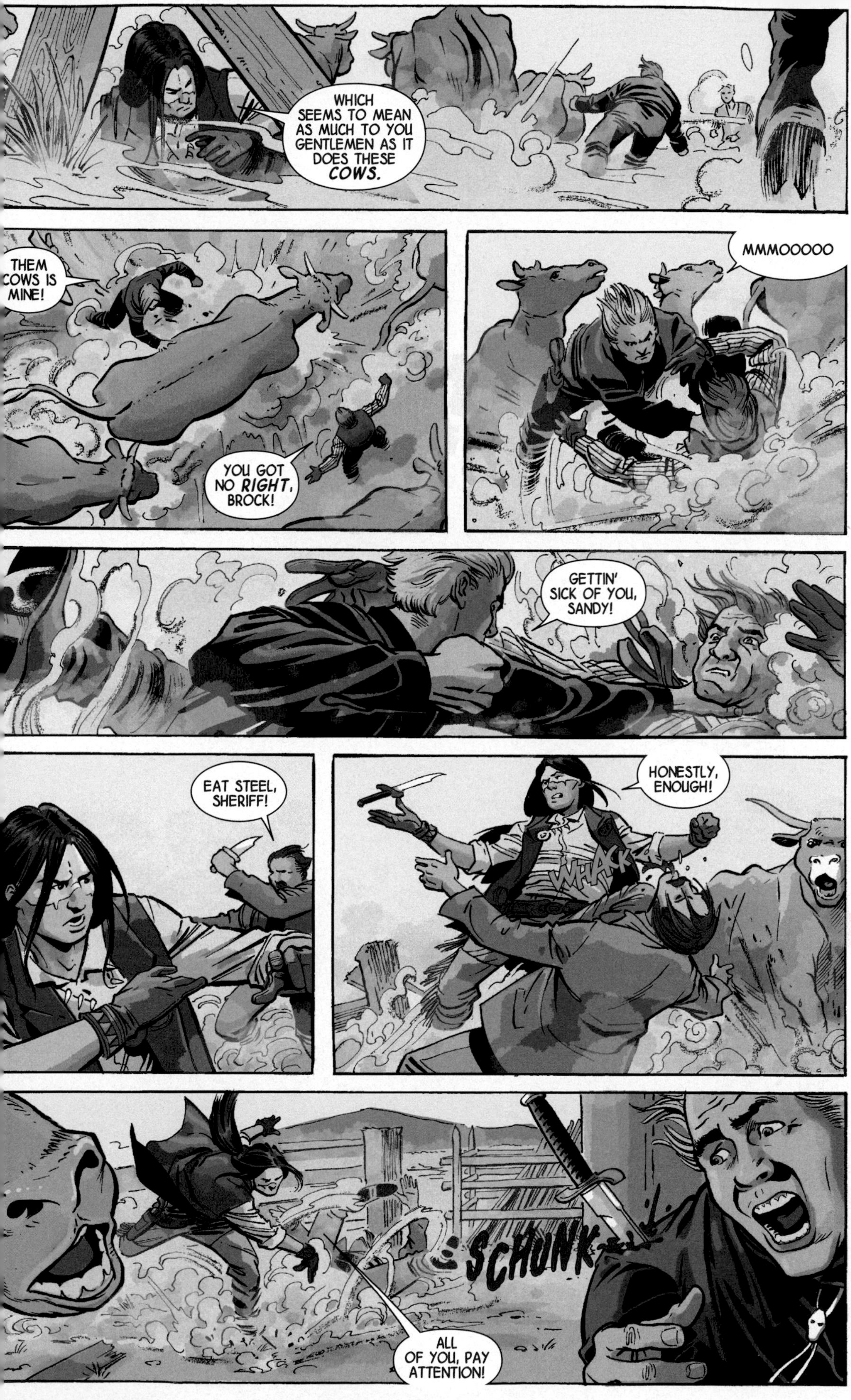
WHICH SEEMS TO MEAN AS MUCH TO YOU GENTLEMEN AS IT DOES THESE COWS.
THEM COWS IS MINE!
YOU GOT NO RIGHT, BROCK!
MMMOOOOO
GETTIN' SICK OF YOU, SANDY!
EAT STEEL, SHERIFF!
HONESTLY, ENOUGH!
WHACK
SCHUNK
ALL OF YOU, PAY ATTENTION!

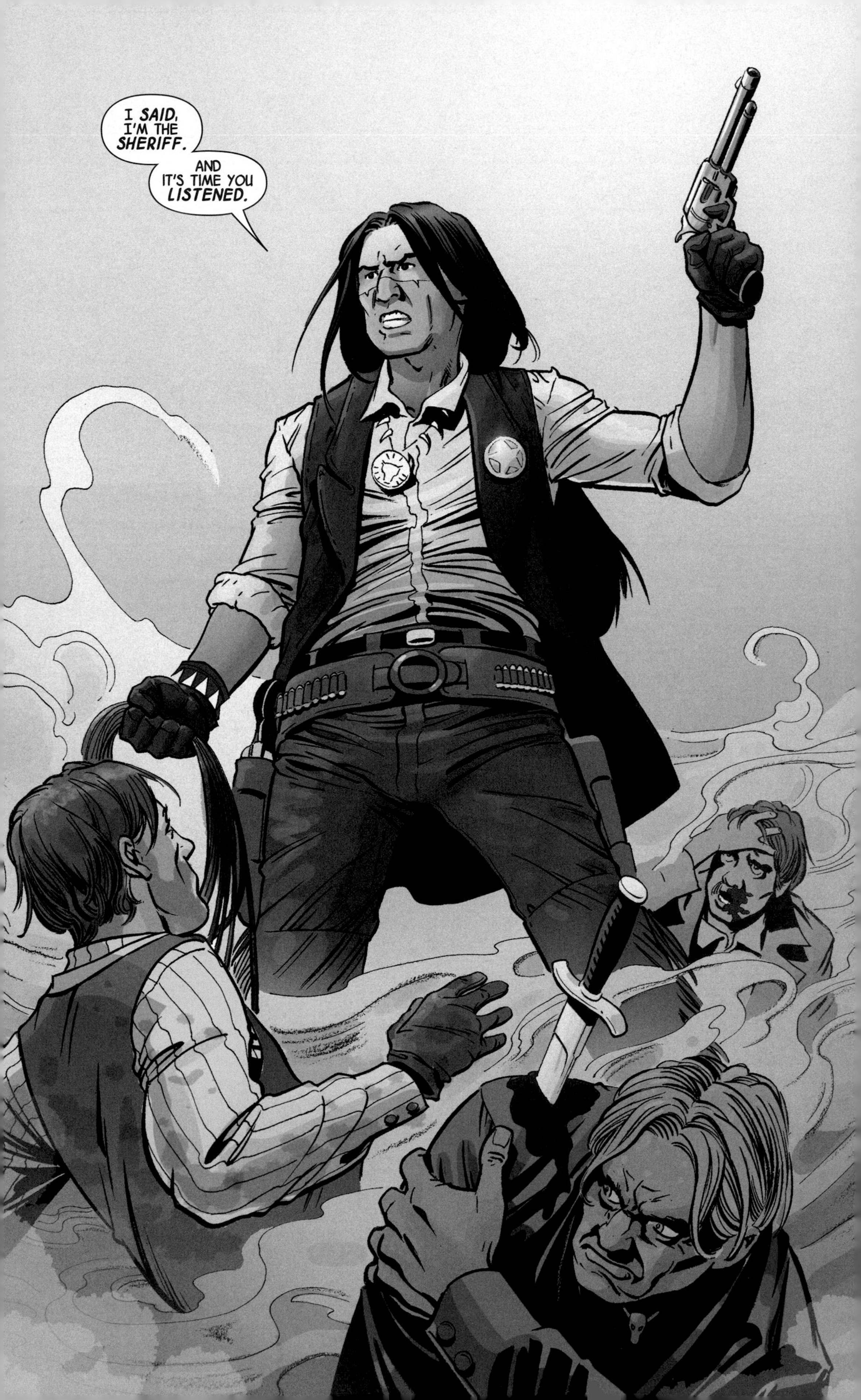

I SAID, I'M THE SHERIFF.
AND IT'S TIME YOU LISTENED.

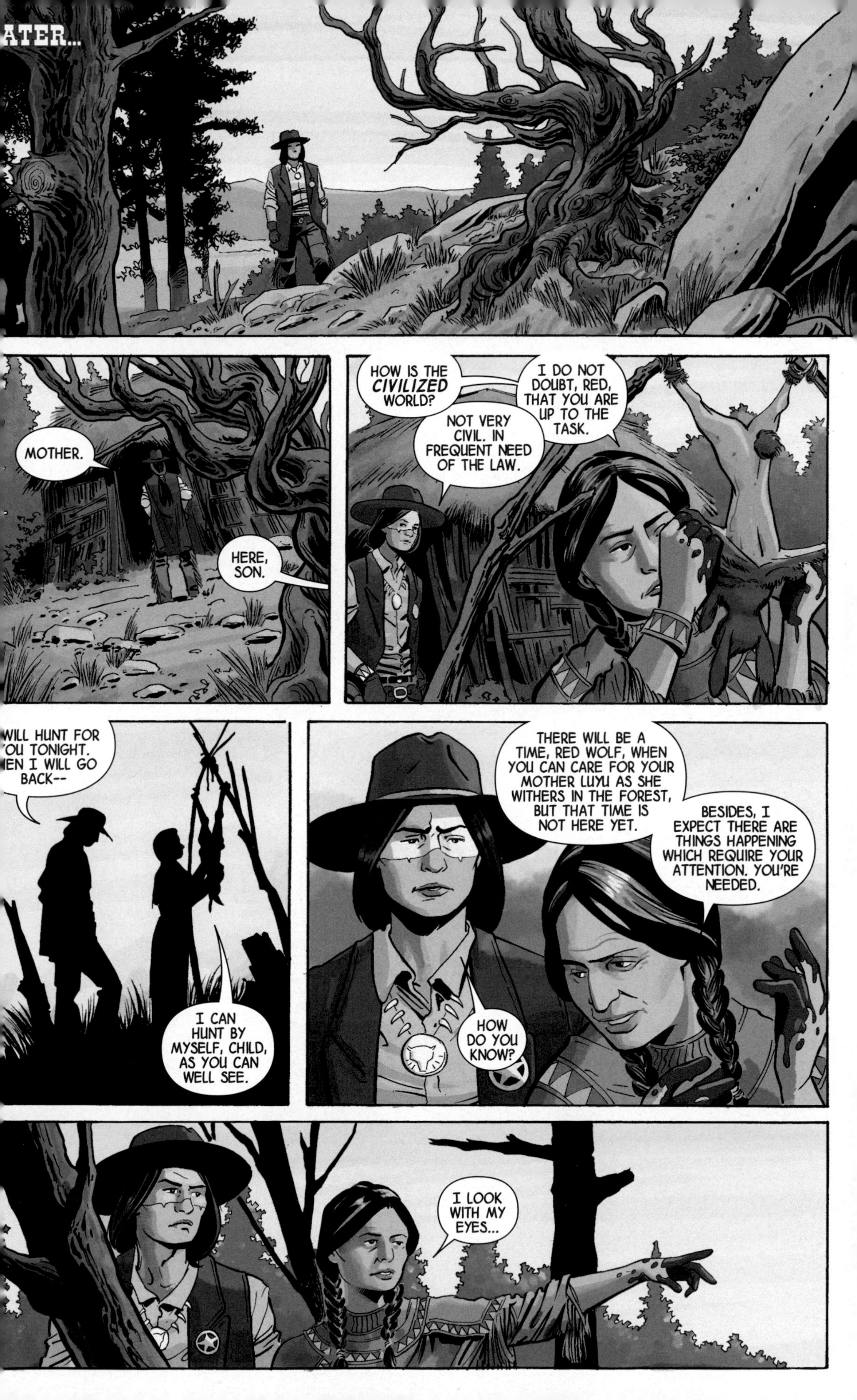
ATER...
MOTHER.
HERE, SON.
HOW IS THE *CIVILIZED* WORLD?
NOT VERY CIVIL. IN FREQUENT NEED OF THE LAW.
I DO NOT DOUBT, RED, THAT YOU ARE UP TO THE TASK.
WILL HUNT FOR 'OU TONIGHT. IEN I WILL GO BACK--
I CAN HUNT BY MYSELF, CHILD, AS YOU CAN WELL SEE.
THERE WILL BE A TIME, RED WOLF, WHEN YOU CAN CARE FOR YOUR MOTHER LUYU AS SHE WITHERS IN THE FOREST, BUT THAT TIME IS NOT HERE YET.
BESIDES, I EXPECT THERE ARE THINGS HAPPENING WHICH REQUIRE YOUR ATTENTION. YOU'RE NEEDED.
HOW DO YOU KNOW?
I LOOK WITH MY EYES...

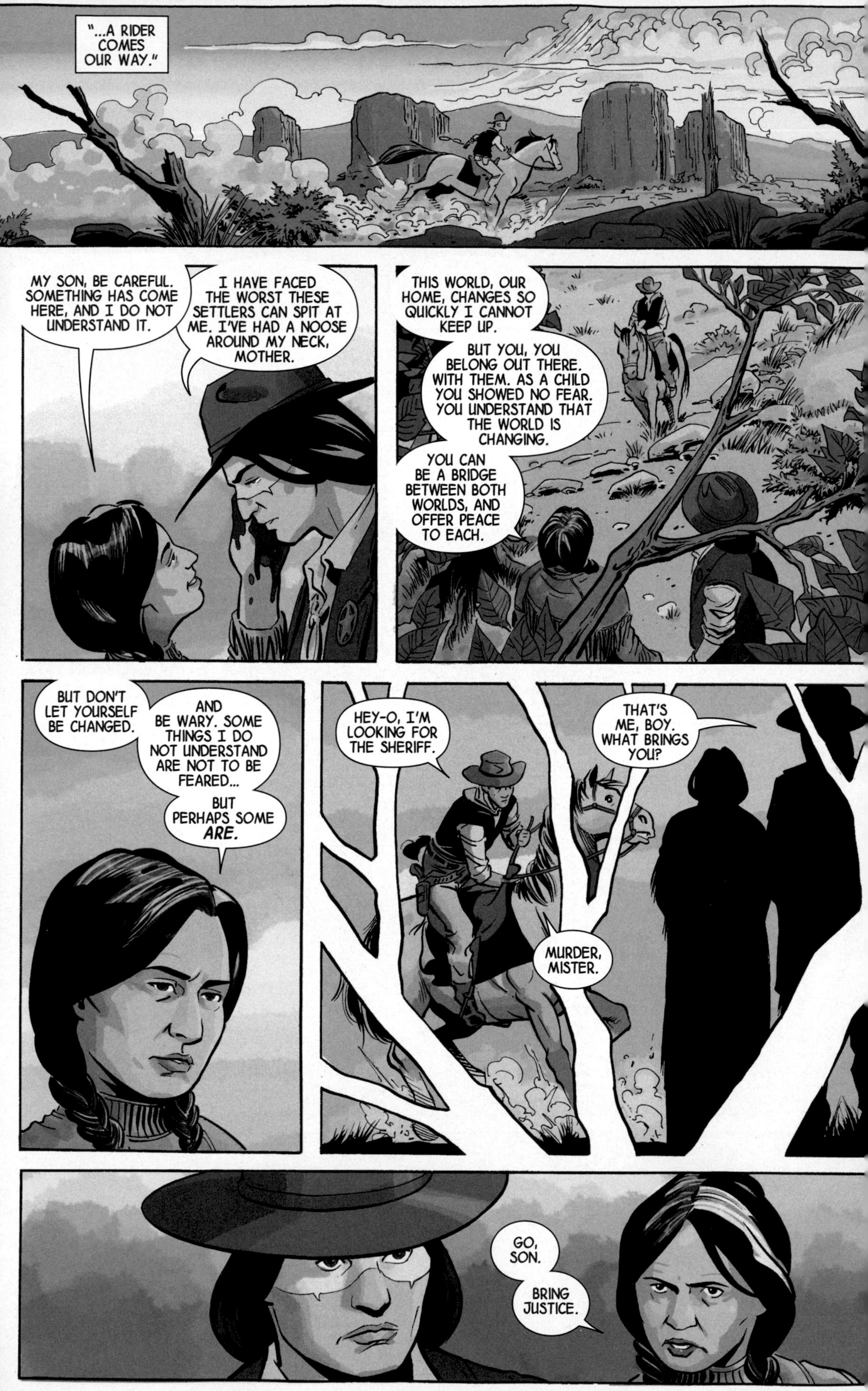
"...A RIDER COMES OUR WAY."
MY SON, BE CAREFUL. SOMETHING HAS COME HERE, AND I DO NOT UNDERSTAND IT.
I HAVE FACED THE WORST THESE SETTLERS CAN SPIT AT ME. I'VE HAD A NOOSE AROUND MY NECK, MOTHER.
THIS WORLD, OUR HOME, CHANGES SO QUICKLY I CANNOT KEEP UP.
BUT YOU, YOU BELONG OUT THERE. WITH THEM. AS A CHILD YOU SHOWED NO FEAR. YOU UNDERSTAND THAT THE WORLD IS CHANGING.
YOU CAN BE A BRIDGE BETWEEN BOTH WORLDS, AND OFFER PEACE TO EACH.
BUT DON'T LET YOURSELF BE CHANGED.
AND BE WARY. SOME THINGS I DO NOT UNDERSTAND ARE NOT TO BE FEARED...
BUT PERHAPS SOME *ARE.*
HEY-O, I'M LOOKING FOR THE SHERIFF.
THAT'S ME, BOY. WHAT BRINGS YOU?
MURDER, MISTER.
GO, SON.
BRING JUSTICE.

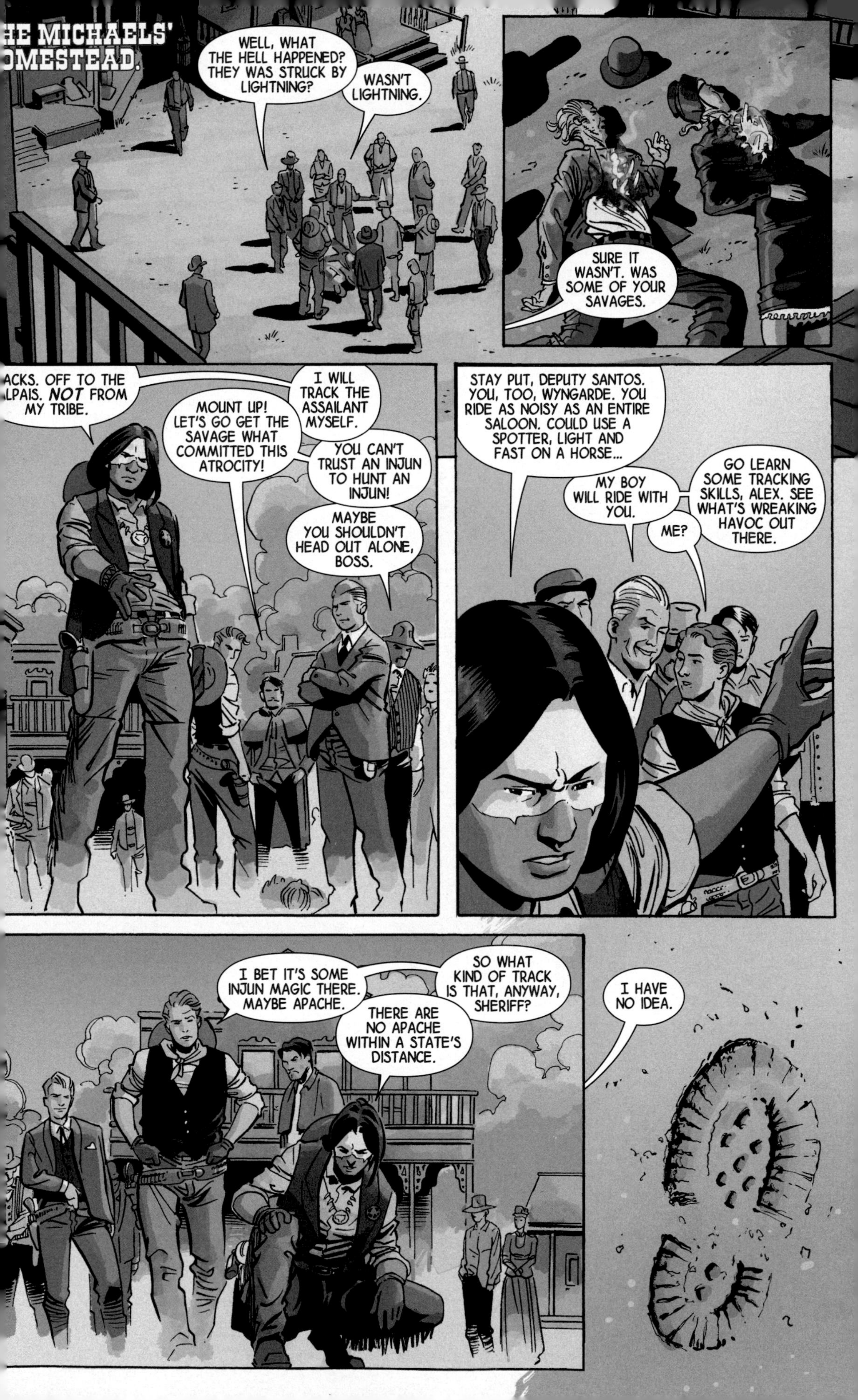
HE MICHAELS'
OMESTEAD.
WELL, WHAT THE HELL HAPPENED? THEY WAS STRUCK BY LIGHTNING?
WASN'T LIGHTNING.
SURE IT WASN'T. WAS SOME OF YOUR SAVAGES.
ACKS. OFF TO THE LPAIS. NOT FROM MY TRIBE.
I WILL TRACK THE ASSAILANT MYSELF.
MOUNT UP! LET'S GO GET THE SAVAGE WHAT COMMITTED THIS ATROCITY!
YOU CAN'T TRUST AN INJUN TO HUNT AN INJUN!
MAYBE YOU SHOULDN'T HEAD OUT ALONE, BOSS.
STAY PUT, DEPUTY SANTOS. YOU, TOO, WYNGARDE. YOU RIDE AS NOISY AS AN ENTIRE SALOON. COULD USE A SPOTTER, LIGHT AND FAST ON A HORSE...
MY BOY WILL RIDE WITH YOU.
GO LEARN SOME TRACKING SKILLS, ALEX. SEE WHAT'S WREAKING HAVOC OUT THERE.
ME?
I BET IT'S SOME INJUN MAGIC THERE. MAYBE APACHE.
SO WHAT KIND OF TRACK IS THAT, ANYWAY, SHERIFF?
THERE ARE NO APACHE WITHIN A STATE'S DISTANCE.
I HAVE NO IDEA.

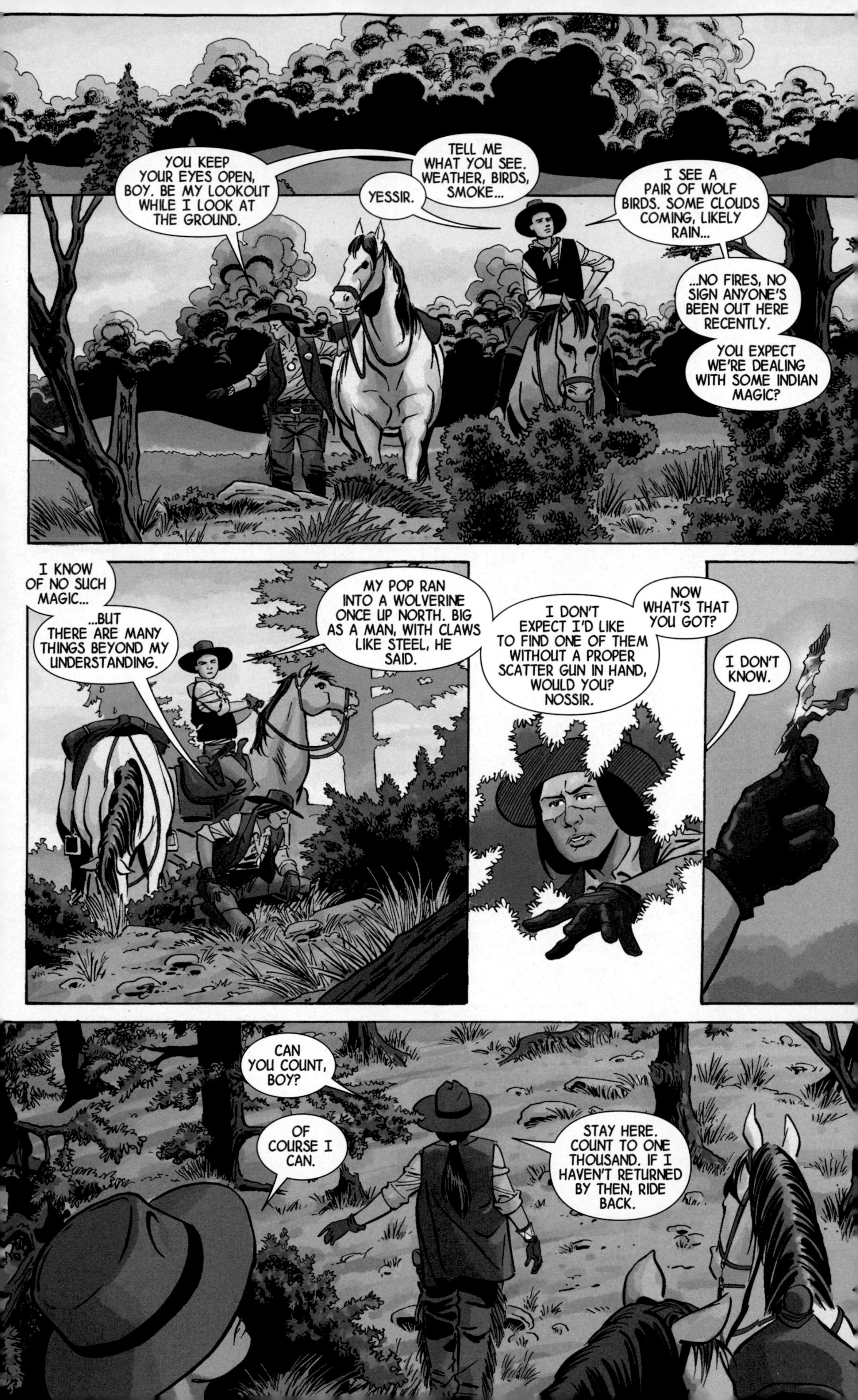

YOU KEEP YOUR EYES OPEN, BOY. BE MY LOOKOUT WHILE I LOOK AT THE GROUND.
TELL ME WHAT YOU SEE. WEATHER, BIRDS, SMOKE...
YESSIR.
I SEE A PAIR OF WOLF BIRDS. SOME CLOUDS COMING, LIKELY RAIN...
...NO FIRES, NO SIGN ANYONE'S BEEN OUT HERE RECENTLY.
YOU EXPECT WE'RE DEALING WITH SOME INDIAN MAGIC?
I KNOW OF NO SUCH MAGIC...
...BUT THERE ARE MANY THINGS BEYOND MY UNDERSTANDING.
MY POP RAN INTO A WOLVERINE ONCE UP NORTH. BIG AS A MAN, WITH CLAWS LIKE STEEL, HE SAID.
I DON'T EXPECT I'D LIKE TO FIND ONE OF THEM WITHOUT A PROPER SCATTER GUN IN HAND, WOULD YOU? NOSSIR.
NOW WHAT'S THAT YOU GOT?
I DON'T KNOW.
CAN YOU COUNT, BOY?
OF COURSE I CAN.
STAY HERE. COUNT TO ONE THOUSAND. IF I HAVEN'T RETURNED BY THEN, RIDE BACK.

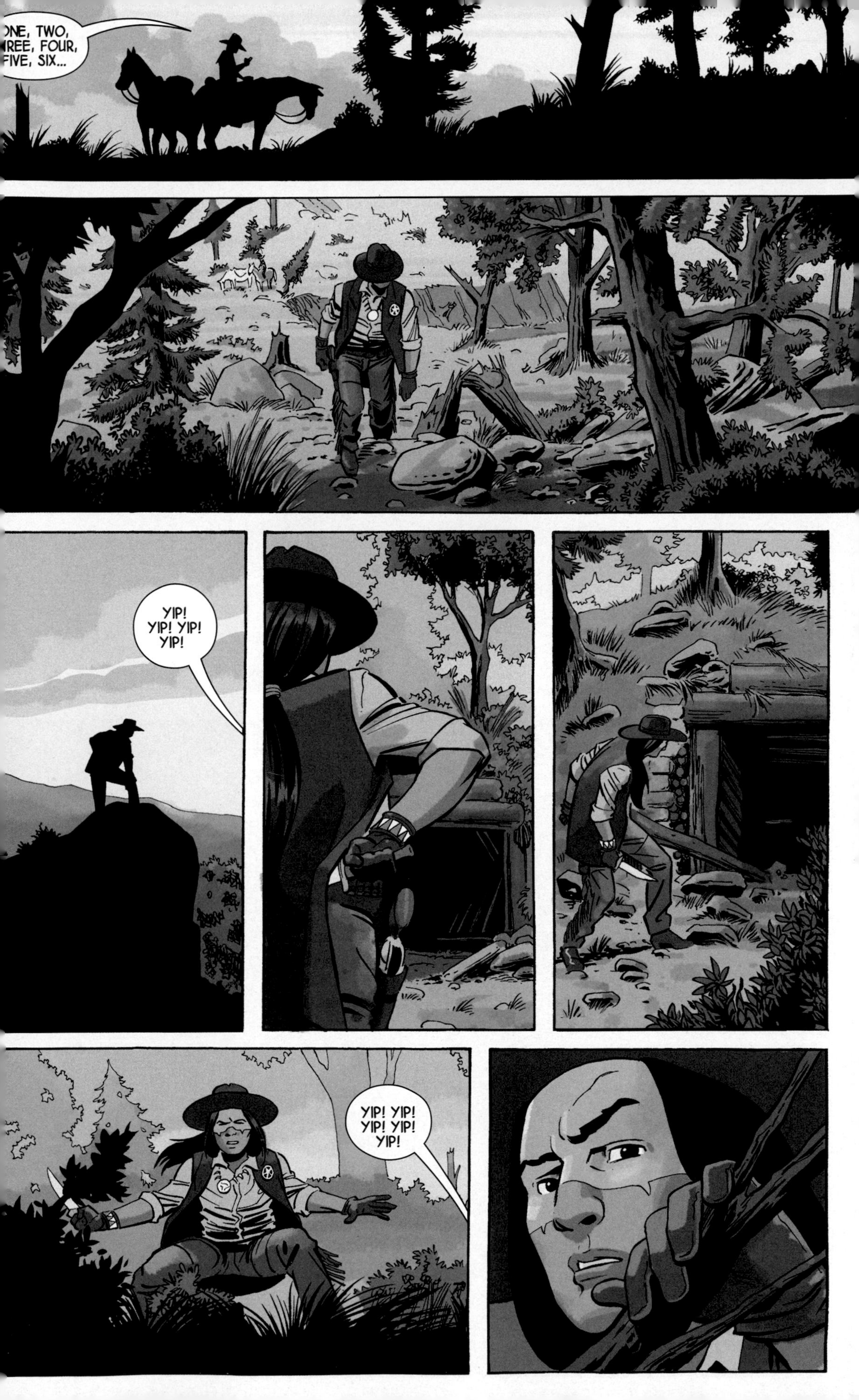
ONE, TWO, THREE, FOUR, FIVE, SIX...
YIP! YIP! YIP! YIP!
YIP! YIP! YIP! YIP! YIP!

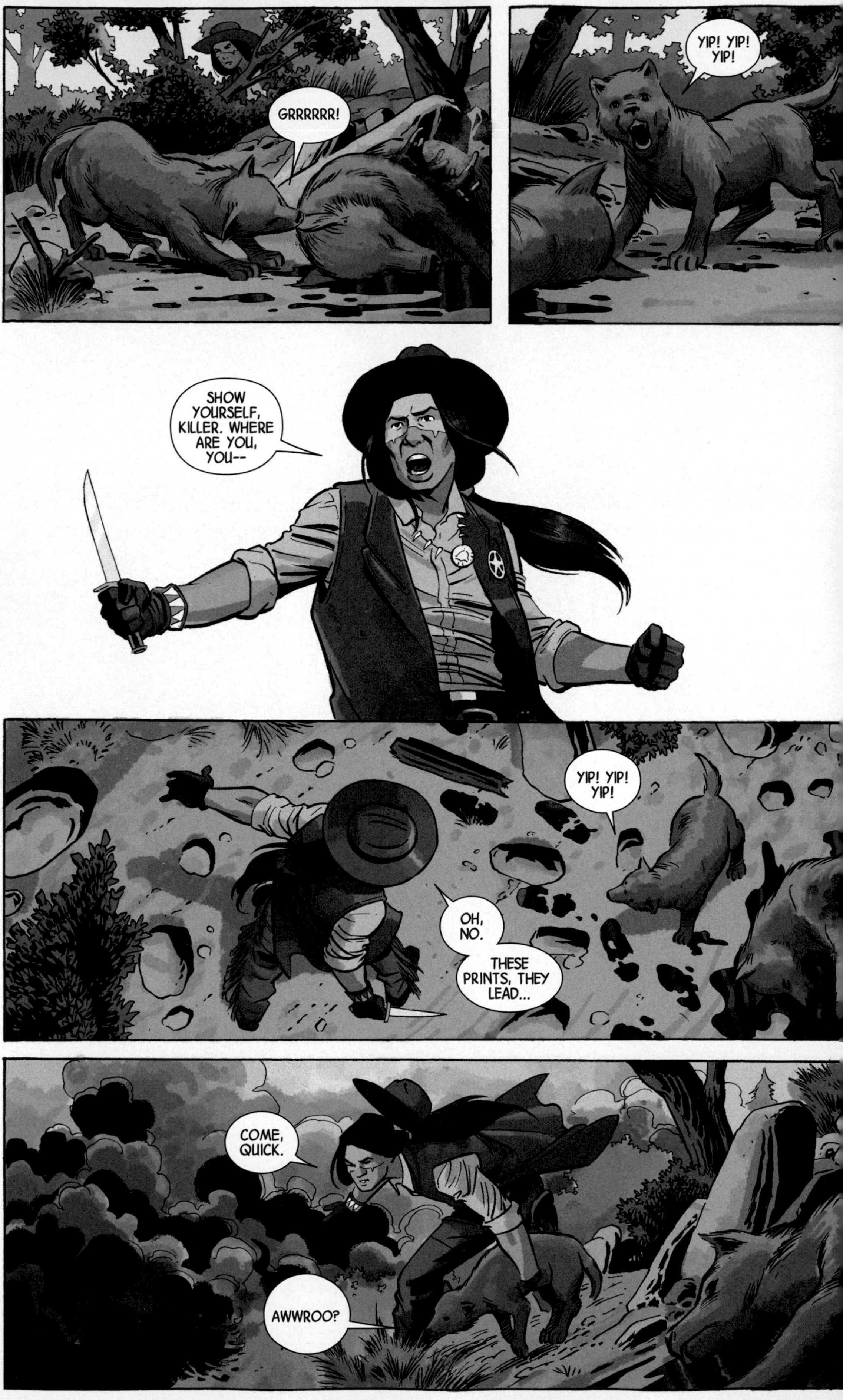
GRRRRRR!
YIP! YIP! YIP!
SHOW YOURSELF, KILLER. WHERE ARE YOU, YOU--
YIP! YIP! YIP!
OH, NO.
THESE PRINTS, THEY LEAD...
COME, QUICK.
AWWROO?

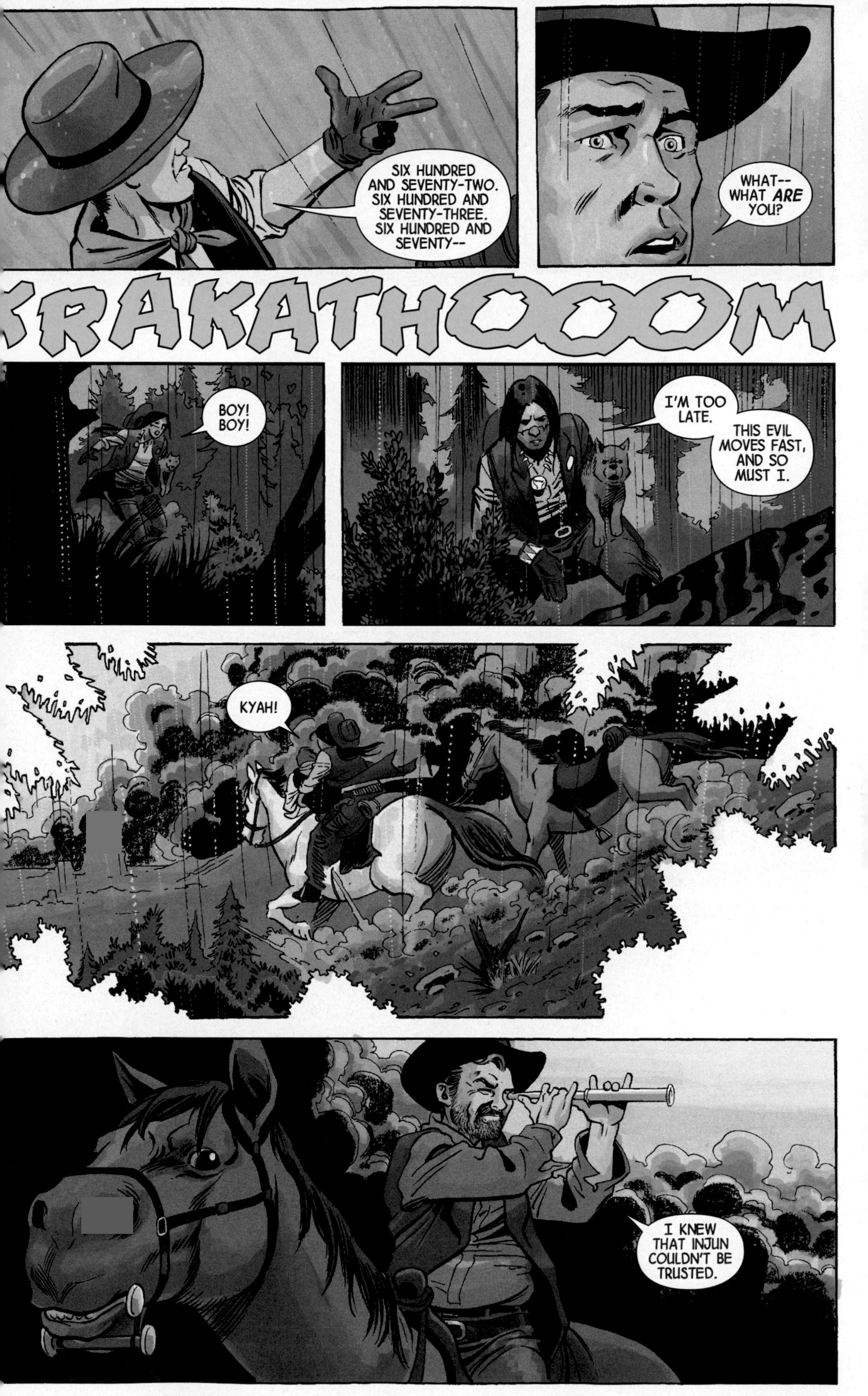
SIX HUNDRED AND SEVENTY-TWO. SIX HUNDRED AND SEVENTY-THREE. SIX HUNDRED AND SEVENTY--
WHAT-- WHAT ARE YOU?
RAKATHOOOM
BOY! BOY!
I'M TOO LATE.
THIS EVIL MOVES FAST, AND SO MUST I.
KYAH!
I KNEW THAT INJUN COULDN'T BE TRUSTED.

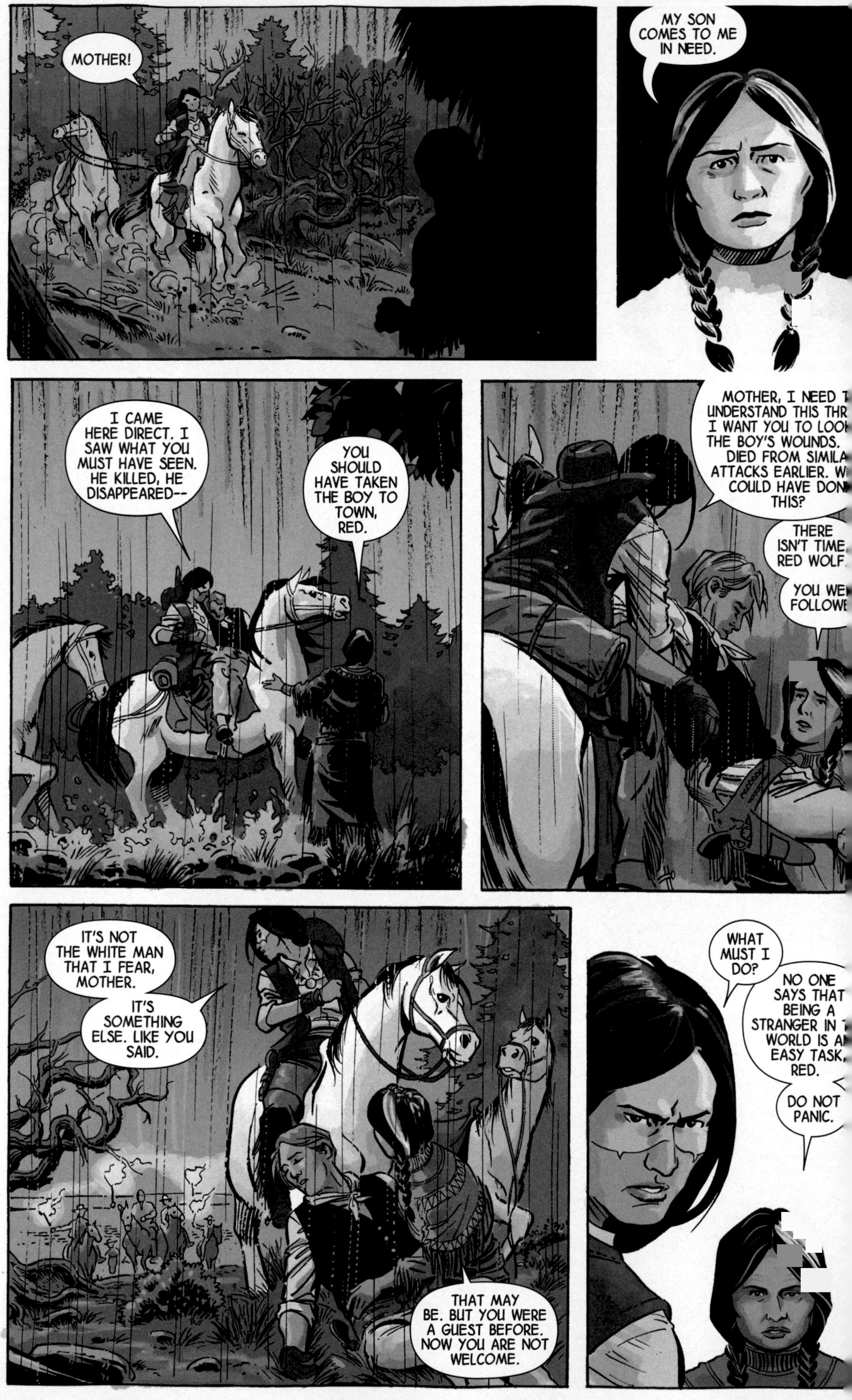
MOTHER!
MY SON COMES TO ME IN NEED.
I CAME HERE DIRECT. I SAW WHAT YOU MUST HAVE SEEN. HE KILLED, HE DISAPPEARED--
YOU SHOULD HAVE TAKEN THE BOY TO TOWN, RED.
MOTHER, I NEED UNDERSTAND THIS I WANT YOU TO THE BOY'S WOUNDS. DIED FROM ATTACKS EARLIER. COULD HAVE THIS?
THERE ISN'T RED
YOU
IT'S NOT THE WHITE MAN THAT I FEAR, MOTHER.
IT'S SOMETHING ELSE. LIKE YOU SAID.
THAT MAY BE. BUT YOU WERE A GUEST BEFORE. NOW YOU ARE NOT WELCOME.
WHAT MUST I DO?
NO ONE SAYS THAT BEING A STRANGER IN WORLD IS EASY RED.
DO NOT PANIC.

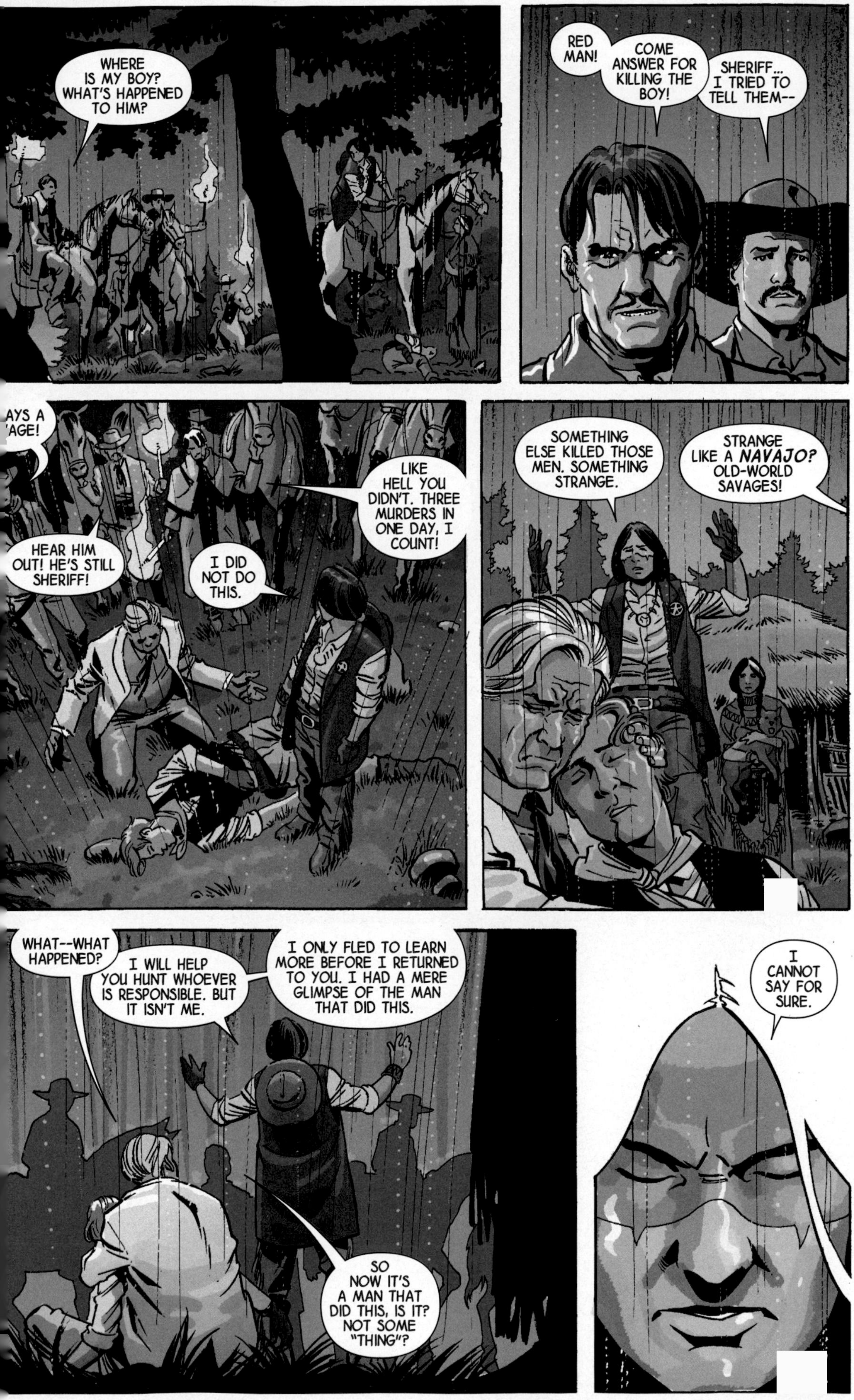
WHERE IS MY BOY? WHAT'S HAPPENED TO HIM?
RED MAN!
COME ANSWER FOR KILLING THE BOY!
SHERIFF... I TRIED TO TELL THEM--
AYS A AGE!
HEAR HIM OUT! HE'S STILL SHERIFF!
LIKE HELL YOU DIDN'T. THREE MURDERS IN ONE DAY, I COUNT!
I DID NOT DO THIS.
SOMETHING ELSE KILLED THOSE MEN. SOMETHING STRANGE.
STRANGE LIKE A NAVAJO? OLD-WORLD SAVAGES!
WHAT--WHAT HAPPENED?
I WILL HELP YOU HUNT WHOEVER IS RESPONSIBLE. BUT IT ISN'T ME.
I ONLY FLED TO LEARN MORE BEFORE I RETURNED TO YOU. I HAD A MERE GLIMPSE OF THE MAN THAT DID THIS.
SO NOW IT'S A MAN THAT DID THIS, IS IT? NOT SOME "THING"?
I CANNOT SAY FOR SURE.

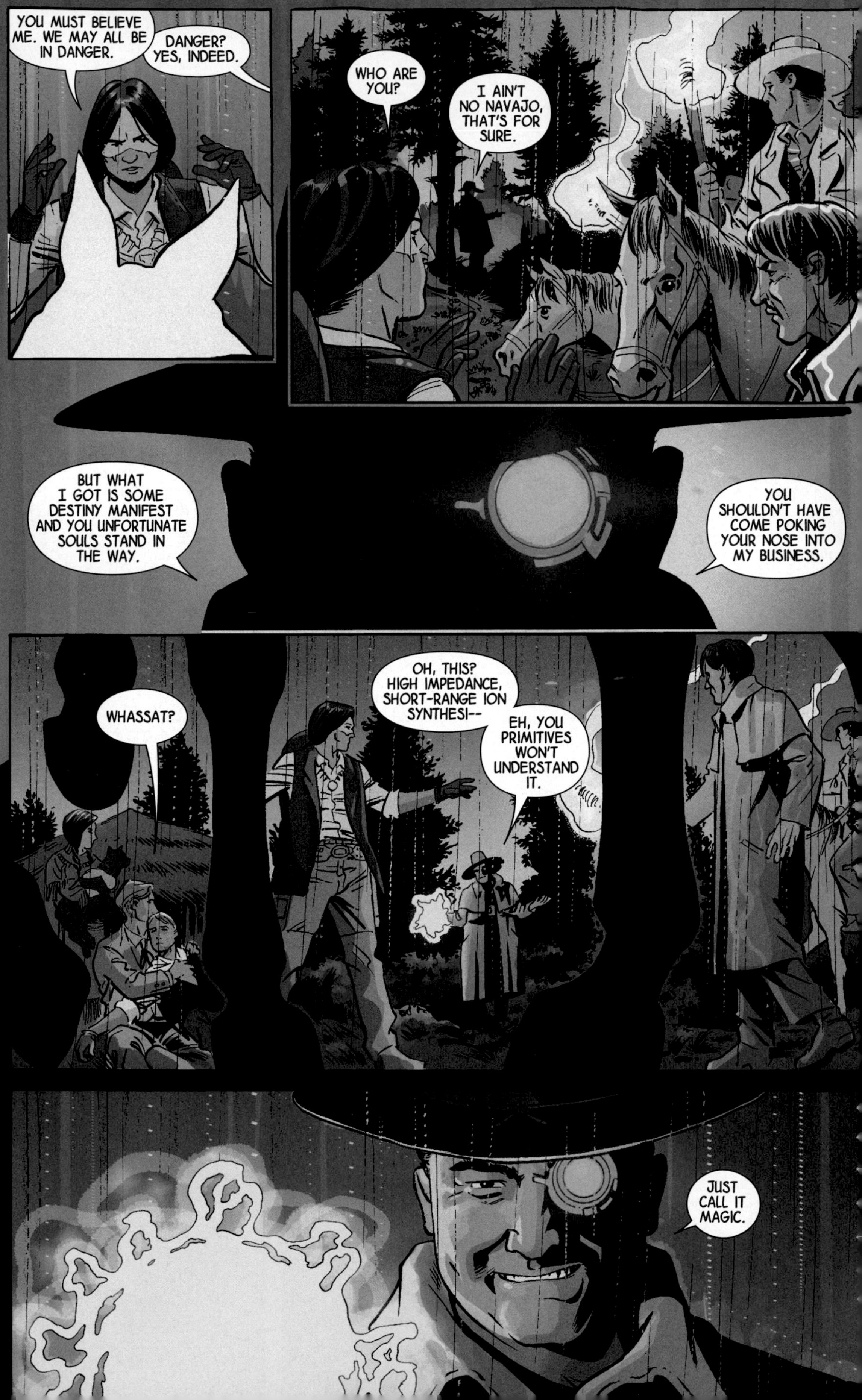
YOU MUST BELIEVE ME. WE MAY ALL BE IN DANGER.
DANGER? YES, INDEED.
WHO ARE YOU?
I AIN'T NO NAVAJO, THAT'S FOR SURE.
BUT WHAT I GOT IS SOME DESTINY MANIFEST AND YOU UNFORTUNATE SOULS STAND IN THE WAY.
YOU SHOULDN'T HAVE COME POKING YOUR NOSE INTO MY BUSINESS.
WHASSAT?
OH, THIS? HIGH IMPEDANCE, SHORT-RANGE ION SYNTHESI--
EH, YOU PRIMITIVES WON'T UNDERSTAND IT.
JUST CALL IT MAGIC.

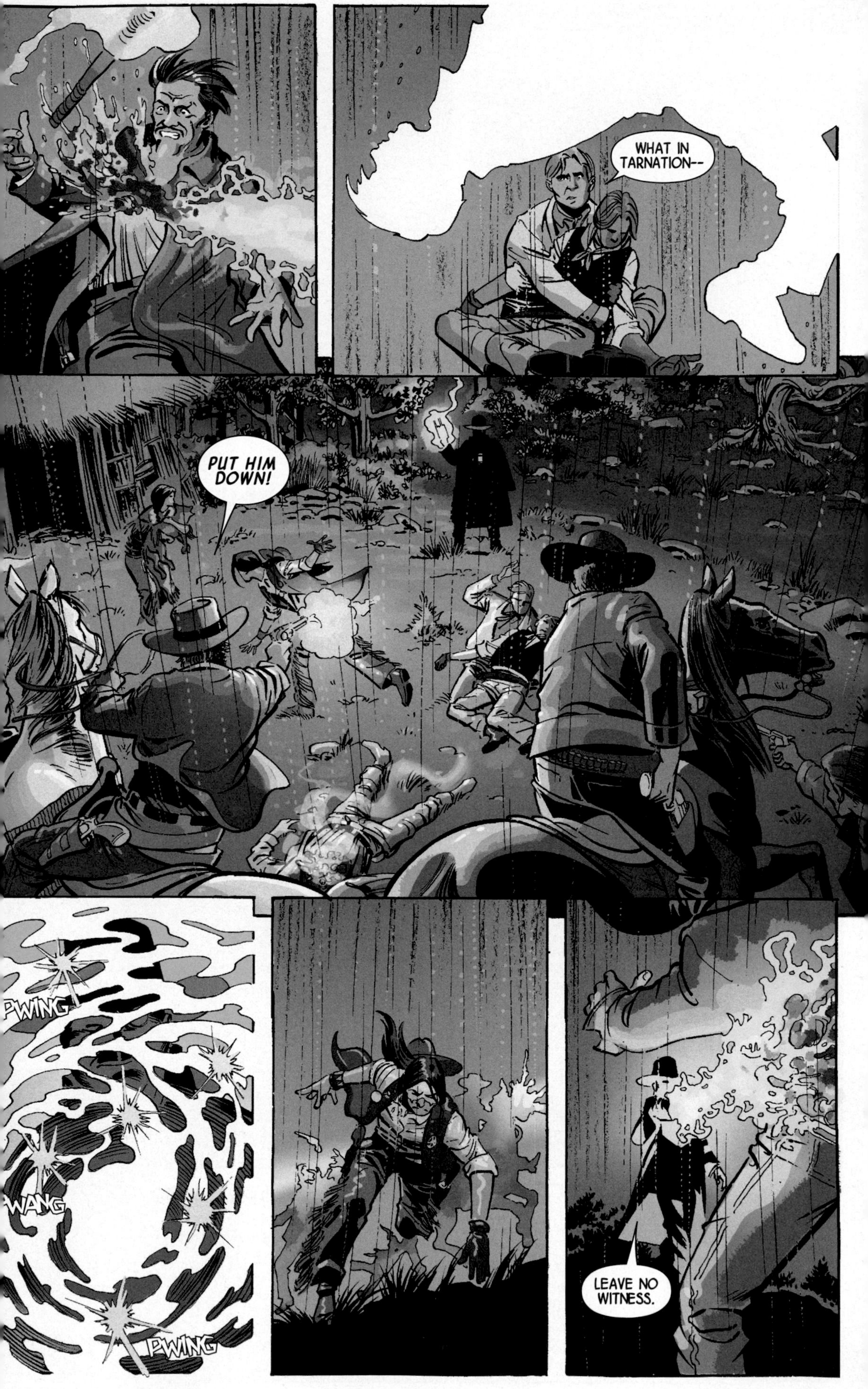
WHAT IN TARNATION--
PUT HIM DOWN!
PWING
WANG
PWING
LEAVE NO WITNESS.

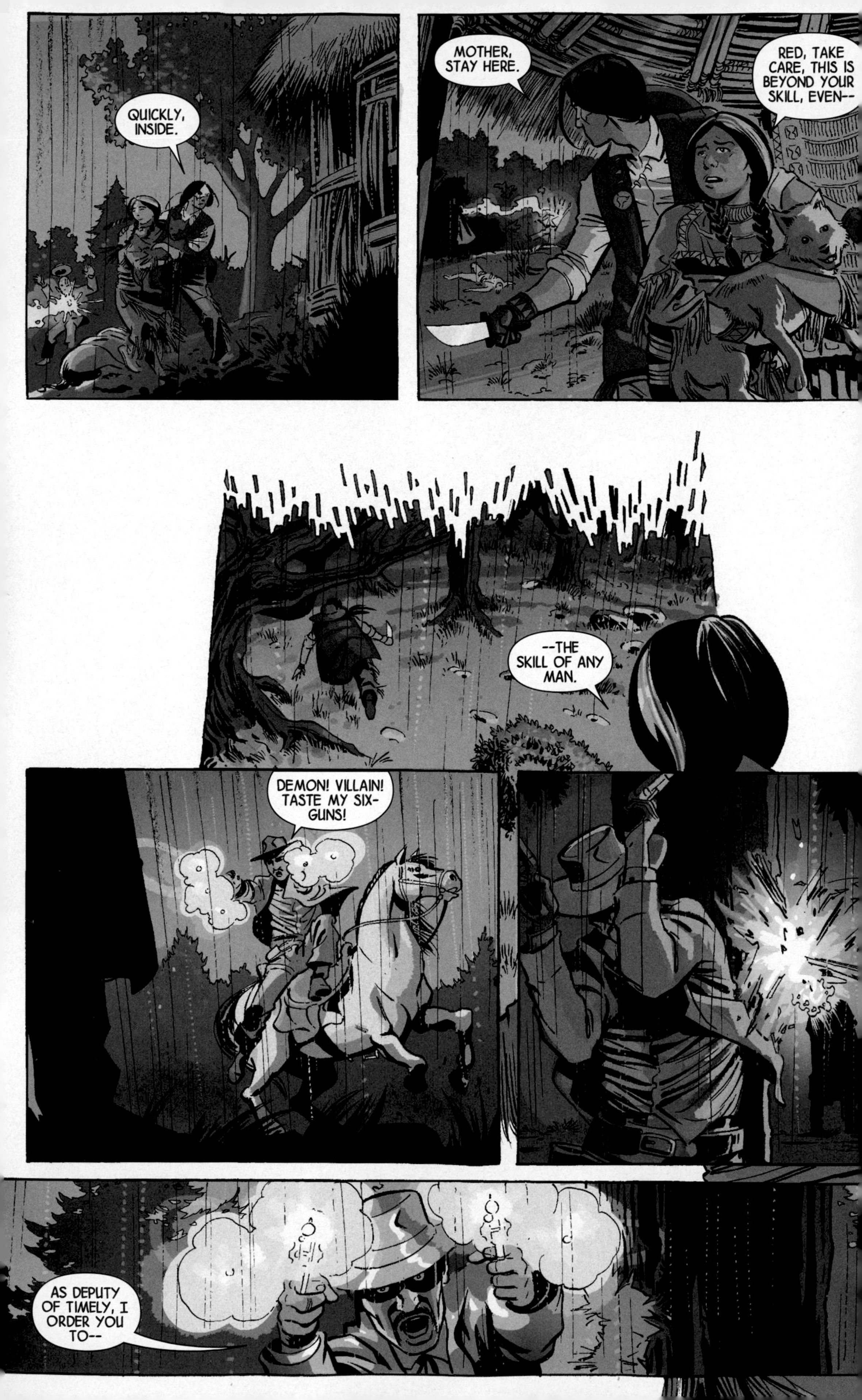
QUICKLY, INSIDE.
MOTHER, STAY HERE.
RED, TAKE CARE, THIS IS BEYOND YOUR SKILL, EVEN--
--THE SKILL OF ANY MAN.
DEMON! VILLAIN! TASTE MY SIX-GUNS!
AS DEPUTY OF TIMELY, I ORDER YOU TO--

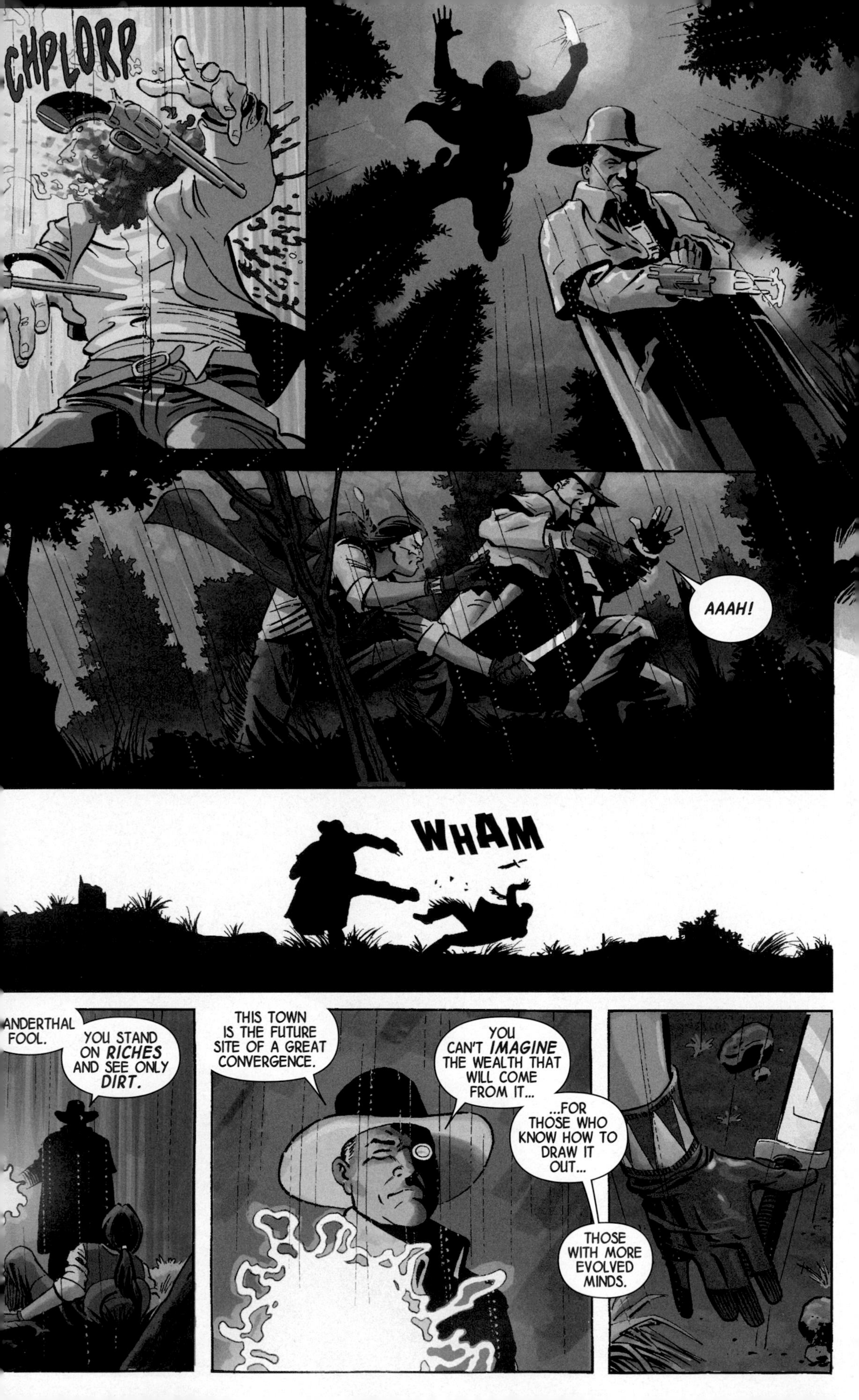
CHPLORP
AAAH!
WHAM
ANDERTHAL FOOL.
YOU STAND ON RICHES AND SEE ONLY DIRT.
THIS TOWN IS THE FUTURE SITE OF A GREAT CONVERGENCE.
YOU CAN'T IMAGINE THE WEALTH THAT WILL COME FROM IT...
...FOR THOSE WHO KNOW HOW TO DRAW IT OUT...
THOSE WITH MORE EVOLVED MINDS.

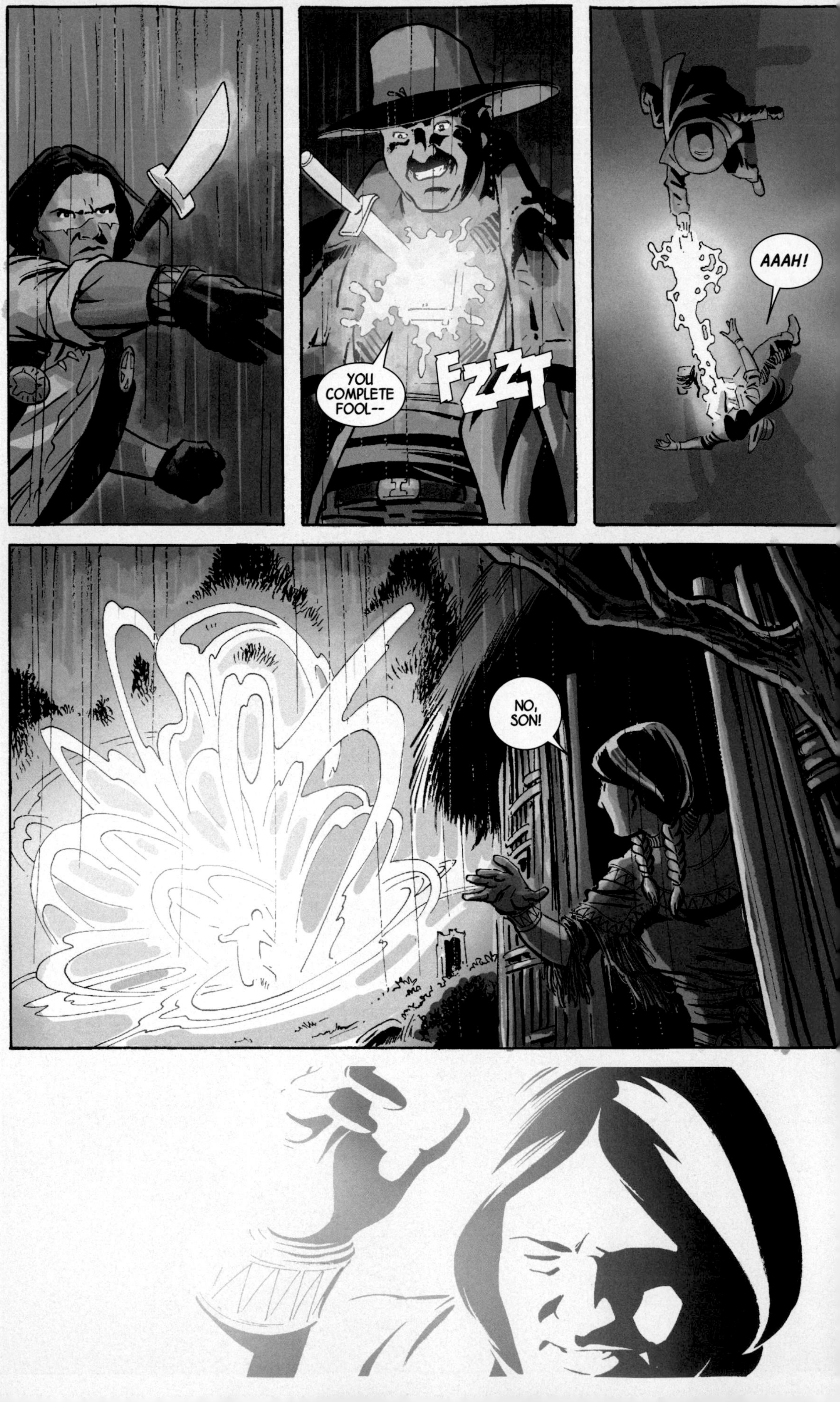
YOU COMPLETE FOOL--
FZZT
AAAH!
NO, SON!

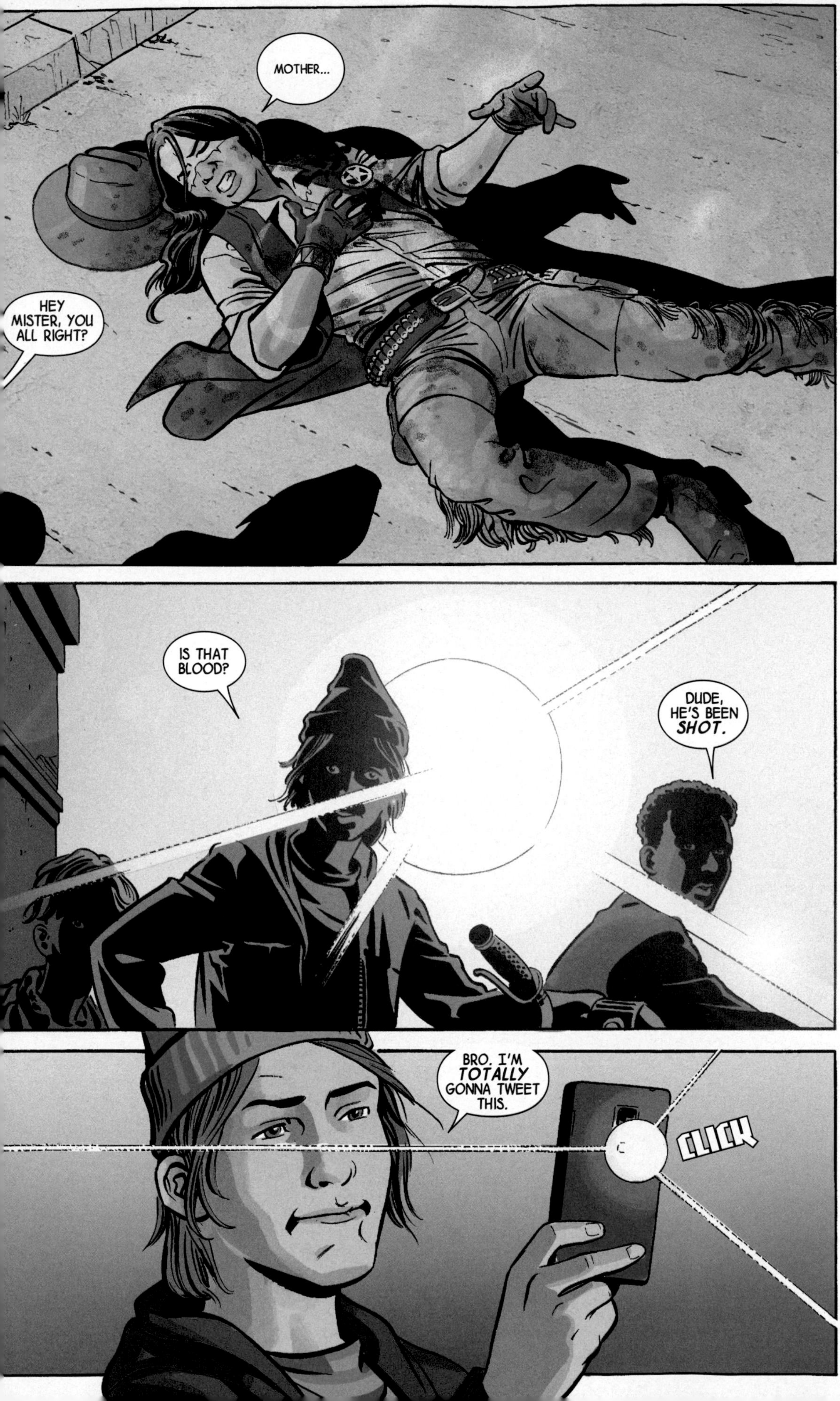
MOTHER...
HEY MISTER, YOU ALL RIGHT?
IS THAT BLOOD?
DUDE, HE'S BEEN *SHOT.*
BRO. I'M *TOTALLY* GONNA TWEET THIS.
CLICK

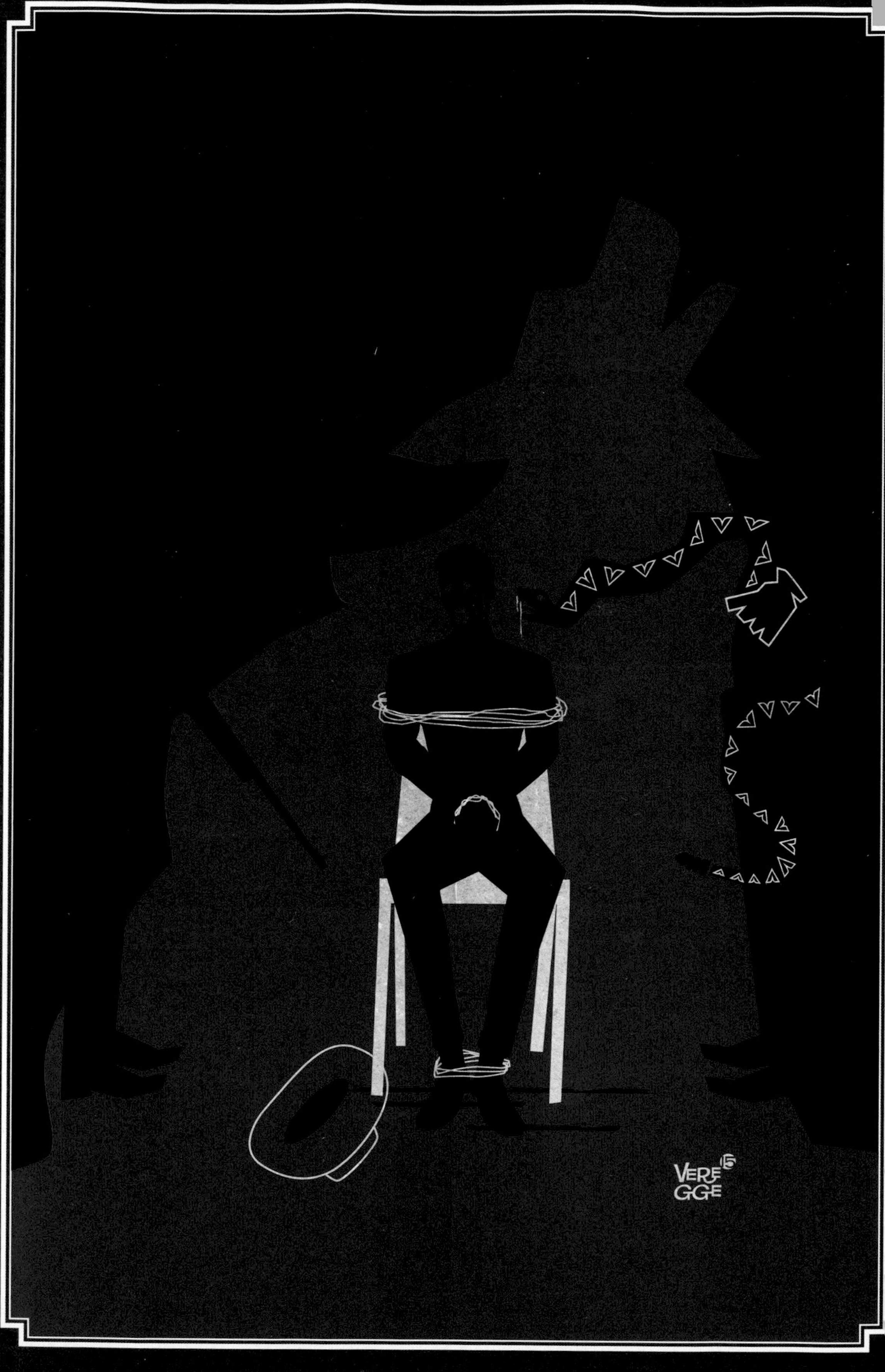
VEREGGE 15

2

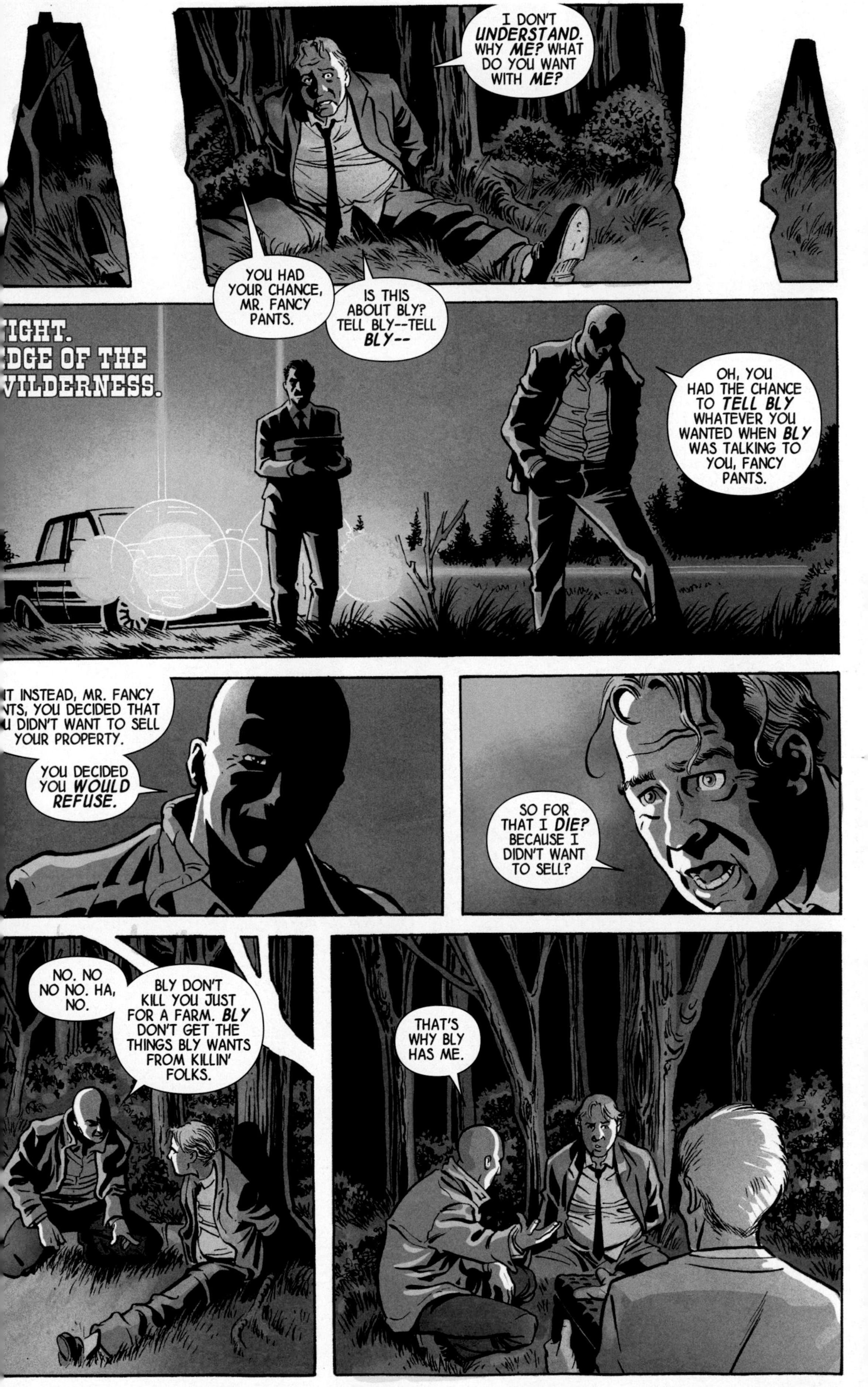
I DON'T UNDERSTAND. WHY ME? WHAT DO YOU WANT WITH ME?
YOU HAD YOUR CHANCE, MR. FANCY PANTS.
IS THIS ABOUT BLY? TELL BLY--TELL BLY--
IGHT. DGE OF THE VILDERNESS.
OH, YOU HAD THE CHANCE TO TELL BLY WHATEVER YOU WANTED WHEN BLY WAS TALKING TO YOU, FANCY PANTS.
IT INSTEAD, MR. FANCY NTS, YOU DECIDED THAT U DIDN'T WANT TO SELL YOUR PROPERTY.
YOU DECIDED YOU WOULD REFUSE.
SO FOR THAT I DIE? BECAUSE I DIDN'T WANT TO SELL?
NO. NO NO NO. HA, NO.
BLY DON'T KILL YOU JUST FOR A FARM. BLY DON'T GET THE THINGS BLY WANTS FROM KILLIN' FOLKS.
THAT'S WHY BLY HAS ME.

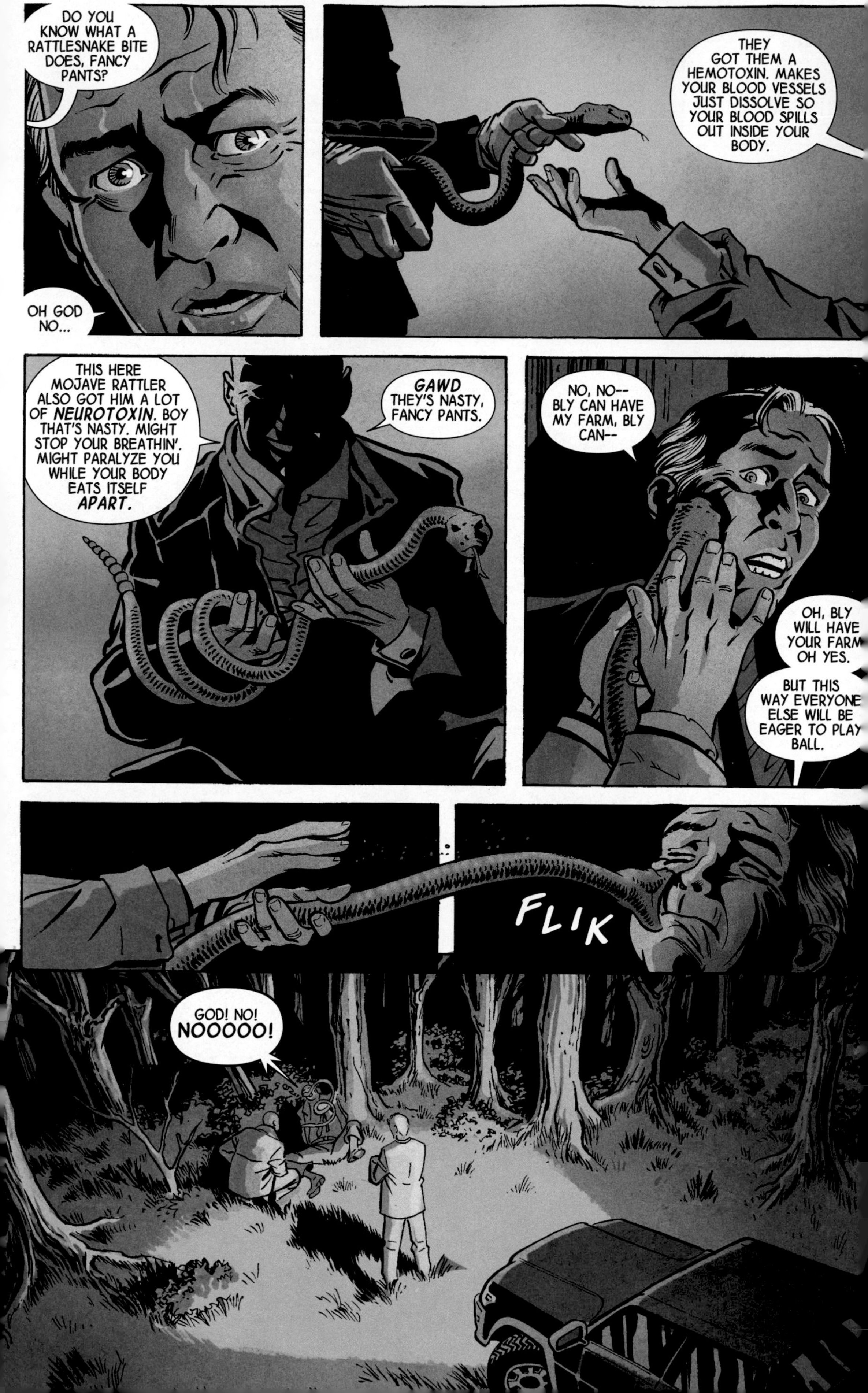
DO YOU KNOW WHAT A RATTLESNAKE BITE DOES, FANCY PANTS?
OH GOD NO...
THEY GOT THEM A HEMOTOXIN. MAKES YOUR BLOOD VESSELS JUST DISSOLVE SO YOUR BLOOD SPILLS OUT INSIDE YOUR BODY.
THIS HERE MOJAVE RATTLER ALSO GOT HIM A LOT OF NEUROTOXIN. BOY THAT'S NASTY. MIGHT STOP YOUR BREATHIN'. MIGHT PARALYZE YOU WHILE YOUR BODY EATS ITSELF APART.
GAWD THEY'S NASTY, FANCY PANTS.
NO, NO-- BLY CAN HAVE MY FARM, BLY CAN--
OH, BLY WILL HAVE YOUR FARM OH YES.
BUT THIS WAY EVERYONE ELSE WILL BE EAGER TO PLAY BALL.
FLIK
GOD! NO! NOOOOO!

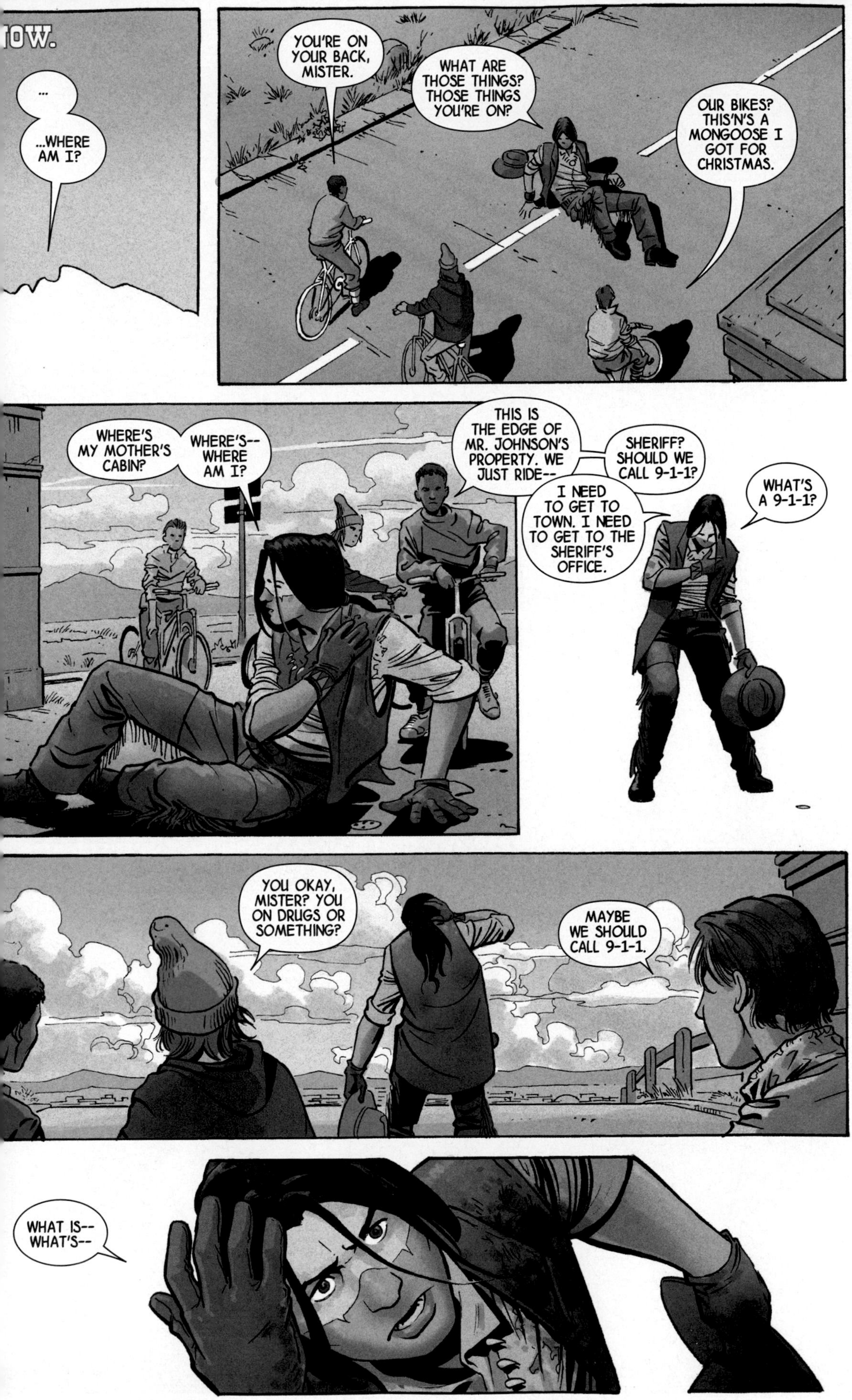

...OW.
...
...WHERE AM I?
YOU'RE ON YOUR BACK, MISTER.
WHAT ARE THOSE THINGS? THOSE THINGS YOU'RE ON?
OUR BIKES? THIS'N'S A MONGOOSE I GOT FOR CHRISTMAS.
WHERE'S MY MOTHER'S CABIN?
WHERE'S-- WHERE AM I?
THIS IS THE EDGE OF MR. JOHNSON'S PROPERTY. WE JUST RIDE--
SHERIFF? SHOULD WE CALL 9-1-1?
I NEED TO GET TO TOWN. I NEED TO GET TO THE SHERIFF'S OFFICE.
WHAT'S A 9-1-1?
YOU OKAY, MISTER? YOU ON DRUGS OR SOMETHING?
MAYBE WE SHOULD CALL 9-1-1.
WHAT IS-- WHAT'S--

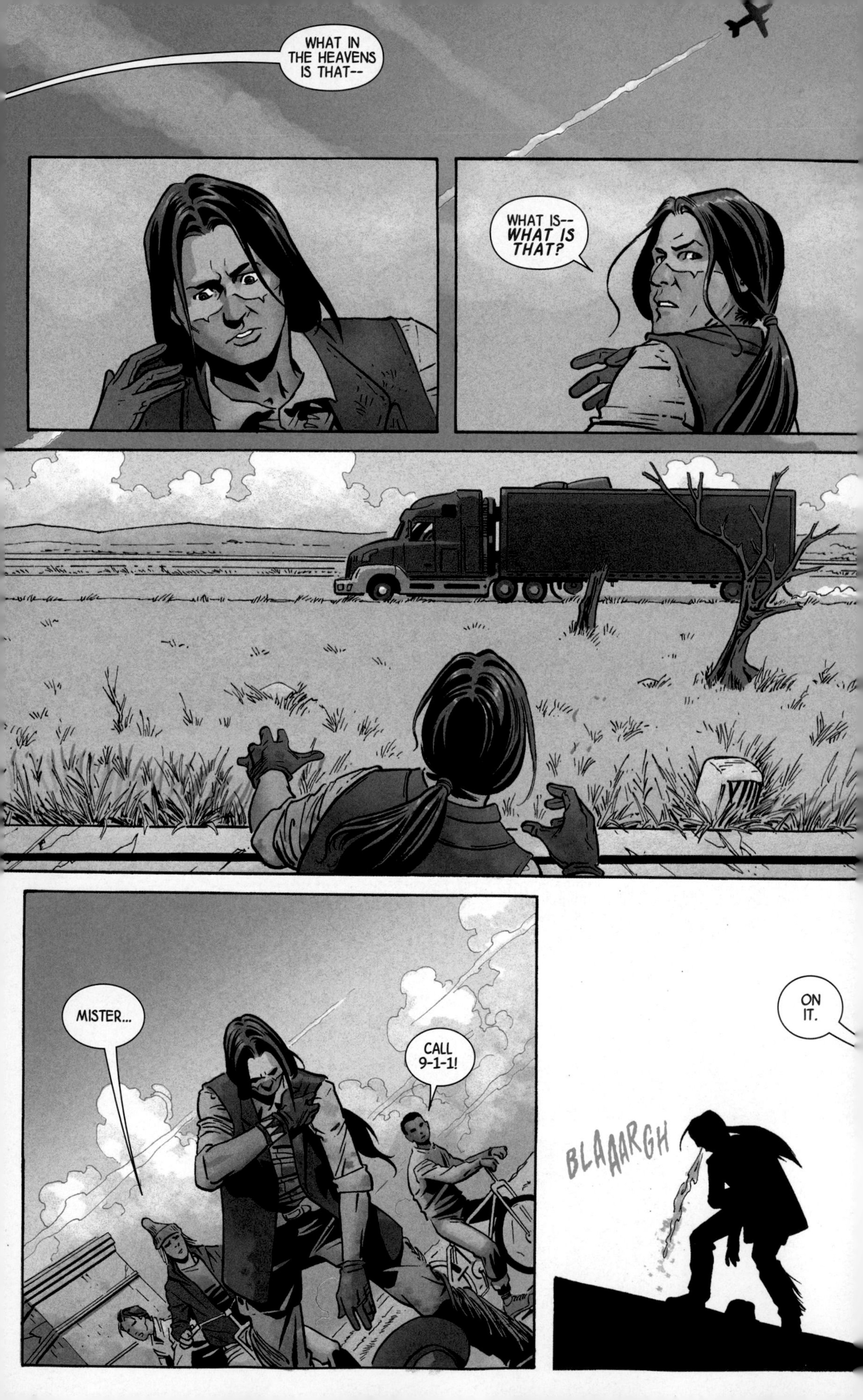
WHAT IN THE HEAVENS IS THAT--
WHAT IS-- WHAT IS THAT?
MISTER...
CALL 9-1-1!
ON IT.
BLAAARGH

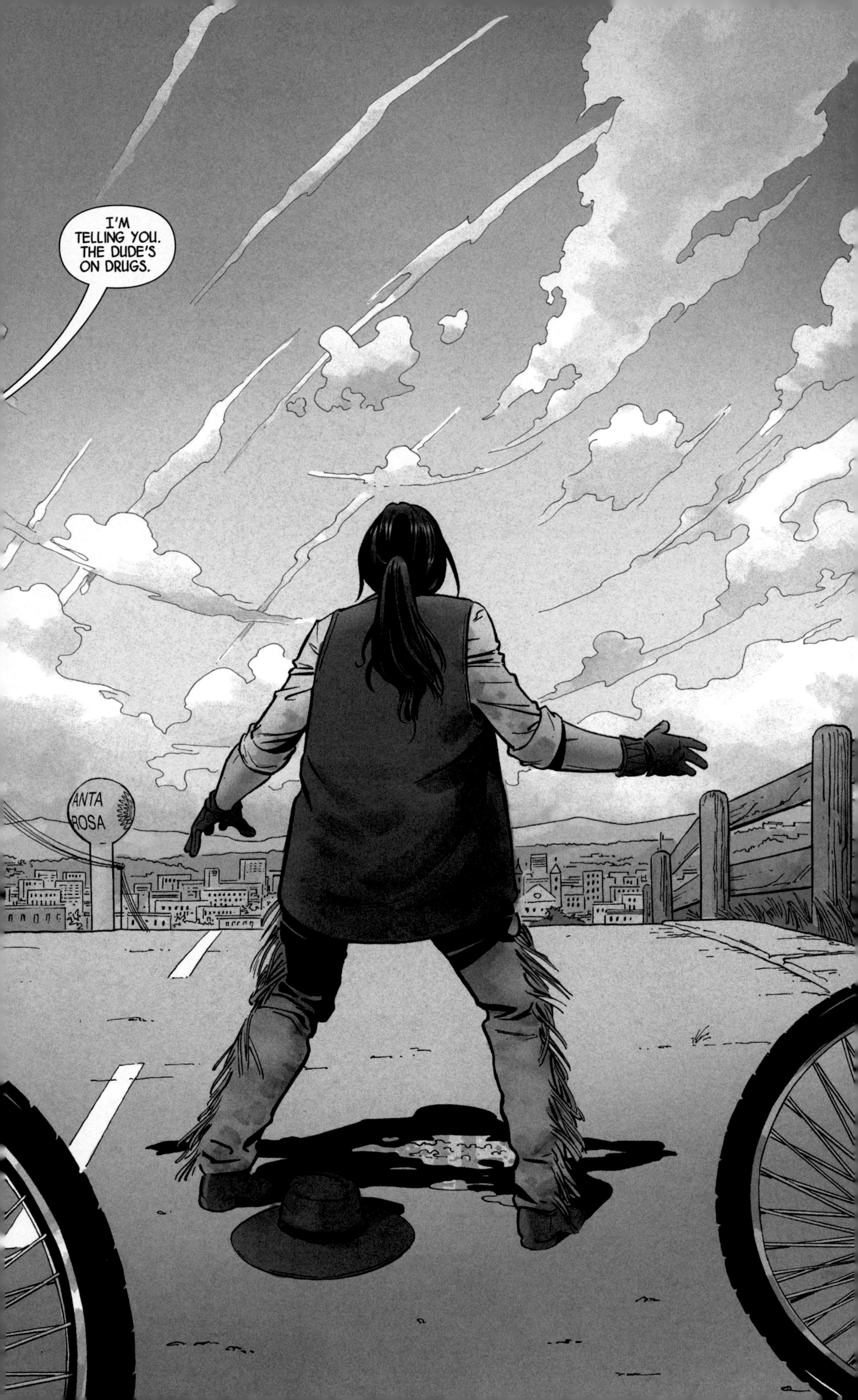
I'M TELLING YOU. THE DUDE'S ON DRUGS.
ANTA ROSA

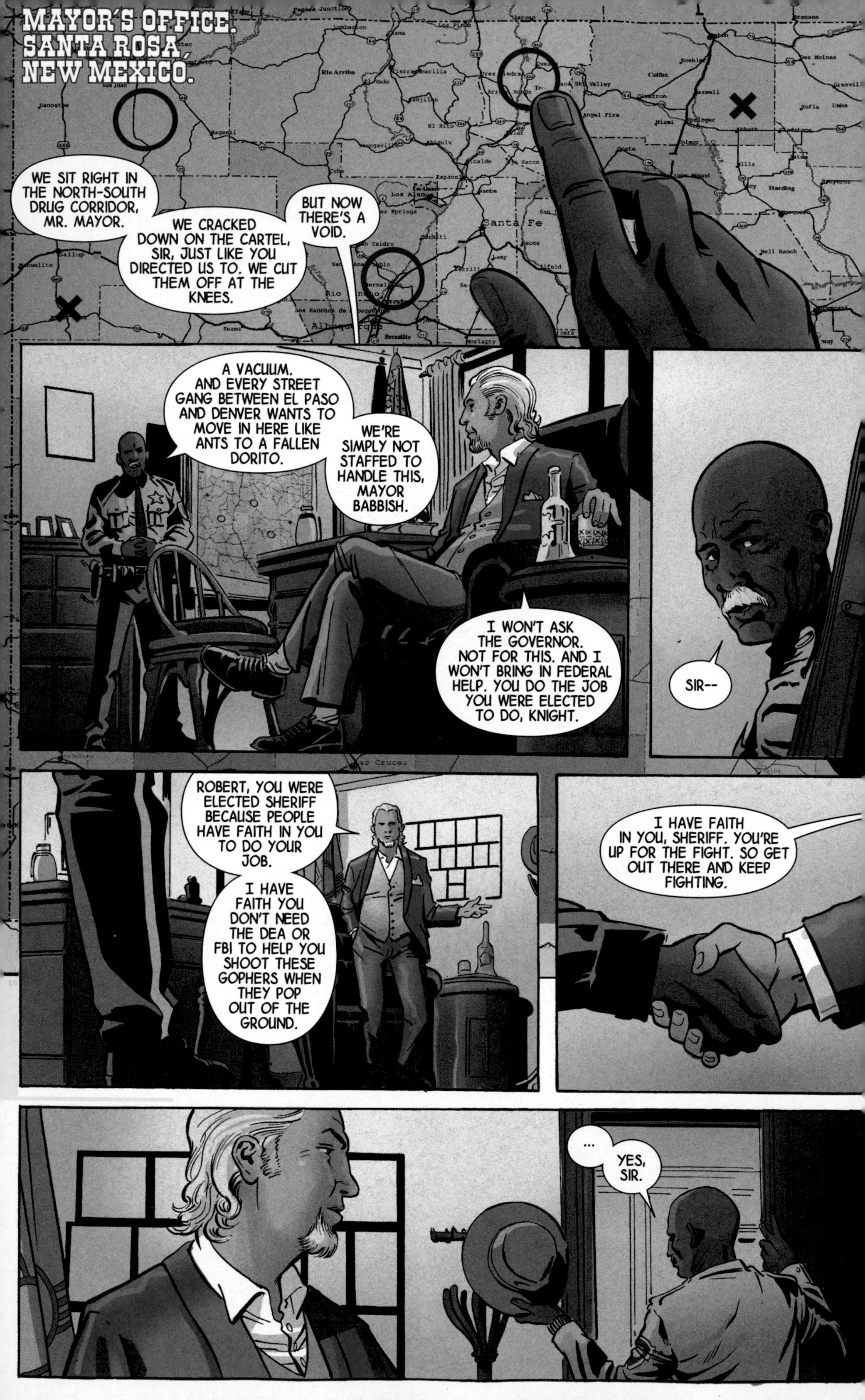
MAYOR'S OFFICE. SANTA ROSA, NEW MEXICO.
WE SIT RIGHT IN THE NORTH-SOUTH DRUG CORRIDOR, MR. MAYOR.
WE CRACKED DOWN ON THE CARTEL, SIR, JUST LIKE YOU DIRECTED US TO. WE CUT THEM OFF AT THE KNEES.
BUT NOW THERE'S A VOID.
A VACUUM. AND EVERY STREET GANG BETWEEN EL PASO AND DENVER WANTS TO MOVE IN HERE LIKE ANTS TO A FALLEN DORITO.
WE'RE SIMPLY NOT STAFFED TO HANDLE THIS, MAYOR BABBISH.
I WON'T ASK THE GOVERNOR. NOT FOR THIS. AND I WON'T BRING IN FEDERAL HELP. YOU DO THE JOB YOU WERE ELECTED TO DO, KNIGHT.
SIR--
ROBERT, YOU WERE ELECTED SHERIFF BECAUSE PEOPLE HAVE FAITH IN YOU TO DO YOUR JOB.
I HAVE FAITH YOU DON'T NEED THE DEA OR FBI TO HELP YOU SHOOT THESE GOPHERS WHEN THEY POP OUT OF THE GROUND.
I HAVE FAITH IN YOU, SHERIFF. YOU'RE UP FOR THE FIGHT. SO GET OUT THERE AND KEEP FIGHTING.
...
YES, SIR.

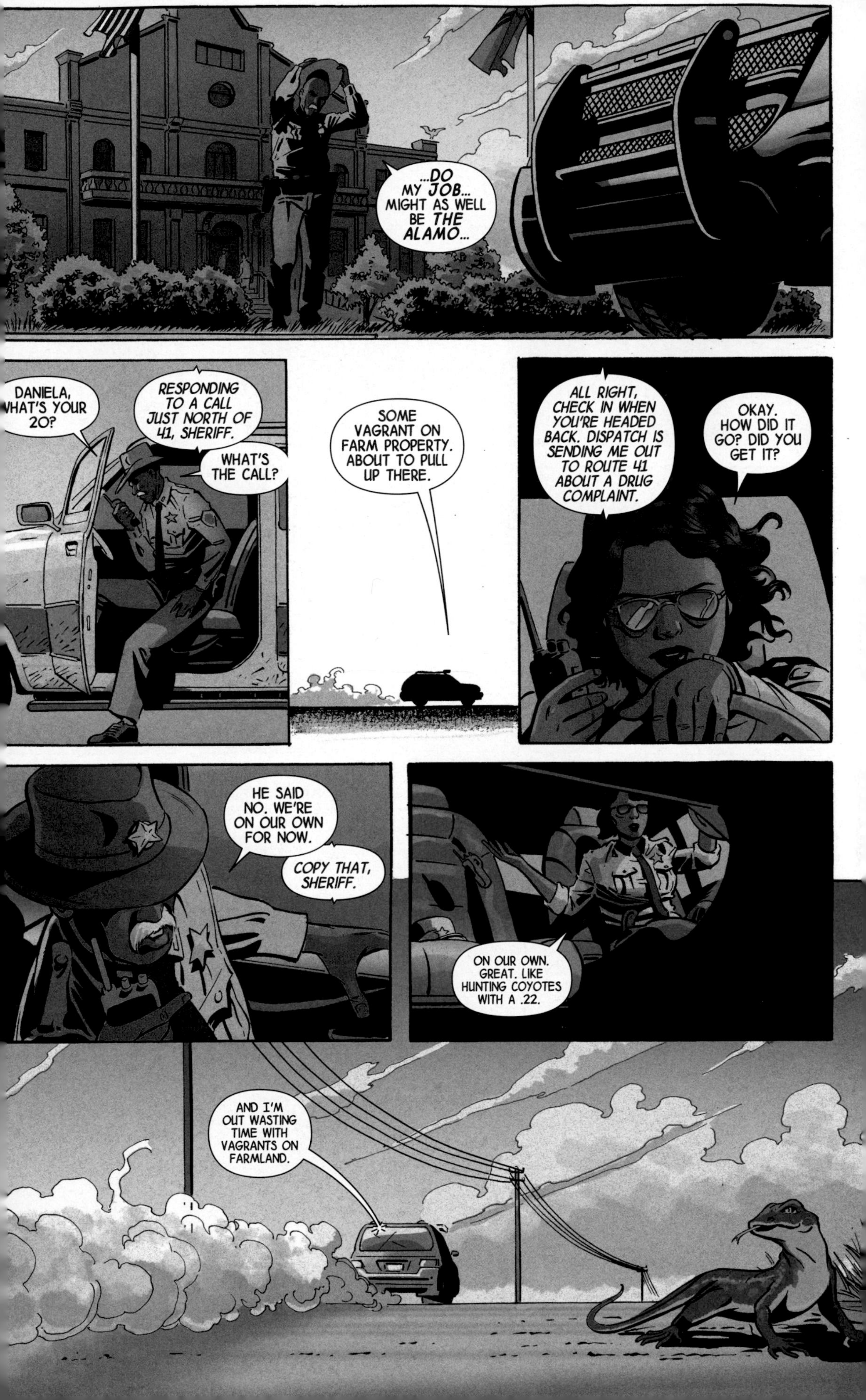
...DO MY JOB... MIGHT AS WELL BE THE ALAMO...
DANIELA, WHAT'S YOUR 20?
RESPONDING TO A CALL JUST NORTH OF 41, SHERIFF.
WHAT'S THE CALL?
SOME VAGRANT ON FARM PROPERTY. ABOUT TO PULL UP THERE.
ALL RIGHT, CHECK IN WHEN YOU'RE HEADED BACK. DISPATCH IS SENDING ME OUT TO ROUTE 41 ABOUT A DRUG COMPLAINT.
OKAY. HOW DID IT GO? DID YOU GET IT?
HE SAID NO. WE'RE ON OUR OWN FOR NOW.
COPY THAT, SHERIFF.
ON OUR OWN. GREAT. LIKE HUNTING COYOTES WITH A .22.
AND I'M OUT WASTING TIME WITH VAGRANTS ON FARMLAND.

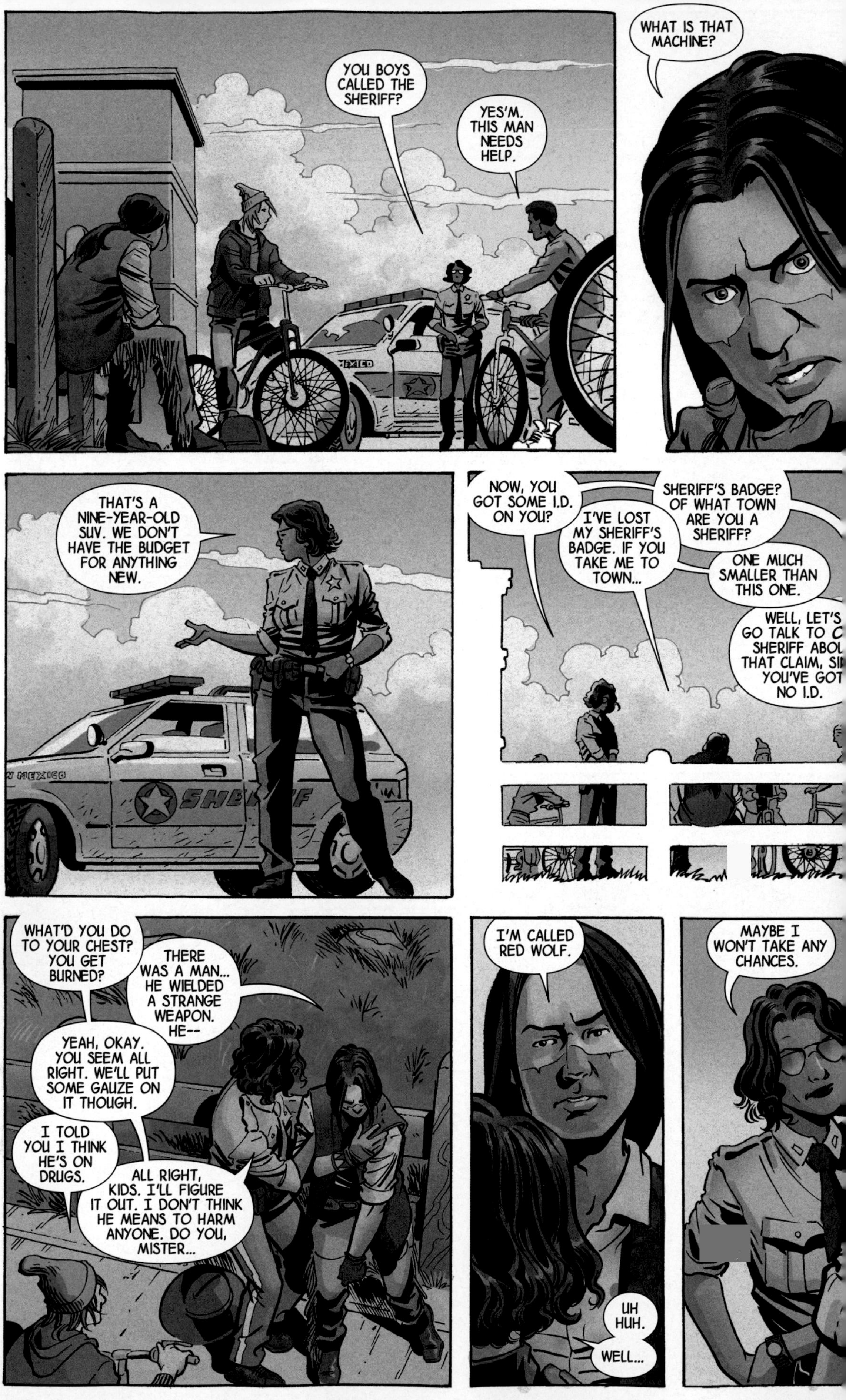
YOU BOYS CALLED THE SHERIFF?
YES'M. THIS MAN NEEDS HELP.
WHAT IS THAT MACHINE?
THAT'S A NINE-YEAR-OLD SUV. WE DON'T HAVE THE BUDGET FOR ANYTHING NEW.
NOW, YOU GOT SOME I.D. ON YOU?
I'VE LOST MY SHERIFF'S BADGE. IF YOU TAKE ME TO TOWN...
SHERIFF'S BADGE? OF WHAT TOWN ARE YOU A SHERIFF?
ONE MUCH SMALLER THAN THIS ONE.
WELL, LET'S GO TALK TO C SHERIFF ABOL THAT CLAIM, SI YOU'VE GOT NO I.D.
WHAT'D YOU DO TO YOUR CHEST? YOU GET BURNED?
THERE WAS A MAN... HE WIELDED A STRANGE WEAPON. HE--
YEAH, OKAY. YOU SEEM ALL RIGHT. WE'LL PUT SOME GAUZE ON IT THOUGH.
I TOLD YOU I THINK HE'S ON DRUGS.
ALL RIGHT, KIDS. I'LL FIGURE IT OUT. I DON'T THINK HE MEANS TO HARM ANYONE. DO YOU, MISTER...
I'M CALLED RED WOLF.
UH HUH.
WELL...
MAYBE I WON'T TAKE ANY CHANCES.

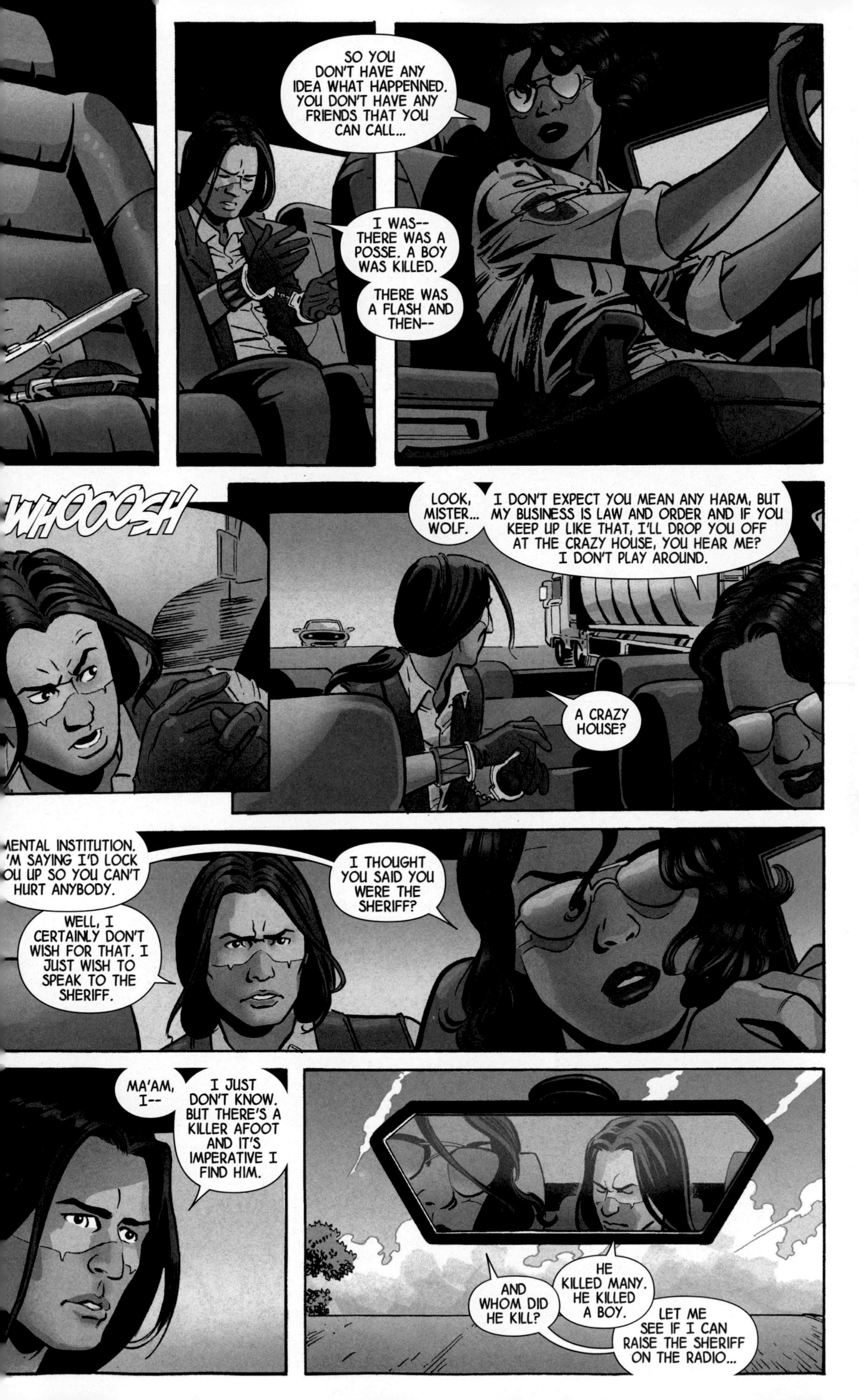
SO YOU DON'T HAVE ANY IDEA WHAT HAPPENNED. YOU DON'T HAVE ANY FRIENDS THAT YOU CAN CALL...
I WAS-- THERE WAS A POSSE. A BOY WAS KILLED.
THERE WAS A FLASH AND THEN--
WHOOOSH
LOOK, MISTER... WOLF.
I DON'T EXPECT YOU MEAN ANY HARM, BUT MY BUSINESS IS LAW AND ORDER AND IF YOU KEEP UP LIKE THAT, I'LL DROP YOU OFF AT THE CRAZY HOUSE, YOU HEAR ME? I DON'T PLAY AROUND.
A CRAZY HOUSE?
MENTAL INSTITUTION. I'M SAYING I'D LOCK YOU UP SO YOU CAN'T HURT ANYBODY.
WELL, I CERTAINLY DON'T WISH FOR THAT. I JUST WISH TO SPEAK TO THE SHERIFF.
I THOUGHT YOU SAID YOU WERE THE SHERIFF?
MA'AM, I--
I JUST DON'T KNOW. BUT THERE'S A KILLER AFOOT AND IT'S IMPERATIVE I FIND HIM.
AND WHOM DID HE KILL?
HE KILLED MANY. HE KILLED A BOY.
LET ME SEE IF I CAN RAISE THE SHERIFF ON THE RADIO...

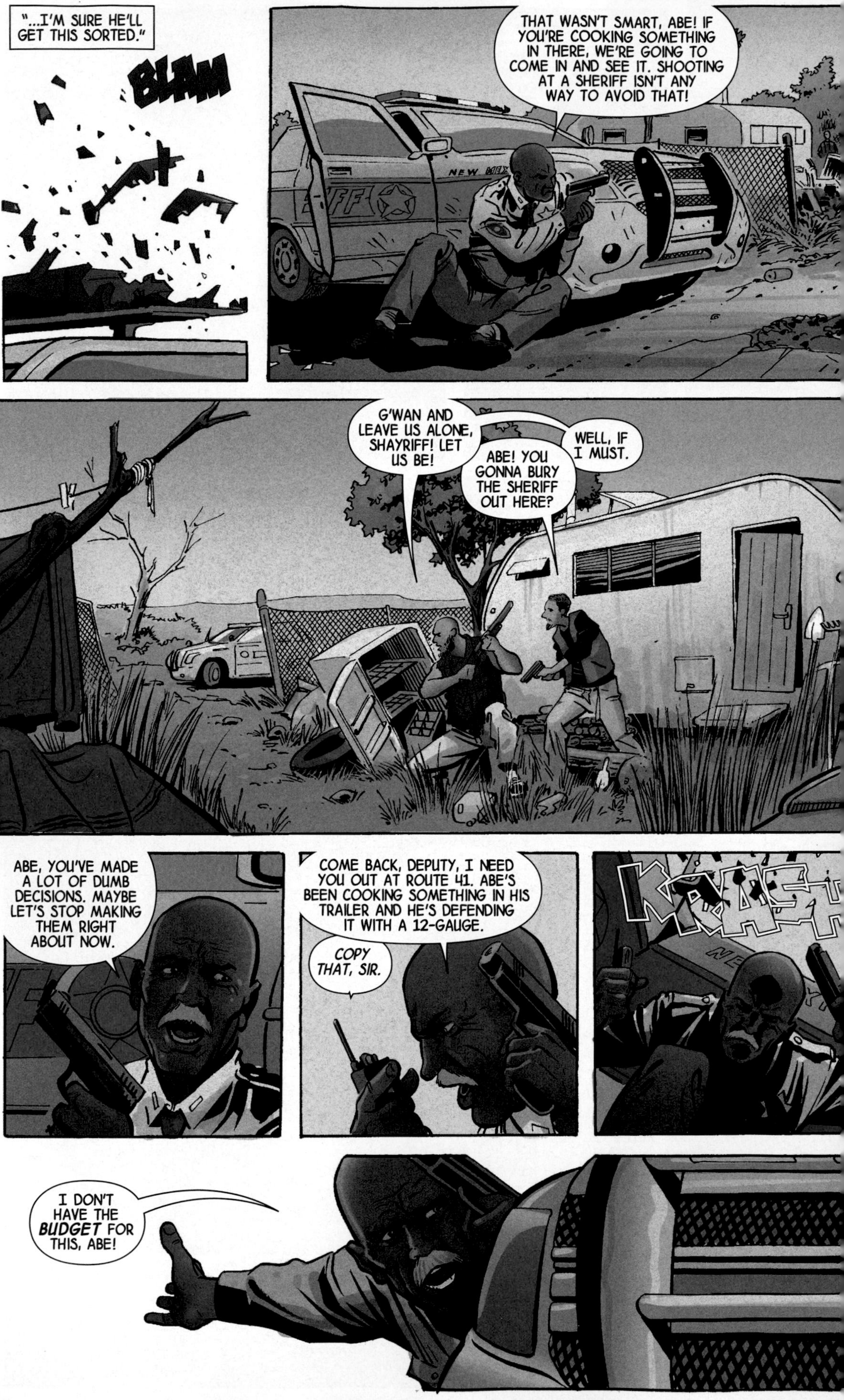
"...I'M SURE HE'LL GET THIS SORTED."
BLAM
THAT WASN'T SMART, ABE! IF YOU'RE COOKING SOMETHING IN THERE, WE'RE GOING TO COME IN AND SEE IT. SHOOTING AT A SHERIFF ISN'T ANY WAY TO AVOID THAT!
G'WAN AND LEAVE US ALONE, SHAYRIFF! LET US BE!
ABE! YOU GONNA BURY THE SHERIFF OUT HERE?
WELL, IF I MUST.
ABE, YOU'VE MADE A LOT OF DUMB DECISIONS. MAYBE LET'S STOP MAKING THEM RIGHT ABOUT NOW.
COME BACK, DEPUTY, I NEED YOU OUT AT ROUTE 41. ABE'S BEEN COOKING SOMETHING IN HIS TRAILER AND HE'S DEFENDING IT WITH A 12-GAUGE.
COPY THAT, SIR.
KRASH
I DON'T HAVE THE BUDGET FOR THIS, ABE!

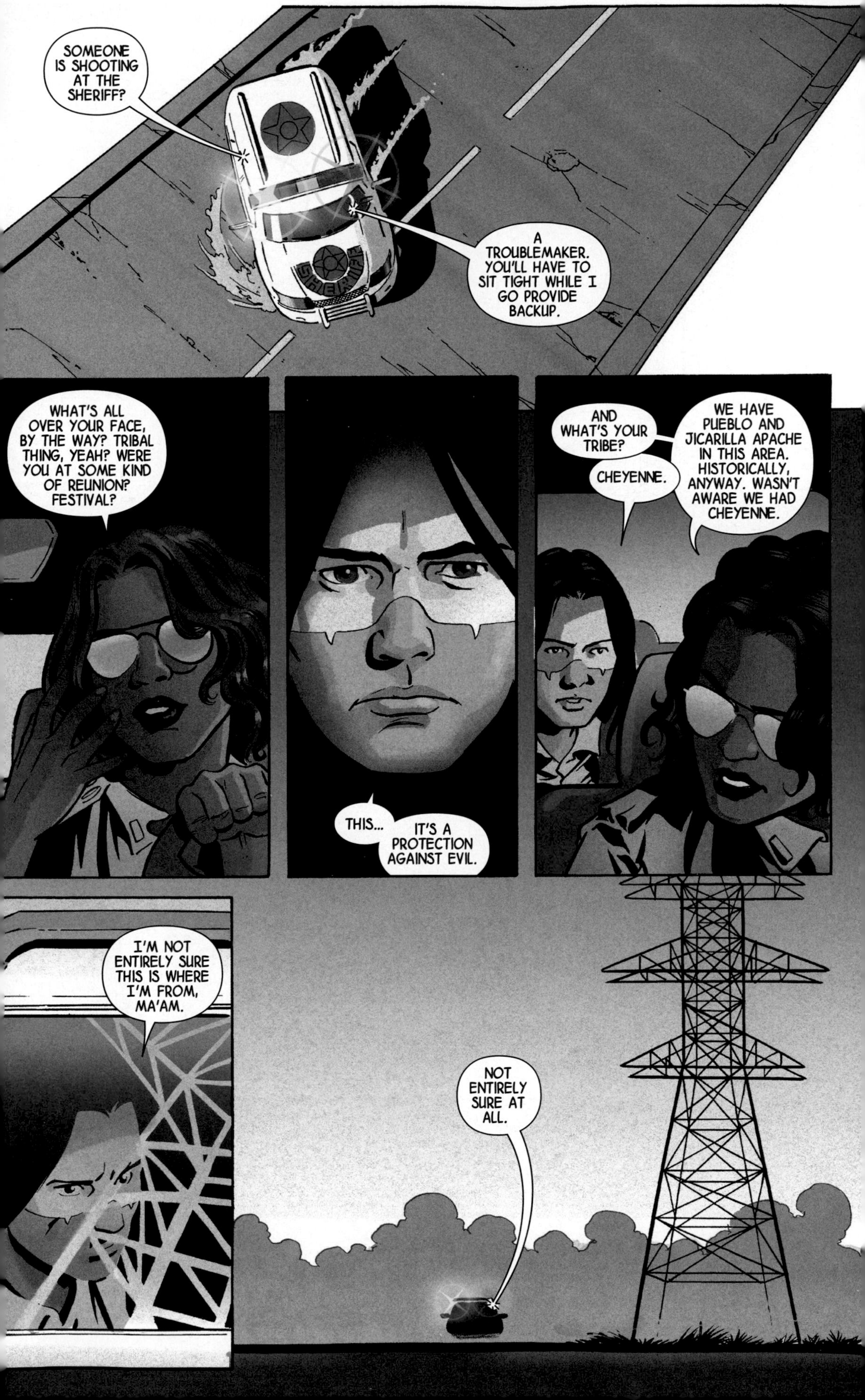
SOMEONE IS SHOOTING AT THE SHERIFF?
A TROUBLEMAKER. YOU'LL HAVE TO SIT TIGHT WHILE I GO PROVIDE BACKUP.
WHAT'S ALL OVER YOUR FACE, BY THE WAY? TRIBAL THING, YEAH? WERE YOU AT SOME KIND OF REUNION? FESTIVAL?
THIS...
IT'S A PROTECTION AGAINST EVIL.
AND WHAT'S YOUR TRIBE?
CHEYENNE.
WE HAVE PUEBLO AND JICARILLA APACHE IN THIS AREA. HISTORICALLY, ANYWAY. WASN'T AWARE WE HAD CHEYENNE.
I'M NOT ENTIRELY SURE THIS IS WHERE I'M FROM, MA'AM.
NOT ENTIRELY SURE AT ALL.

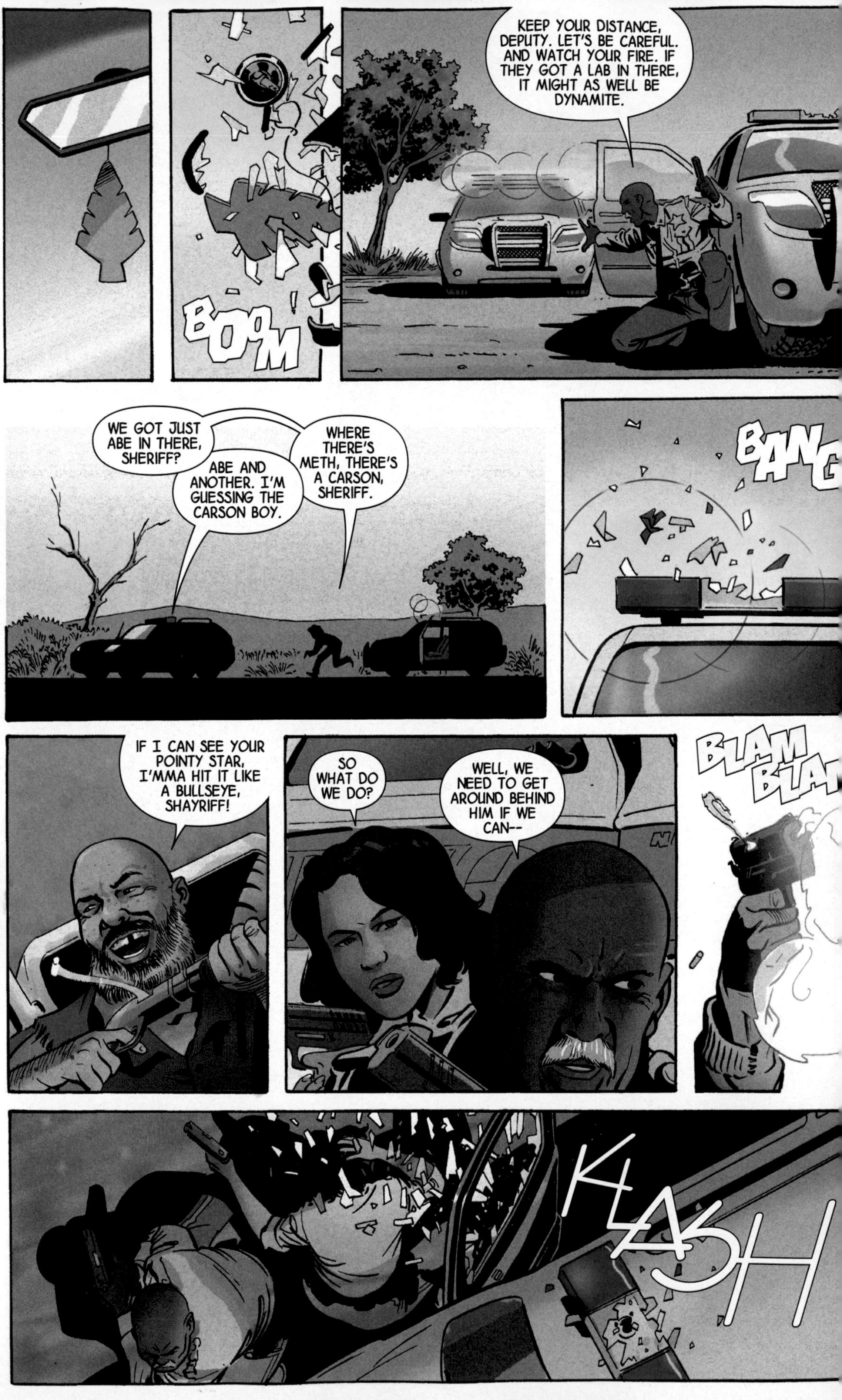
BOOM
KEEP YOUR DISTANCE, DEPUTY. LET'S BE CAREFUL. AND WATCH YOUR FIRE. IF THEY GOT A LAB IN THERE, IT MIGHT AS WELL BE DYNAMITE.
WE GOT JUST ABE IN THERE, SHERIFF?
ABE AND ANOTHER. I'M GUESSING THE CARSON BOY.
WHERE THERE'S METH, THERE'S A CARSON, SHERIFF.
BANG
IF I CAN SEE YOUR POINTY STAR, I'MMA HIT IT LIKE A BULLSEYE, SHAYRIFF!
SO WHAT DO WE DO?
WELL, WE NEED TO GET AROUND BEHIND HIM IF WE CAN--
BLAM
KLASH

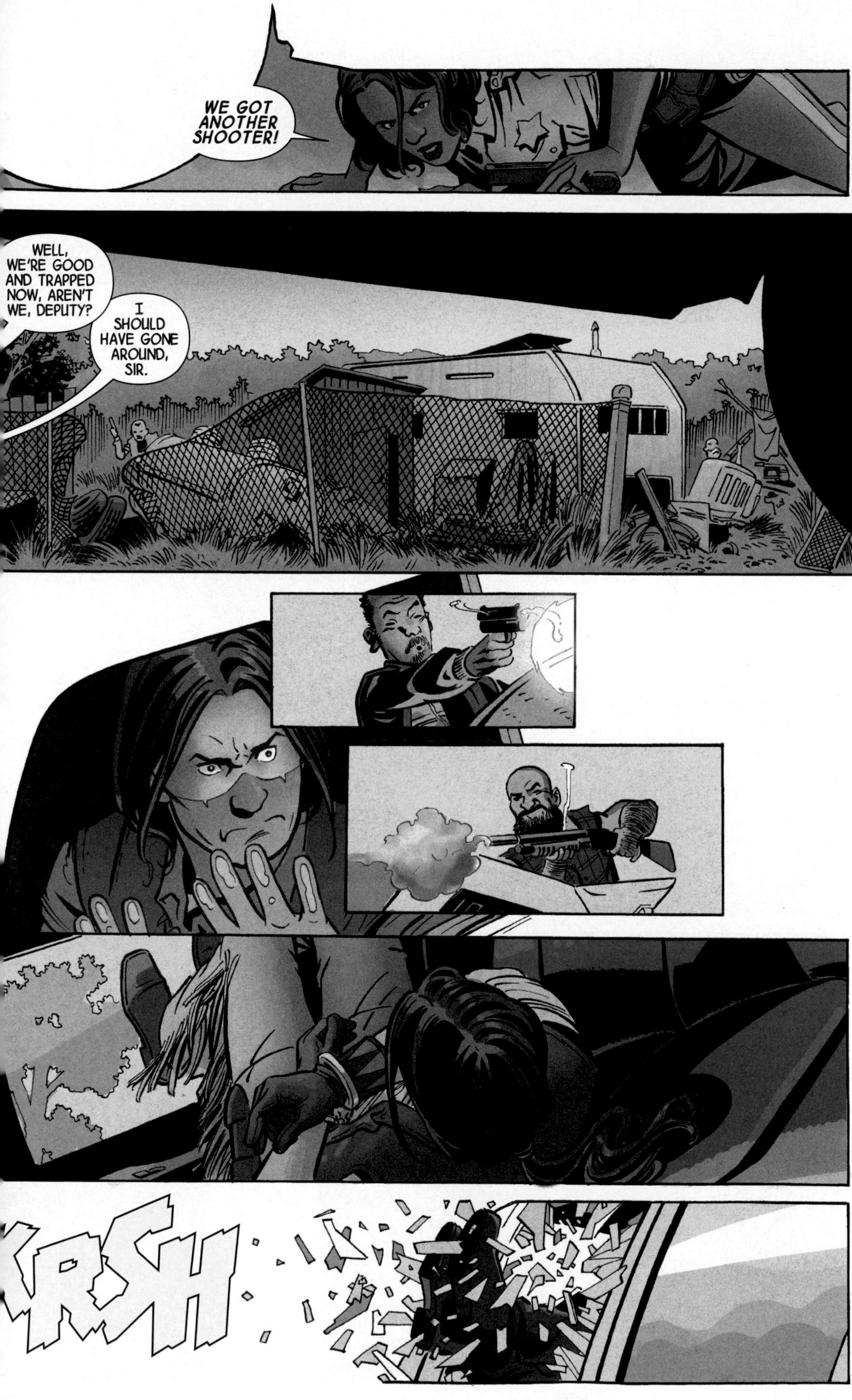
WE GOT ANOTHER SHOOTER!
WELL, WE'RE GOOD AND TRAPPED NOW, AREN'T WE, DEPUTY?
I SHOULD HAVE GONE AROUND, SIR.
KRSH

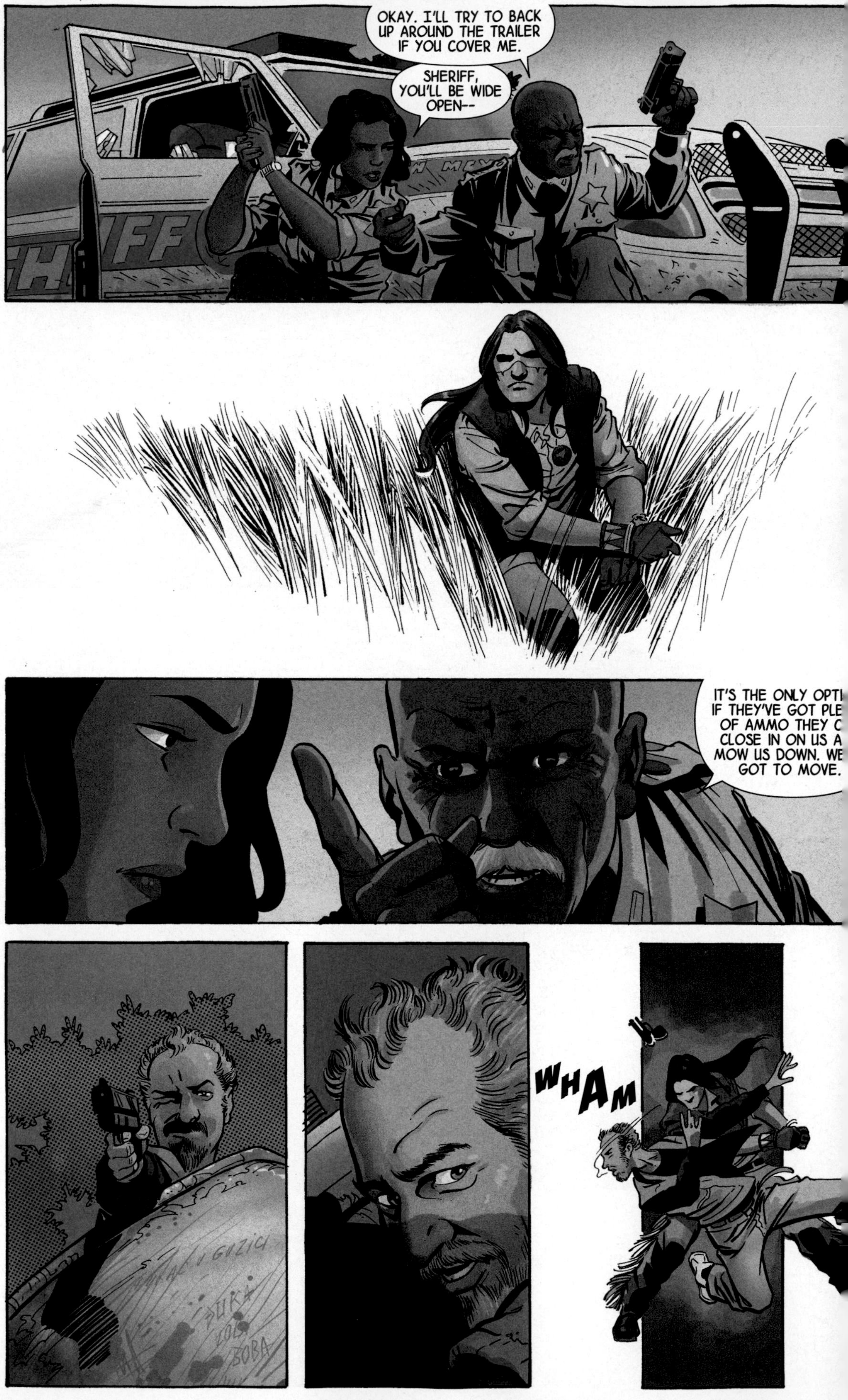
OKAY. I'LL TRY TO BACK UP AROUND THE TRAILER IF YOU COVER ME.
SHERIFF, YOU'LL BE WIDE OPEN--
IT'S THE ONLY OPTI
IF THEY'VE GOT PLE
OF AMMO THEY C
CLOSE IN ON US A
MOW US DOWN. WE
GOT TO MOVE.
WHAM

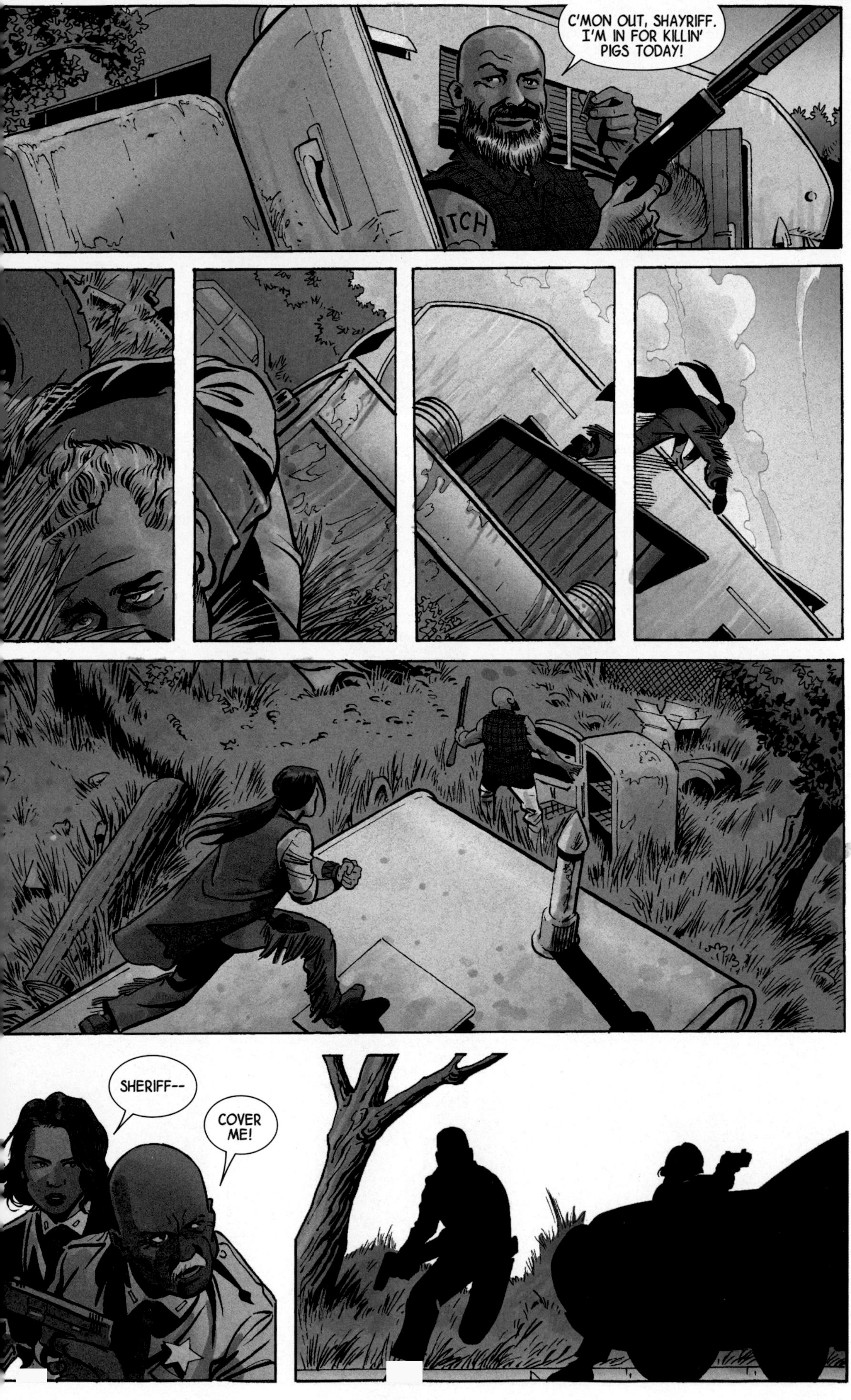
C'MON OUT, SHAYRIFF. I'M IN FOR KILLIN' PIGS TODAY!
ITCH
SHERIFF--
COVER ME!

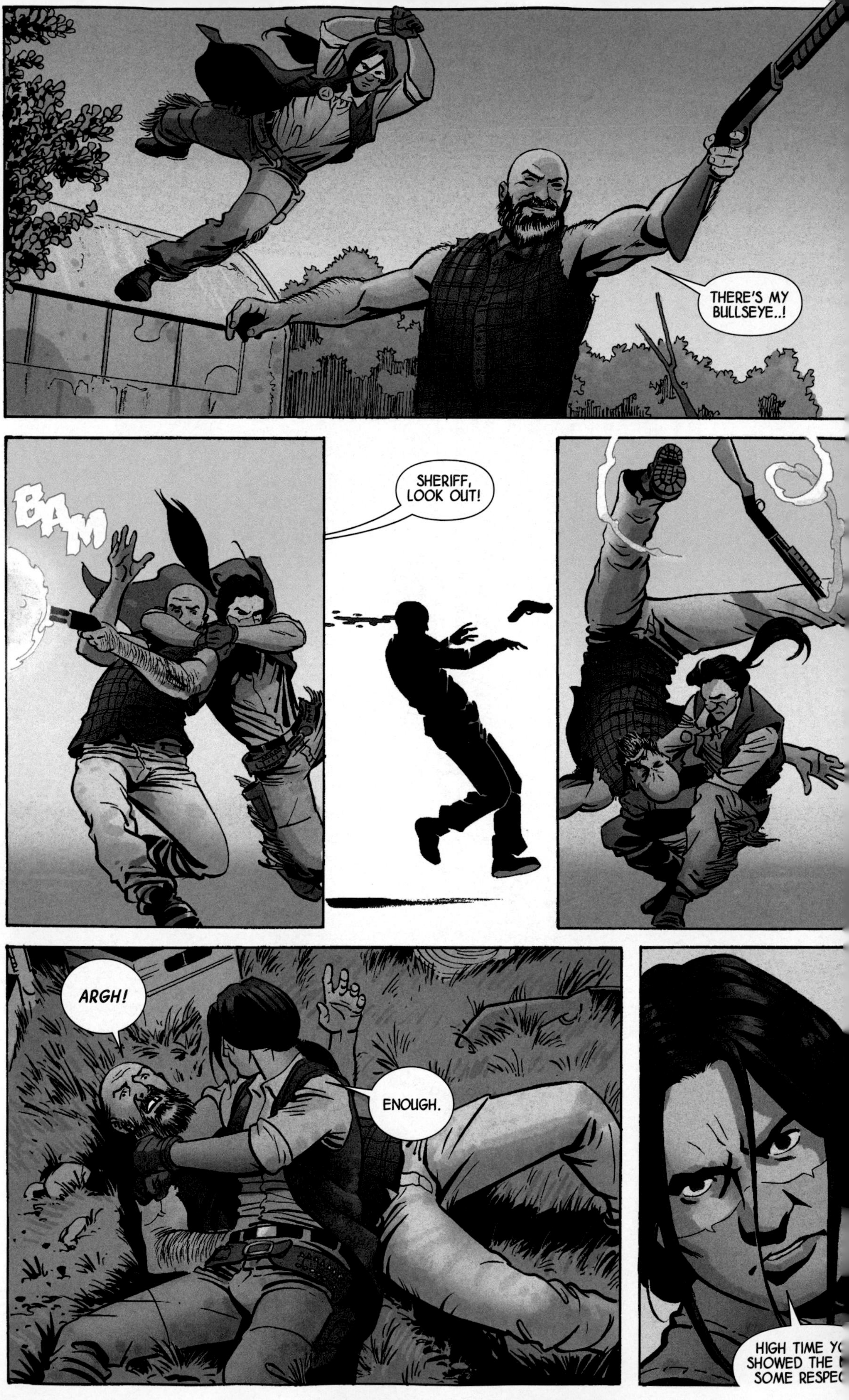
THERE'S MY BULLSEYE..!
BAM
SHERIFF, LOOK OUT!
ARGH!
ENOUGH.
HIGH TIME
SHOWED THE
SOME

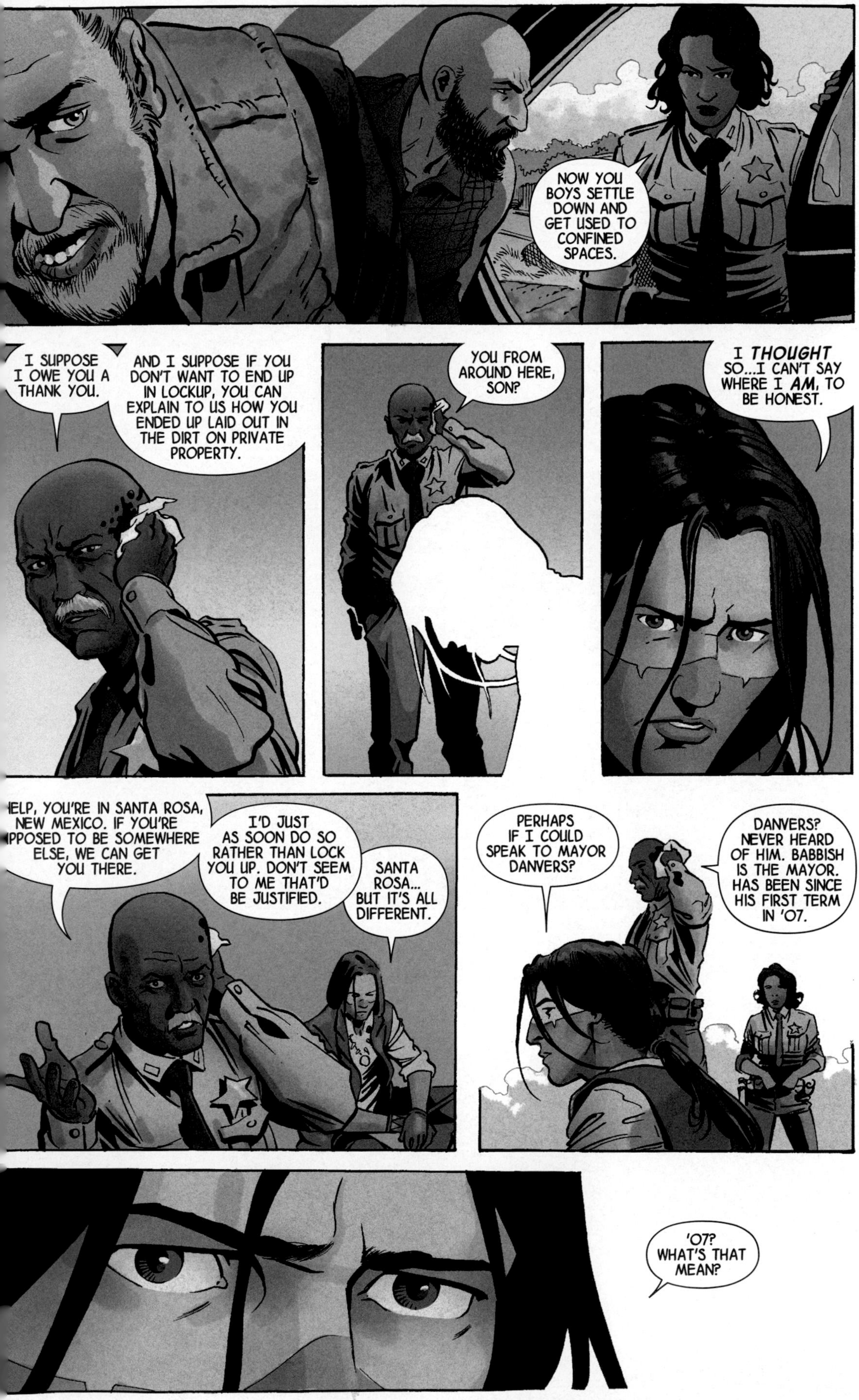
NOW YOU BOYS SETTLE DOWN AND GET USED TO CONFINED SPACES.
I SUPPOSE I OWE YOU A THANK YOU.
AND I SUPPOSE IF YOU DON'T WANT TO END UP IN LOCKUP, YOU CAN EXPLAIN TO US HOW YOU ENDED UP LAID OUT IN THE DIRT ON PRIVATE PROPERTY.
YOU FROM AROUND HERE, SON?
I THOUGHT SO...I CAN'T SAY WHERE I AM, TO BE HONEST.
IELP, YOU'RE IN SANTA ROSA, NEW MEXICO. IF YOU'RE IPPOSED TO BE SOMEWHERE ELSE, WE CAN GET YOU THERE.
I'D JUST AS SOON DO SO RATHER THAN LOCK YOU UP. DON'T SEEM TO ME THAT'D BE JUSTIFIED.
SANTA ROSA... BUT IT'S ALL DIFFERENT.
PERHAPS IF I COULD SPEAK TO MAYOR DANVERS?
DANVERS? NEVER HEARD OF HIM. BABBISH IS THE MAYOR. HAS BEEN SINCE HIS FIRST TERM IN '07.
'07? WHAT'S THAT MEAN?

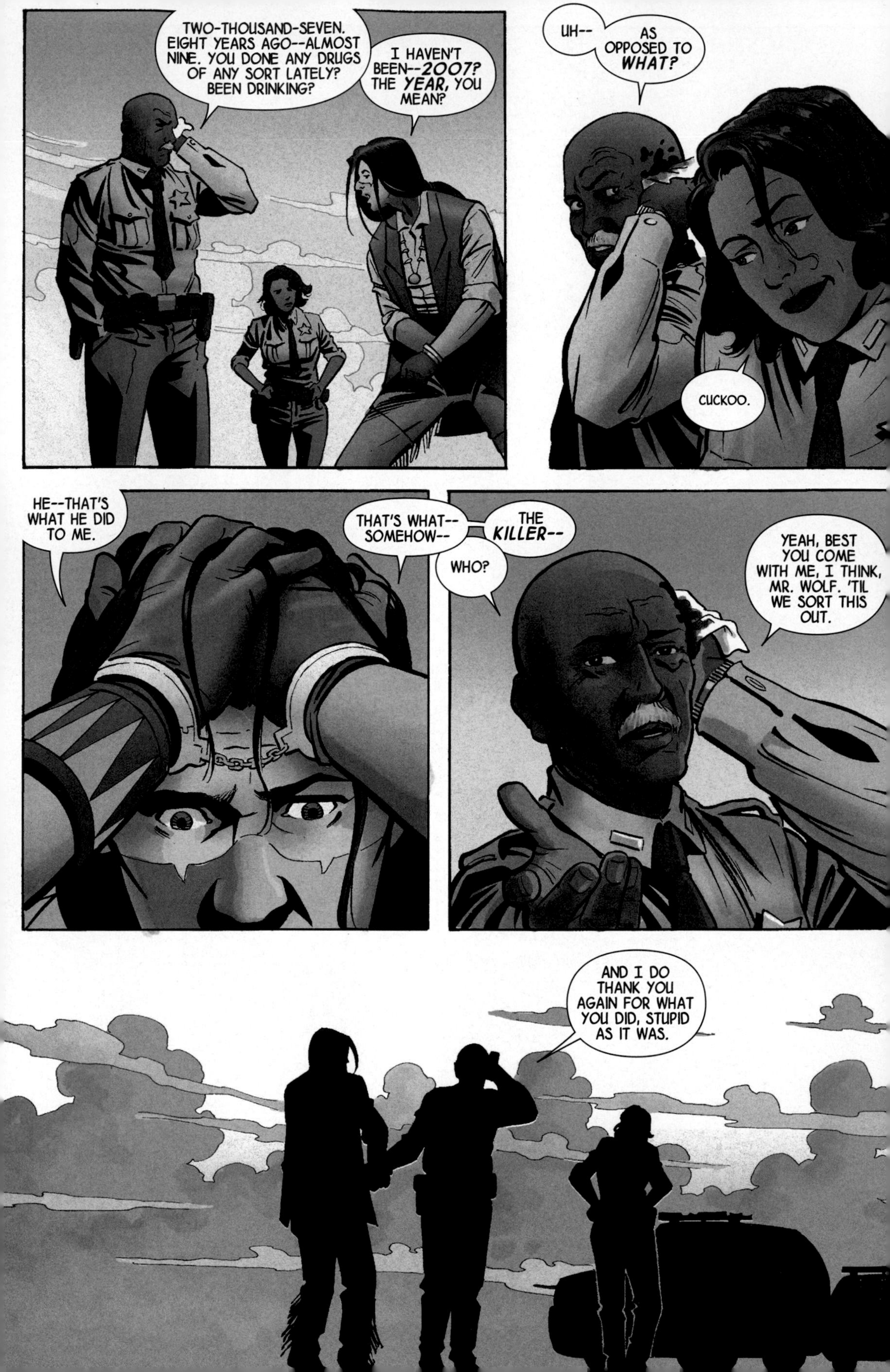
TWO-THOUSAND-SEVEN. EIGHT YEARS AGO--ALMOST NINE. YOU DONE ANY DRUGS OF ANY SORT LATELY? BEEN DRINKING?
I HAVEN'T BEEN--2007? THE YEAR, YOU MEAN?
UH--
AS OPPOSED TO WHAT?
CUCKOO.
HE--THAT'S WHAT HE DID TO ME.
THAT'S WHAT-- SOMEHOW--
THE KILLER--
WHO?
YEAH, BEST YOU COME WITH ME, I THINK, MR. WOLF. 'TIL WE SORT THIS OUT.
AND I DO THANK YOU AGAIN FOR WHAT YOU DID, STUPID AS IT WAS.

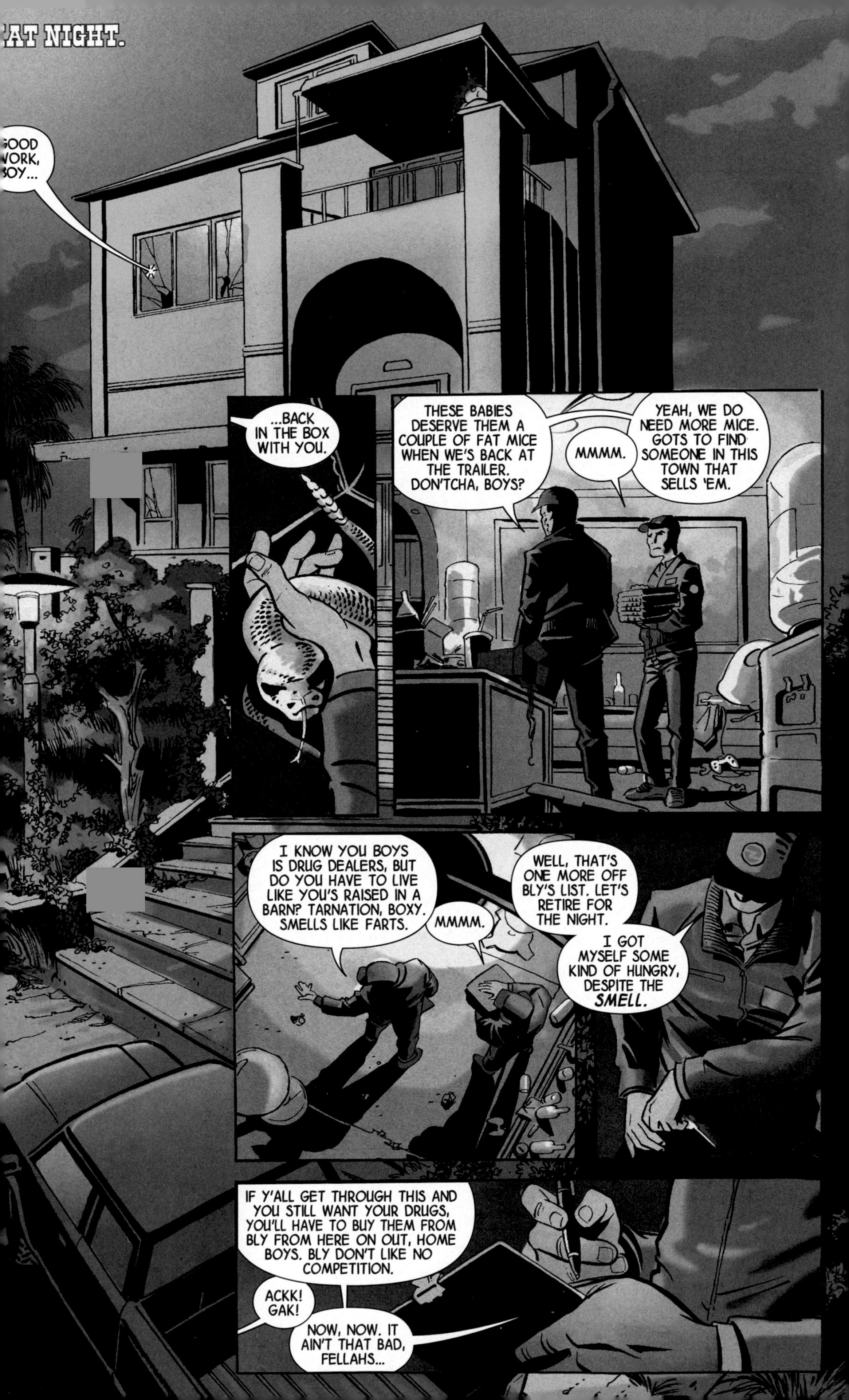
AT NIGHT.
GOOD WORK, BOY...
...BACK IN THE BOX WITH YOU.
THESE BABIES DESERVE THEM A COUPLE OF FAT MICE WHEN WE'S BACK AT THE TRAILER. DON'TCHA, BOYS?
MMMM.
YEAH, WE DO NEED MORE MICE. GOTS TO FIND SOMEONE IN THIS TOWN THAT SELLS 'EM.
I KNOW YOU BOYS IS DRUG DEALERS, BUT DO YOU HAVE TO LIVE LIKE YOU'S RAISED IN A BARN? TARNATION, BOXY. SMELLS LIKE FARTS.
MMMM.
WELL, THAT'S ONE MORE OFF BLY'S LIST. LET'S RETIRE FOR THE NIGHT.
I GOT MYSELF SOME KIND OF HUNGRY, DESPITE THE SMELL.
IF Y'ALL GET THROUGH THIS AND YOU STILL WANT YOUR DRUGS, YOU'LL HAVE TO BUY THEM FROM BLY FROM HERE ON OUT, HOME BOYS. BLY DON'T LIKE NO COMPETITION.
ACKK! GAK!
NOW, NOW. IT AIN'T THAT BAD, FELLAHS...

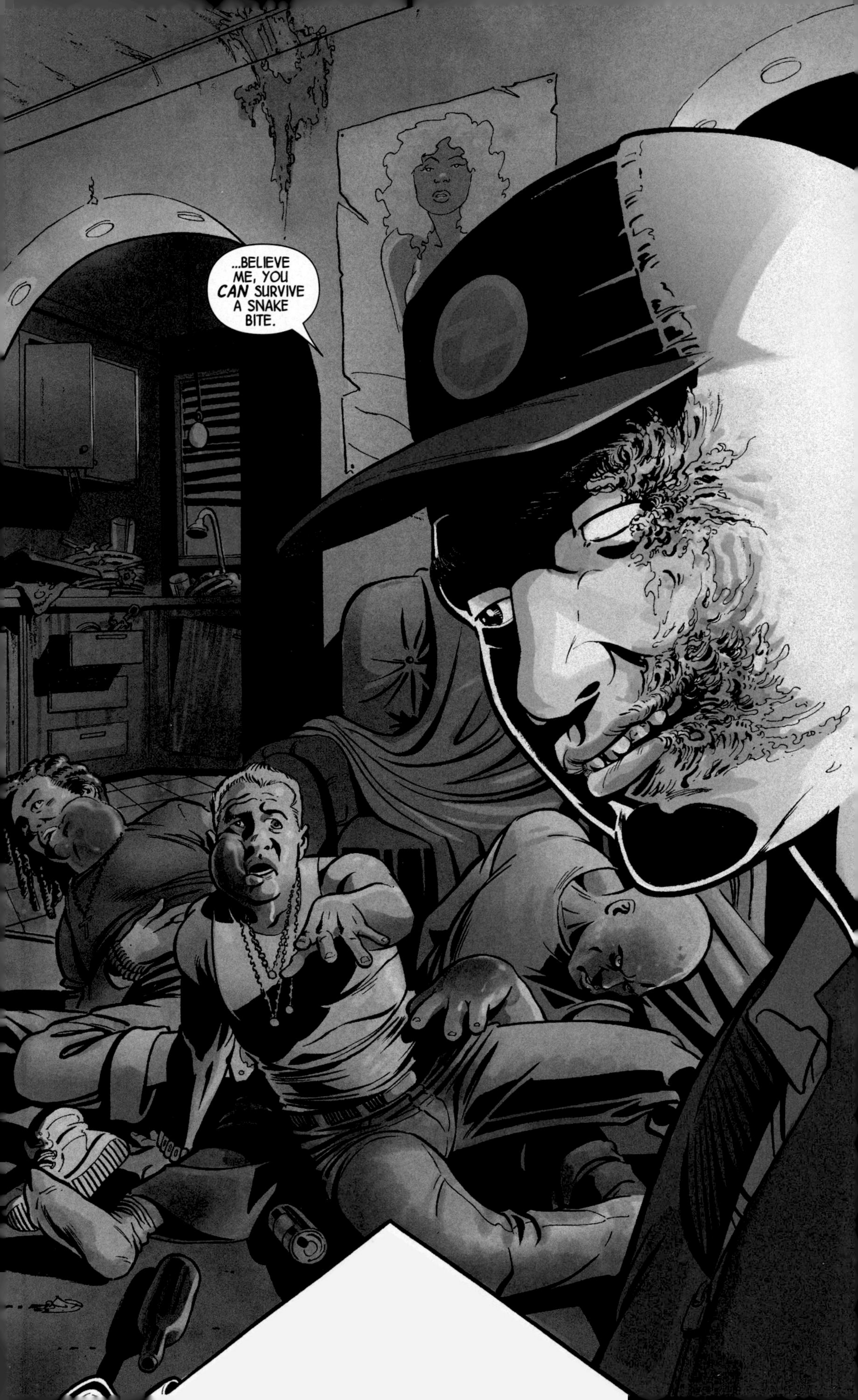
...BELIEVE ME, YOU CAN SURVIVE A SNAKE BITE.

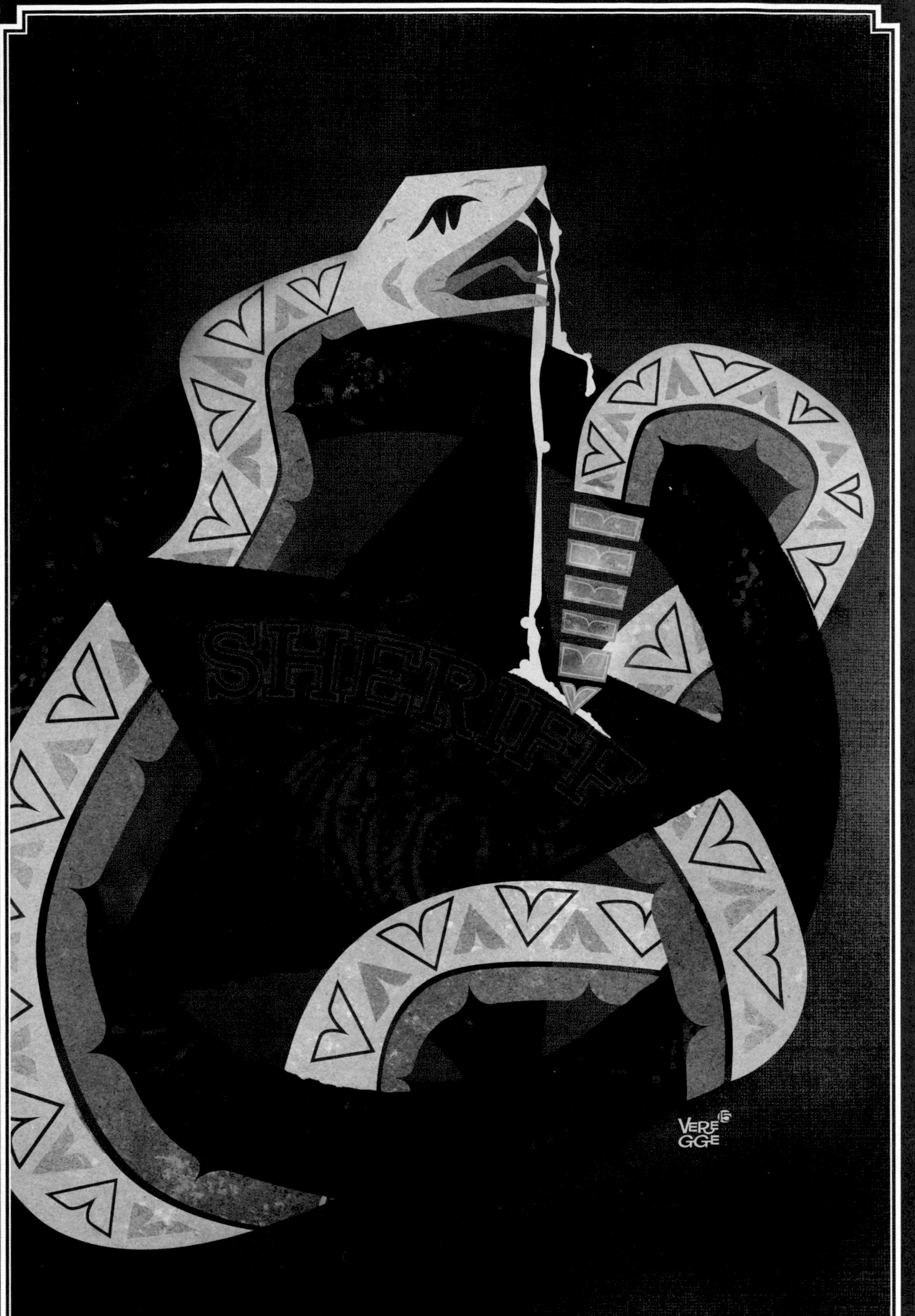
SHERIFF
VEREGGE

3

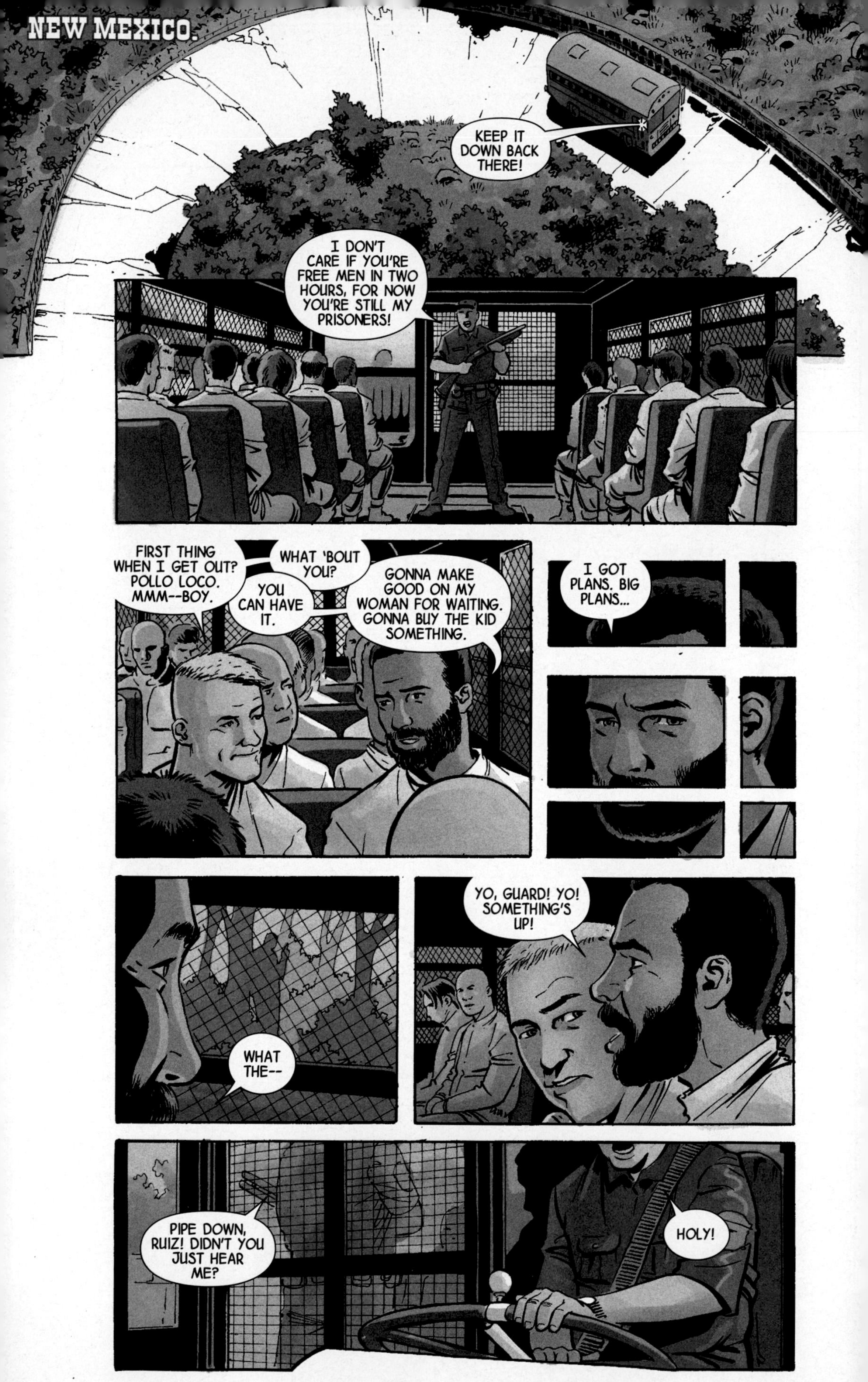
NEW MEXICO.
KEEP IT DOWN BACK THERE!
I DON'T CARE IF YOU'RE FREE MEN IN TWO HOURS, FOR NOW YOU'RE STILL MY PRISONERS!
FIRST THING WHEN I GET OUT? POLLO LOCO. MMM--BOY.
WHAT 'BOUT YOU?
YOU CAN HAVE IT.
GONNA MAKE GOOD ON MY WOMAN FOR WAITING. GONNA BUY THE KID SOMETHING.
I GOT PLANS. BIG PLANS...
WHAT THE--
YO, GUARD! YO! SOMETHING'S UP!
PIPE DOWN, RUIZ! DIDN'T YOU JUST HEAR ME?
HOLY!

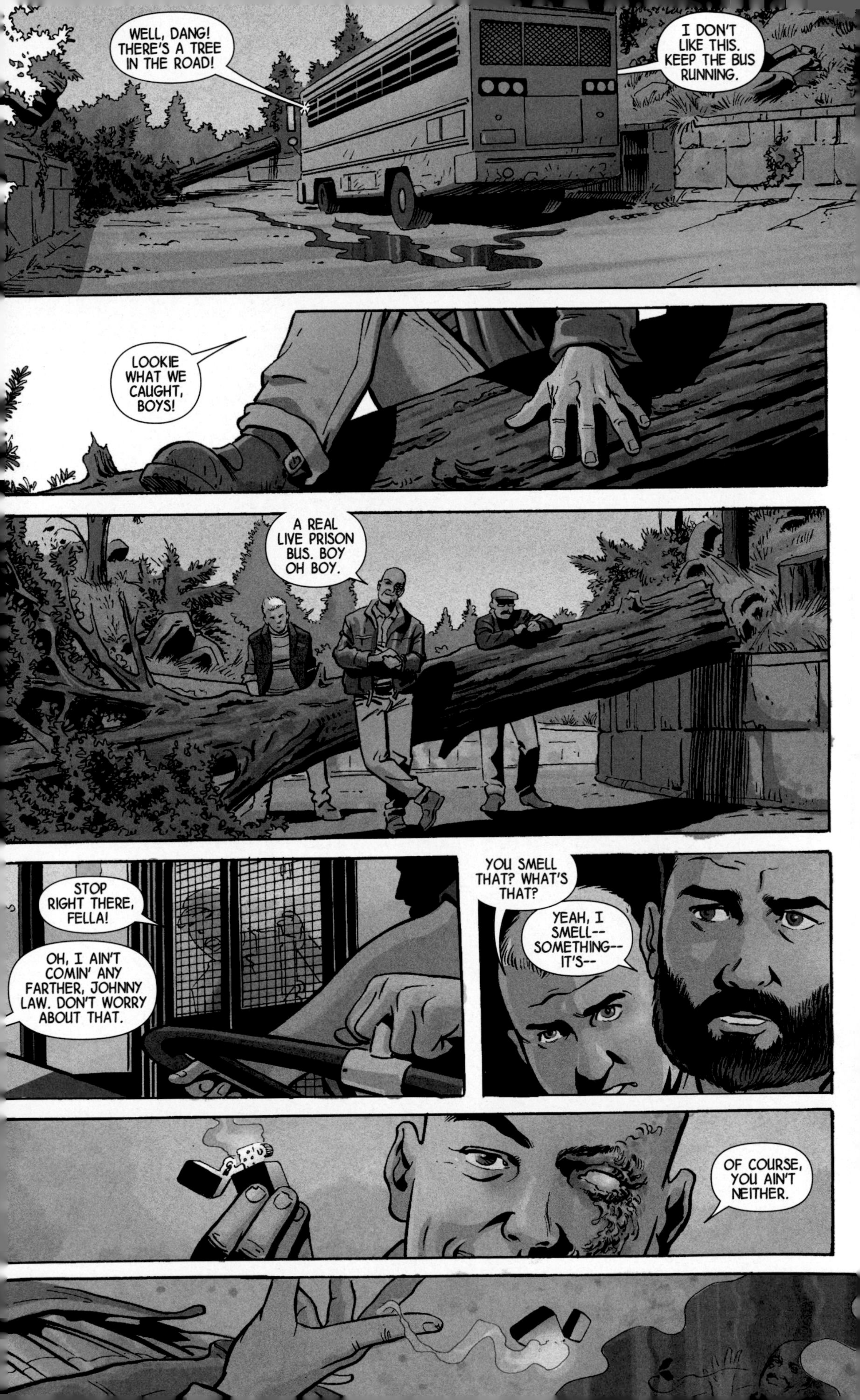
WELL, DANG! THERE'S A TREE IN THE ROAD!
I DON'T LIKE THIS. KEEP THE BUS RUNNING.
LOOKIE WHAT WE CAUGHT, BOYS!
A REAL LIVE PRISON BUS. BOY OH BOY.
STOP RIGHT THERE, FELLA!
OH, I AIN'T COMIN' ANY FARTHER, JOHNNY LAW. DON'T WORRY ABOUT THAT.
YOU SMELL THAT? WHAT'S THAT?
YEAH, I SMELL-- SOMETHING-- IT'S--
OF COURSE, YOU AIN'T NEITHER.

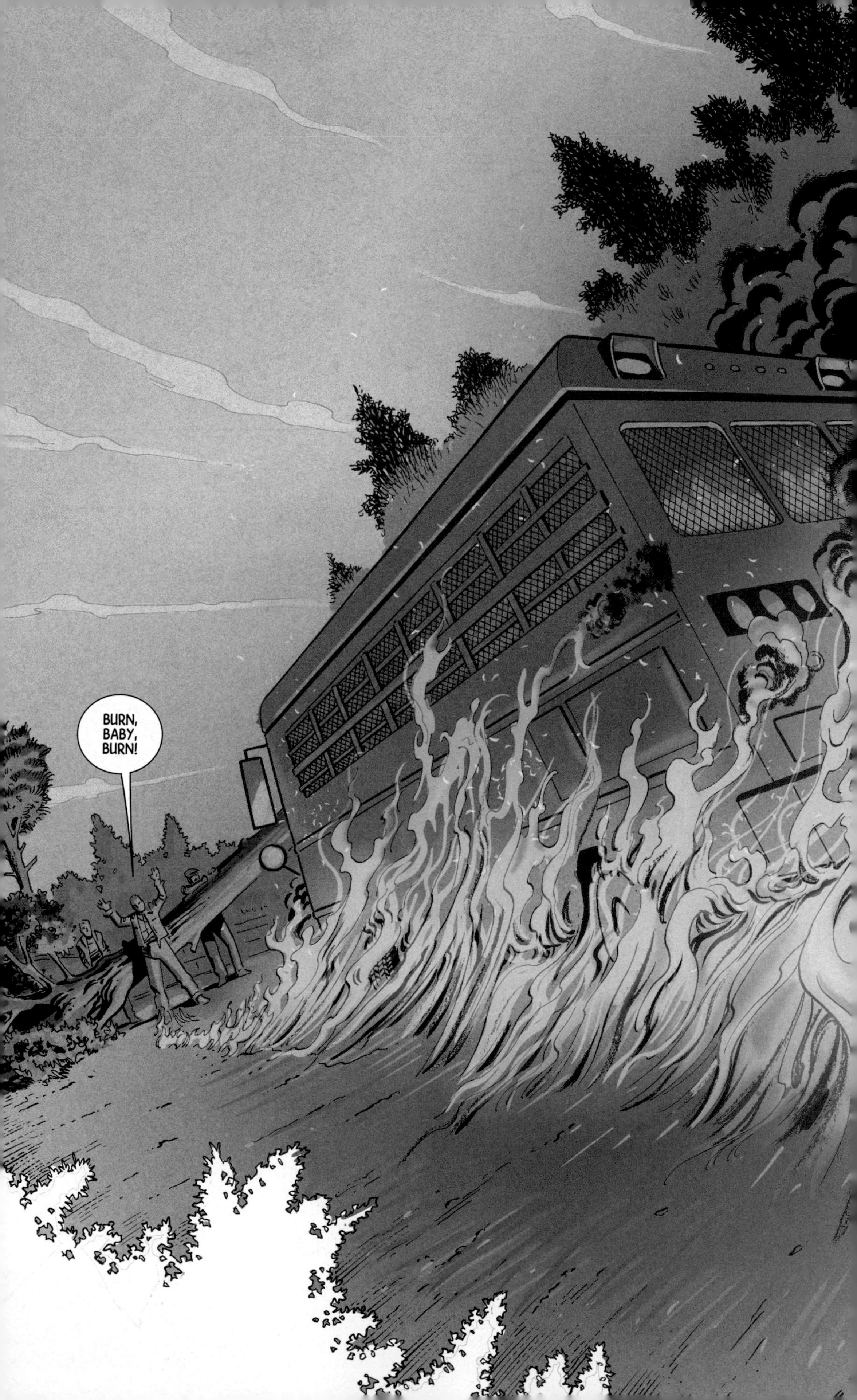
BURN, BABY, BURN!

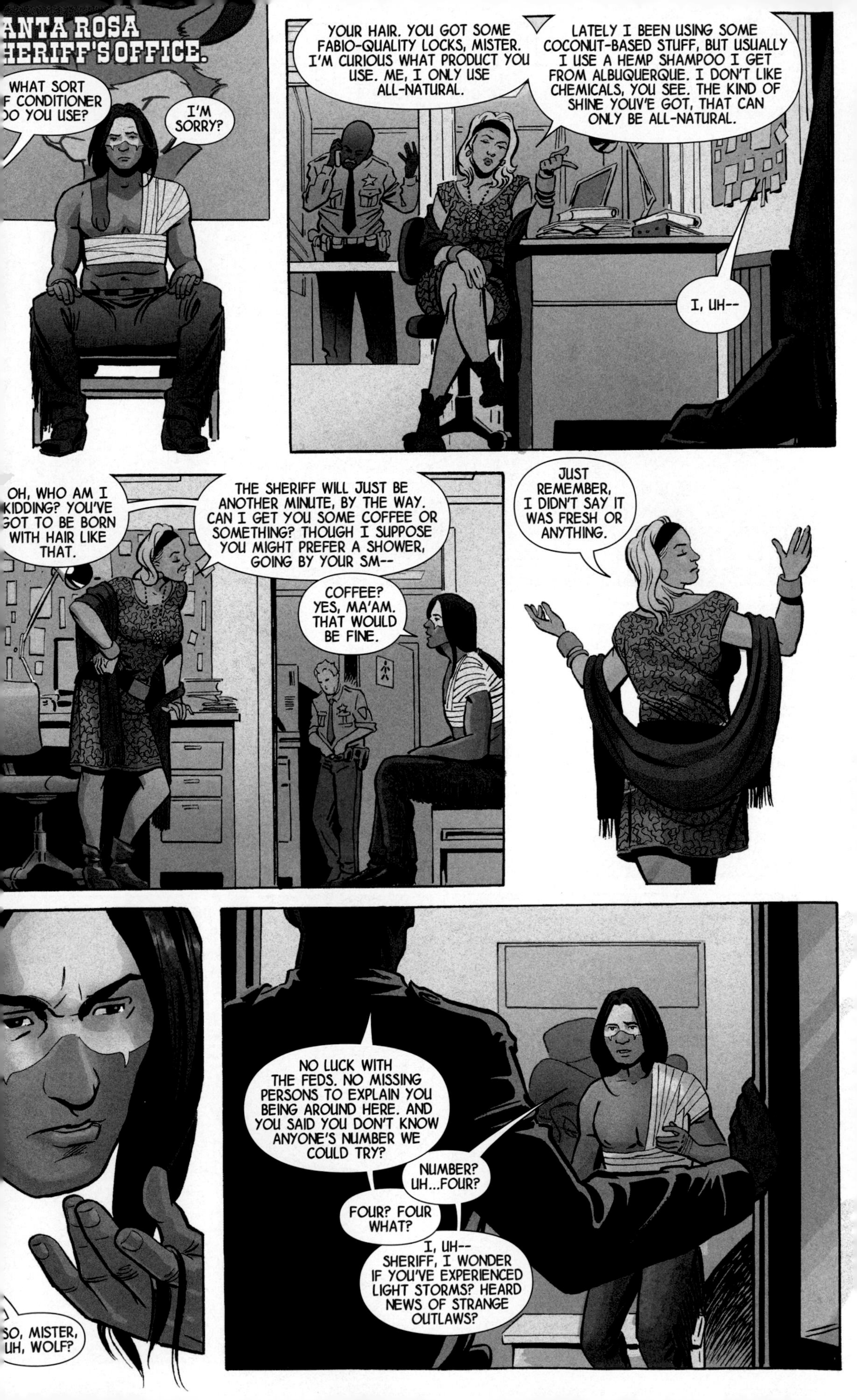
ANTA ROSA
HERIFF'S OFFICE.
WHAT SORT
F CONDITIONER
OO YOU USE?
I'M SORRY?
YOUR HAIR. YOU GOT SOME FABIO-QUALITY LOCKS, MISTER. I'M CURIOUS WHAT PRODUCT YOU USE. ME, I ONLY USE ALL-NATURAL.
LATELY I BEEN USING SOME COCONUT-BASED STUFF, BUT USUALLY I USE A HEMP SHAMPOO I GET FROM ALBUQUERQUE. I DON'T LIKE CHEMICALS, YOU SEE. THE KIND OF SHINE YOUV'E GOT, THAT CAN ONLY BE ALL-NATURAL.
I, UH--
OH, WHO AM I KIDDING? YOU'VE GOT TO BE BORN WITH HAIR LIKE THAT.
THE SHERIFF WILL JUST BE ANOTHER MINUTE, BY THE WAY. CAN I GET YOU SOME COFFEE OR SOMETHING? THOUGH I SUPPOSE YOU MIGHT PREFER A SHOWER, GOING BY YOUR SM--
COFFEE? YES, MA'AM. THAT WOULD BE FINE.
JUST REMEMBER, I DIDN'T SAY IT WAS FRESH OR ANYTHING.
SO, MISTER, UH, WOLF?
NO LUCK WITH THE FEDS. NO MISSING PERSONS TO EXPLAIN YOU BEING AROUND HERE. AND YOU SAID YOU DON'T KNOW ANYONE'S NUMBER WE COULD TRY?
NUMBER? UH...FOUR?
FOUR? FOUR WHAT?
I, UH-- SHERIFF, I WONDER IF YOU'VE EXPERIENCED LIGHT STORMS? HEARD NEWS OF STRANGE OUTLAWS?

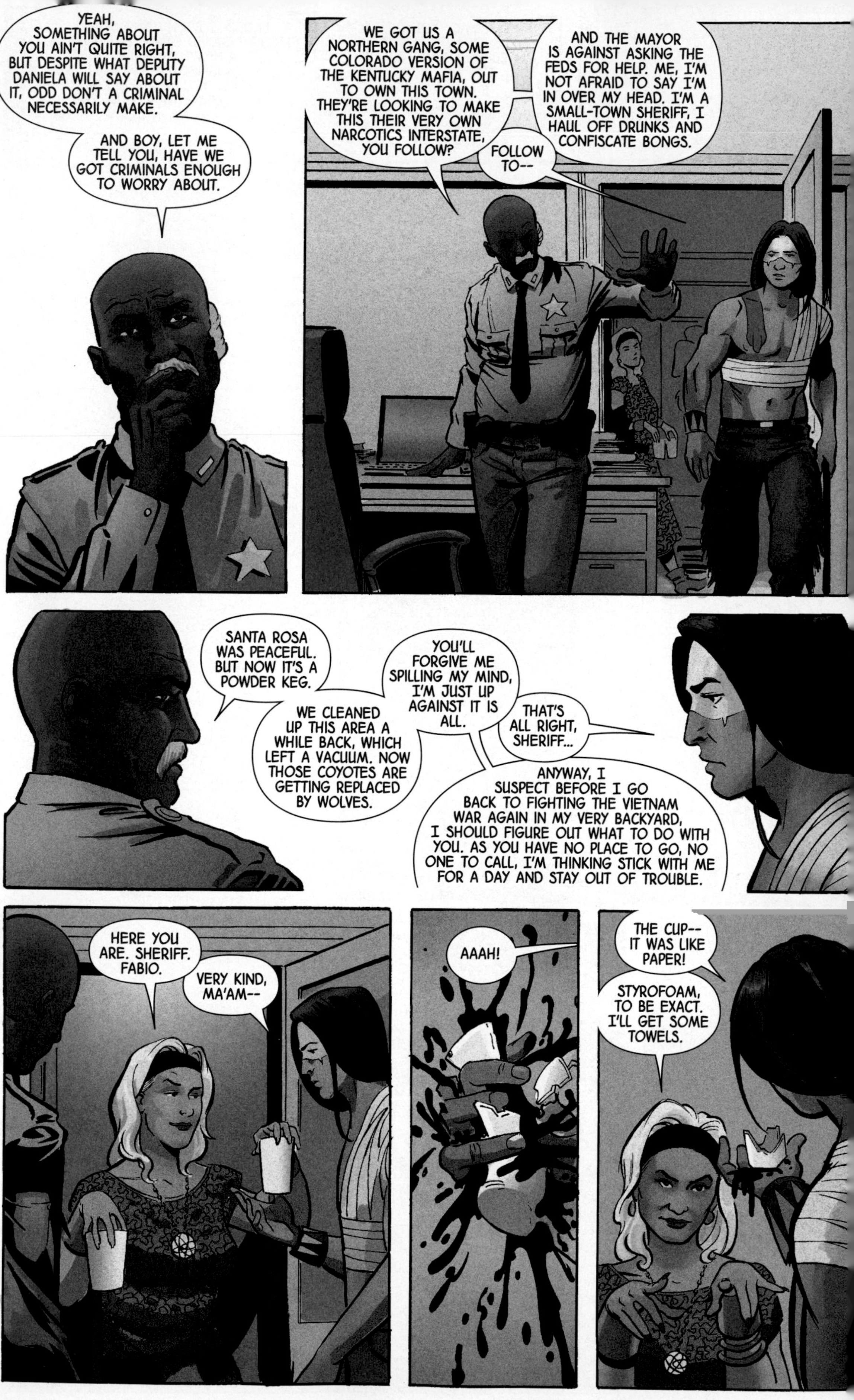
YEAH, SOMETHING ABOUT YOU AIN'T QUITE RIGHT, BUT DESPITE WHAT DEPUTY DANIELA WILL SAY ABOUT IT, ODD DON'T A CRIMINAL NECESSARILY MAKE.
AND BOY, LET ME TELL YOU, HAVE WE GOT CRIMINALS ENOUGH TO WORRY ABOUT.
WE GOT US A NORTHERN GANG, SOME COLORADO VERSION OF THE KENTUCKY MAFIA, OUT TO OWN THIS TOWN. THEY'RE LOOKING TO MAKE THIS THEIR VERY OWN NARCOTICS INTERSTATE, YOU FOLLOW?
FOLLOW TO--
AND THE MAYOR IS AGAINST ASKING THE FEDS FOR HELP. ME, I'M NOT AFRAID TO SAY I'M IN OVER MY HEAD. I'M A SMALL-TOWN SHERIFF, I HAUL OFF DRUNKS AND CONFISCATE BONGS.
SANTA ROSA WAS PEACEFUL. BUT NOW IT'S A POWDER KEG.
WE CLEANED UP THIS AREA A WHILE BACK, WHICH LEFT A VACUUM. NOW THOSE COYOTES ARE GETTING REPLACED BY WOLVES.
YOU'LL FORGIVE ME SPILLING MY MIND, I'M JUST UP AGAINST IT IS ALL.
THAT'S ALL RIGHT, SHERIFF...
ANYWAY, I SUSPECT BEFORE I GO BACK TO FIGHTING THE VIETNAM WAR AGAIN IN MY VERY BACKYARD, I SHOULD FIGURE OUT WHAT TO DO WITH YOU. AS YOU HAVE NO PLACE TO GO, NO ONE TO CALL, I'M THINKING STICK WITH ME FOR A DAY AND STAY OUT OF TROUBLE.
HERE YOU ARE. SHERIFF. FABIO.
VERY KIND, MA'AM--
AAAH!
THE CUP-- IT WAS LIKE PAPER!
STYROFOAM, TO BE EXACT. I'LL GET SOME TOWELS.

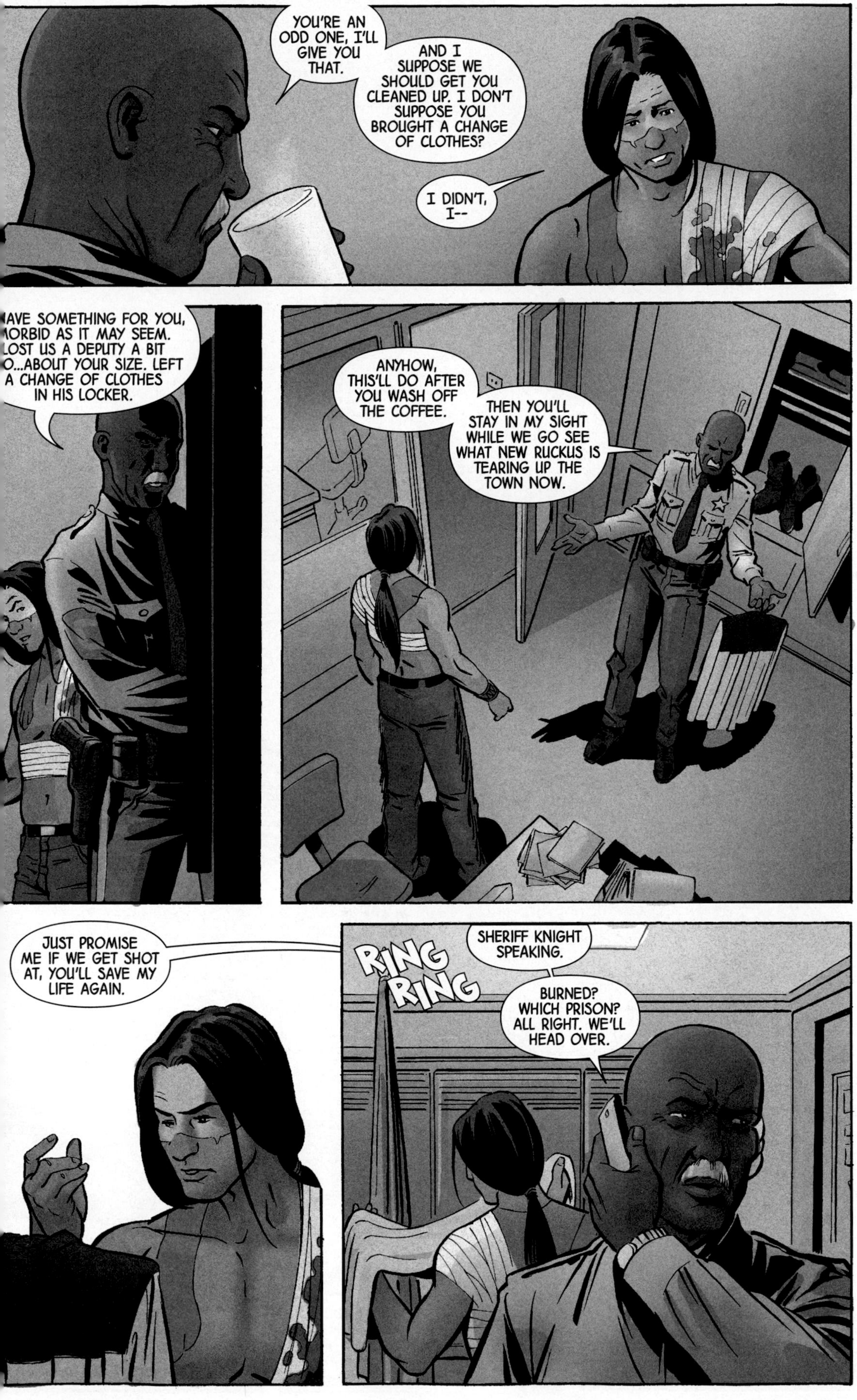
YOU'RE AN ODD ONE, I'LL GIVE YOU THAT.
AND I SUPPOSE WE SHOULD GET YOU CLEANED UP. I DON'T SUPPOSE YOU BROUGHT A CHANGE OF CLOTHES?
I DIDN'T, I--
AVE SOMETHING FOR YOU, MORBID AS IT MAY SEEM. LOST US A DEPUTY A BIT O...ABOUT YOUR SIZE. LEFT A CHANGE OF CLOTHES IN HIS LOCKER.
ANYHOW, THIS'LL DO AFTER YOU WASH OFF THE COFFEE.
THEN YOU'LL STAY IN MY SIGHT WHILE WE GO SEE WHAT NEW RUCKUS IS TEARING UP THE TOWN NOW.
JUST PROMISE ME IF WE GET SHOT AT, YOU'LL SAVE MY LIFE AGAIN.
RING RING
SHERIFF KNIGHT SPEAKING.
BURNED? WHICH PRISON? ALL RIGHT. WE'LL HEAD OVER.

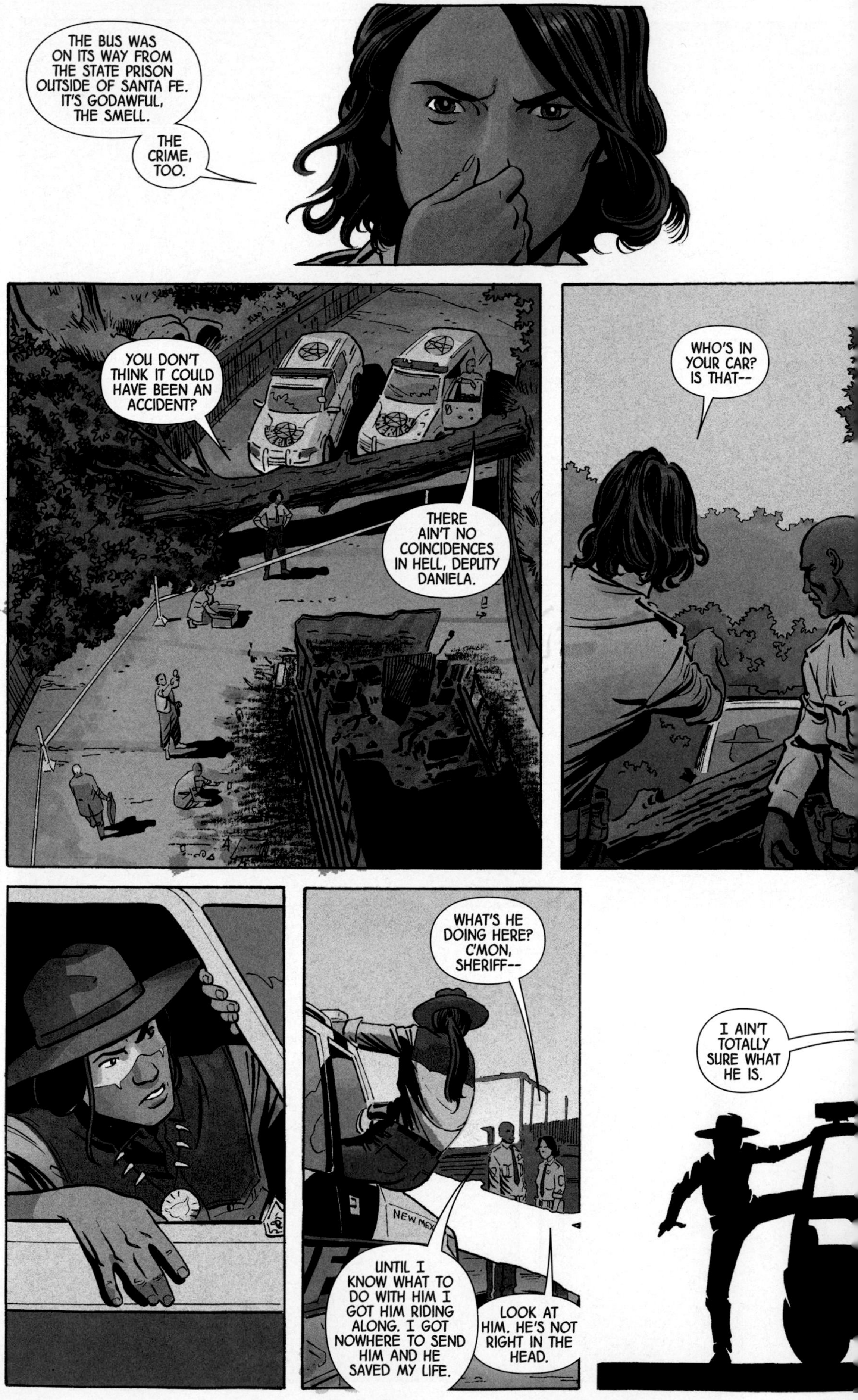
THE BUS WAS ON ITS WAY FROM THE STATE PRISON OUTSIDE OF SANTA FE. IT'S GODAWFUL, THE SMELL.
THE CRIME, TOO.
YOU DON'T THINK IT COULD HAVE BEEN AN ACCIDENT?
THERE AIN'T NO COINCIDENCES IN HELL, DEPUTY DANIELA.
WHO'S IN YOUR CAR? IS THAT--
WHAT'S HE DOING HERE? C'MON, SHERIFF--
UNTIL I KNOW WHAT TO DO WITH HIM I GOT HIM RIDING ALONG. I GOT NOWHERE TO SEND HIM AND HE SAVED MY LIFE.
LOOK AT HIM. HE'S NOT RIGHT IN THE HEAD.
I AIN'T TOTALLY SURE WHAT HE IS.
NEW MEX

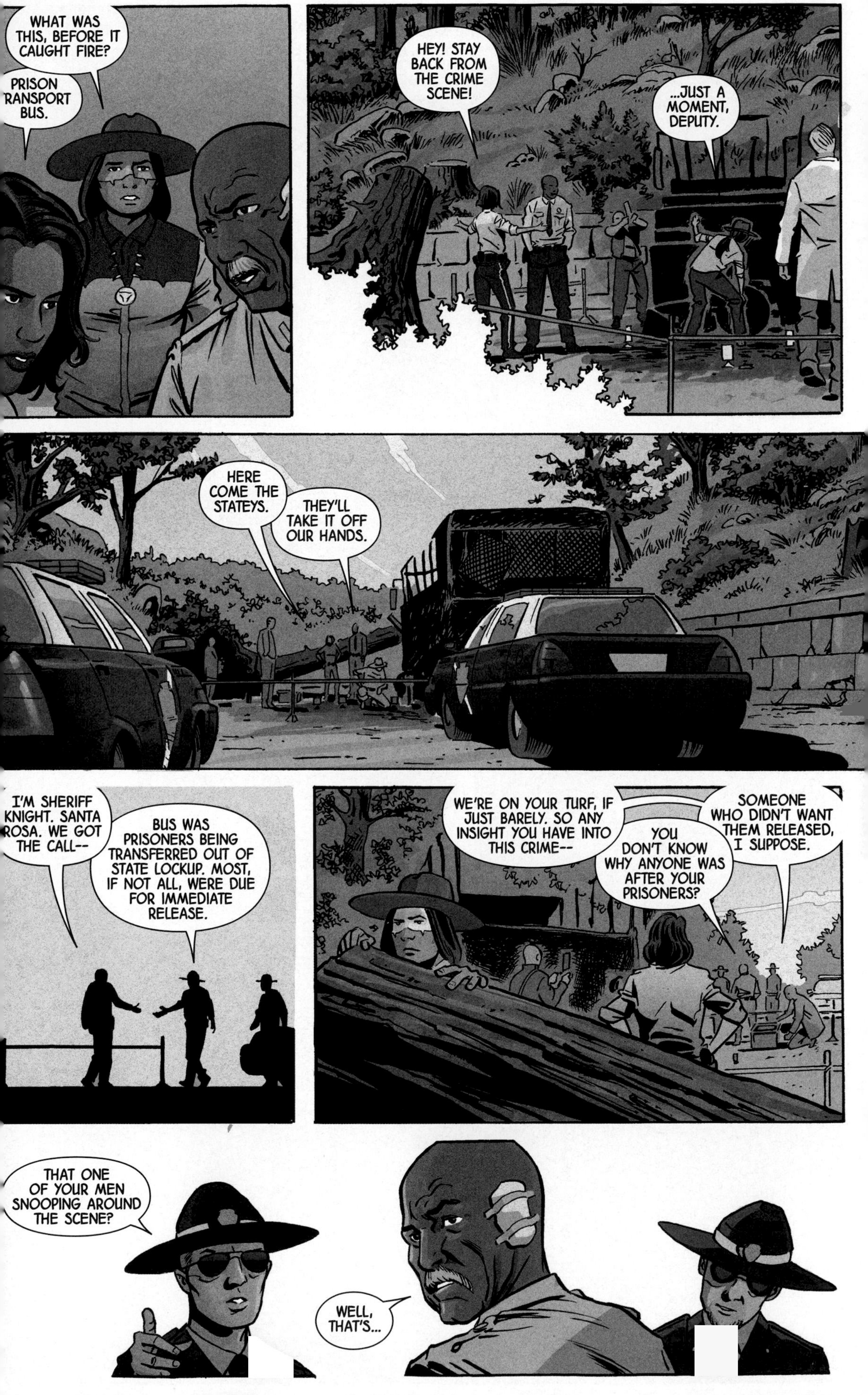
WHAT WAS THIS, BEFORE IT CAUGHT FIRE?
PRISON RANSPORT BUS.
HEY! STAY BACK FROM THE CRIME SCENE!
...JUST A MOMENT, DEPUTY.
HERE COME THE STATEYS.
THEY'LL TAKE IT OFF OUR HANDS.
I'M SHERIFF KNIGHT. SANTA ROSA. WE GOT THE CALL--
BUS WAS PRISONERS BEING TRANSFERRED OUT OF STATE LOCKUP. MOST, IF NOT ALL, WERE DUE FOR IMMEDIATE RELEASE.
WE'RE ON YOUR TURF, IF JUST BARELY. SO ANY INSIGHT YOU HAVE INTO THIS CRIME--
YOU DON'T KNOW WHY ANYONE WAS AFTER YOUR PRISONERS?
SOMEONE WHO DIDN'T WANT THEM RELEASED, I SUPPOSE.
THAT ONE OF YOUR MEN SNOOPING AROUND THE SCENE?
WELL, THAT'S...

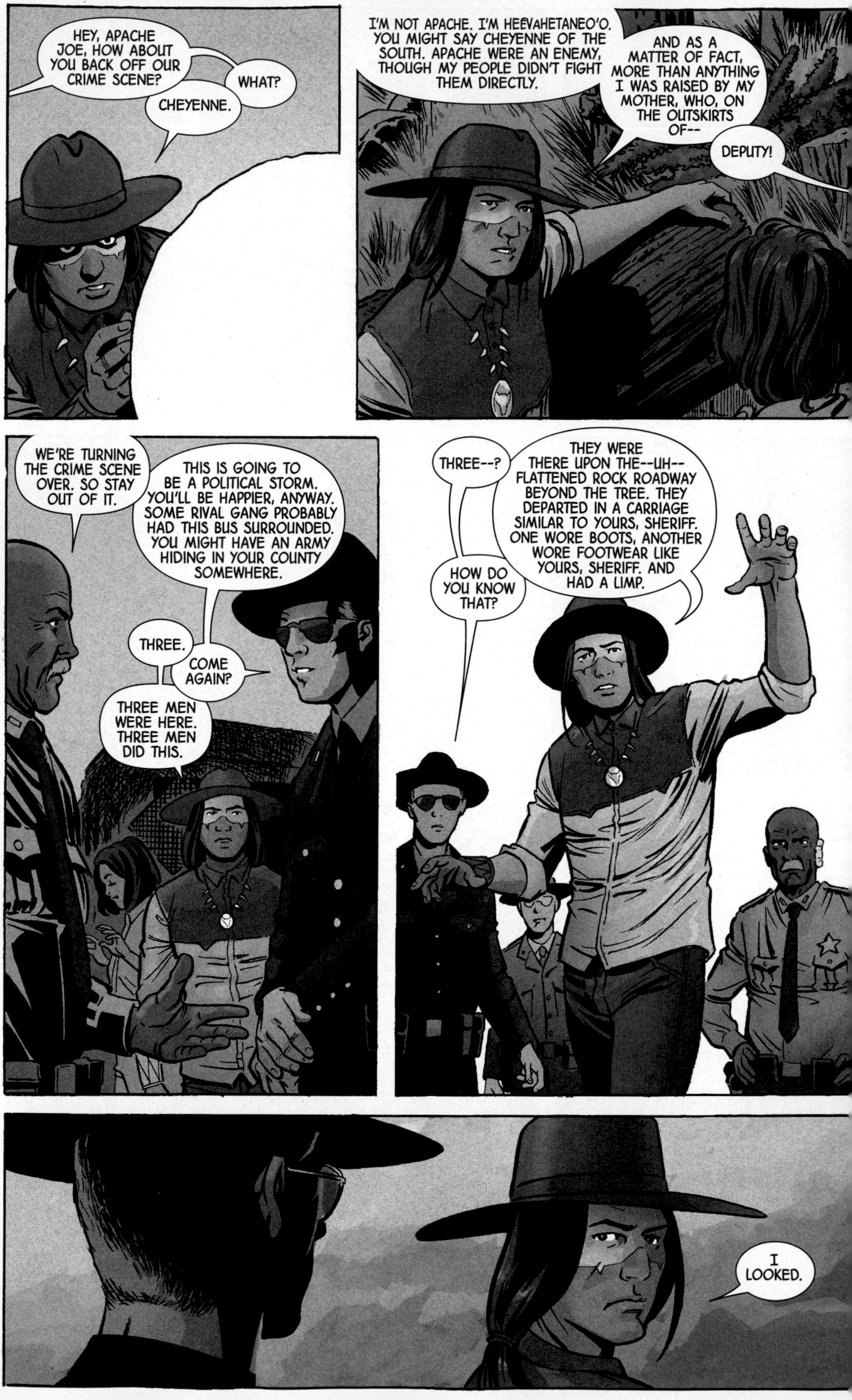
HEY, APACHE JOE, HOW ABOUT YOU BACK OFF OUR CRIME SCENE?
WHAT?
CHEYENNE.
I'M NOT APACHE. I'M HEEVAHETANEO'O. YOU MIGHT SAY CHEYENNE OF THE SOUTH. APACHE WERE AN ENEMY, THOUGH MY PEOPLE DIDN'T FIGHT THEM DIRECTLY.
AND AS A MATTER OF FACT, MORE THAN ANYTHING I WAS RAISED BY MY MOTHER, WHO, ON THE OUTSKIRTS OF--
DEPUTY!
WE'RE TURNING THE CRIME SCENE OVER. SO STAY OUT OF IT.
THIS IS GOING TO BE A POLITICAL STORM. YOU'LL BE HAPPIER, ANYWAY. SOME RIVAL GANG PROBABLY HAD THIS BUS SURROUNDED. YOU MIGHT HAVE AN ARMY HIDING IN YOUR COUNTY SOMEWHERE.
THREE.
COME AGAIN?
THREE MEN WERE HERE. THREE MEN DID THIS.
THREE--?
THEY WERE THERE UPON THE--UH--FLATTENED ROCK ROADWAY BEYOND THE TREE. THEY DEPARTED IN A CARRIAGE SIMILAR TO YOURS, SHERIFF. ONE WORE BOOTS, ANOTHER WORE FOOTWEAR LIKE YOURS, SHERIFF. AND HAD A LIMP.
HOW DO YOU KNOW THAT?
I LOOKED.

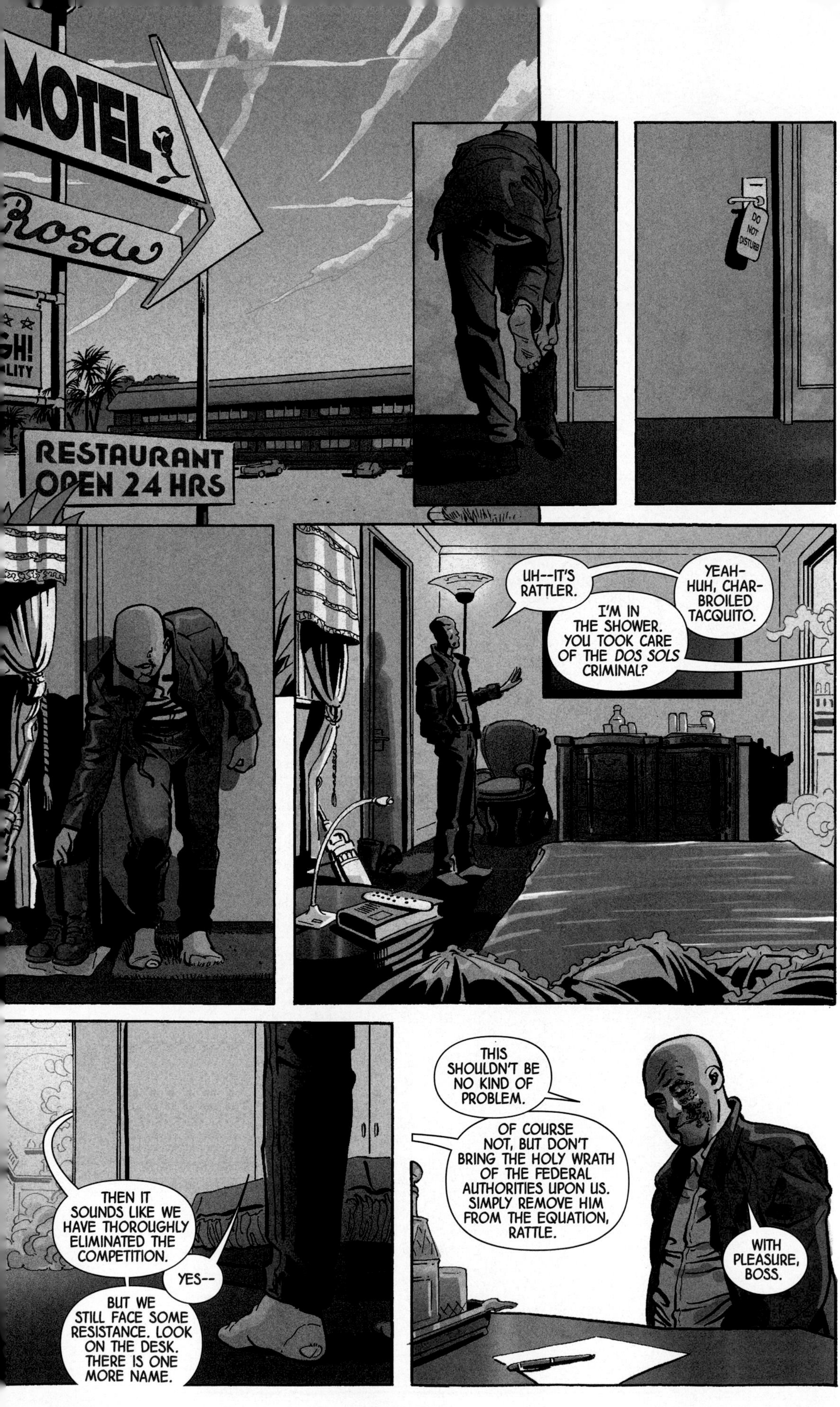
MOTEL
Rosa
RESTAURANT OPEN 24 HRS
DO NOT DISTURB
UH--IT'S RATTLER.
YEAH-HUH, CHAR-BROILED TACQUITO.
I'M IN THE SHOWER. YOU TOOK CARE OF THE *DOS SOLS* CRIMINAL?
THEN IT SOUNDS LIKE WE HAVE THOROUGHLY ELIMINATED THE COMPETITION.
YES--
BUT WE STILL FACE SOME RESISTANCE. LOOK ON THE DESK. THERE IS ONE MORE NAME.
THIS SHOULDN'T BE NO KIND OF PROBLEM.
OF COURSE NOT, BUT DON'T BRING THE HOLY WRATH OF THE FEDERAL AUTHORITIES UPON US. SIMPLY REMOVE HIM FROM THE EQUATION, RATTLE.
WITH PLEASURE, BOSS.

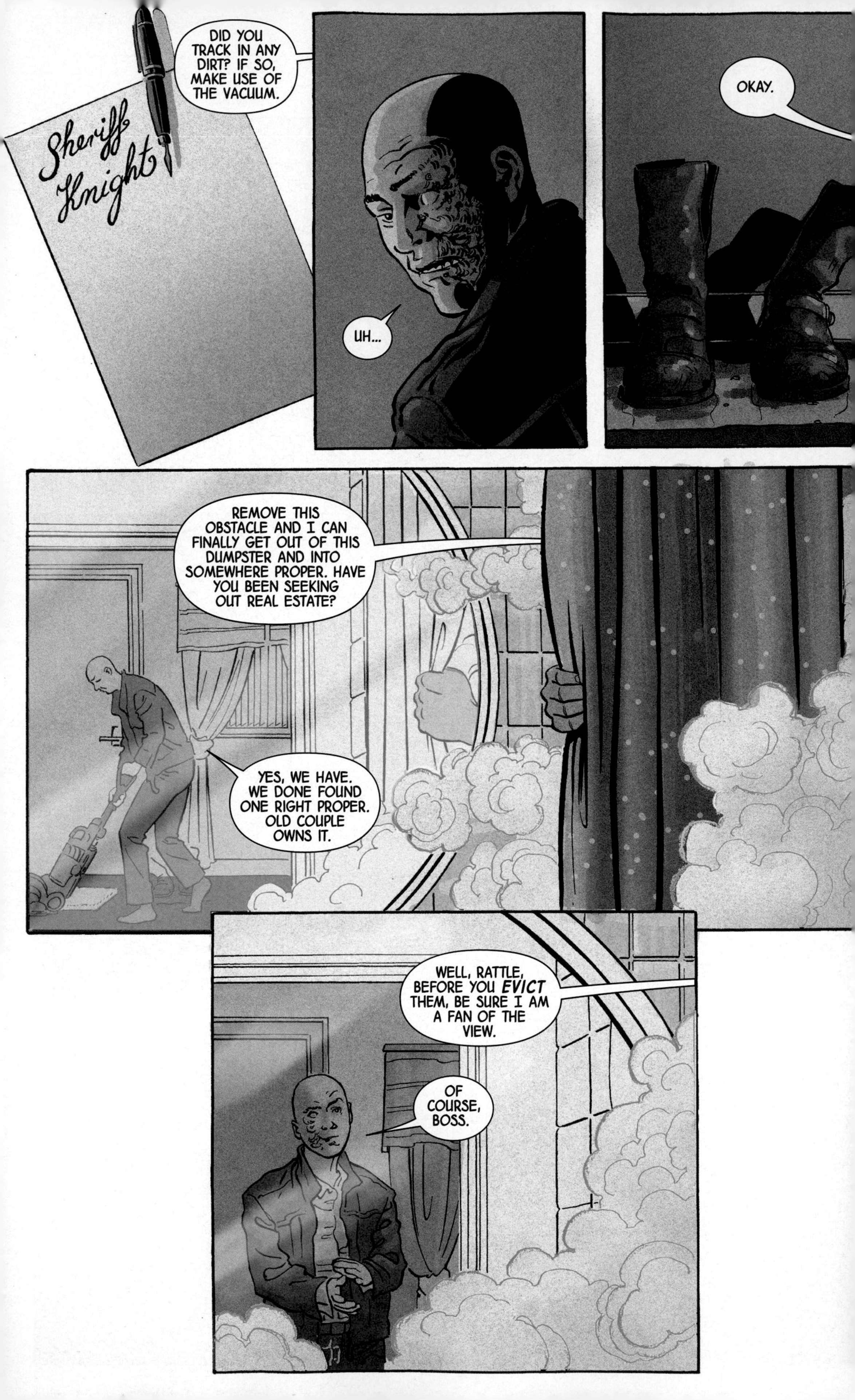

Sheriff Knight
DID YOU TRACK IN ANY DIRT? IF SO, MAKE USE OF THE VACUUM.
UH...
OKAY.
REMOVE THIS OBSTACLE AND I CAN FINALLY GET OUT OF THIS DUMPSTER AND INTO SOMEWHERE PROPER. HAVE YOU BEEN SEEKING OUT REAL ESTATE?
YES, WE HAVE. WE DONE FOUND ONE RIGHT PROPER. OLD COUPLE OWNS IT.
WELL, RATTLE, BEFORE YOU EVICT THEM, BE SURE I AM A FAN OF THE VIEW.
OF COURSE, BOSS.

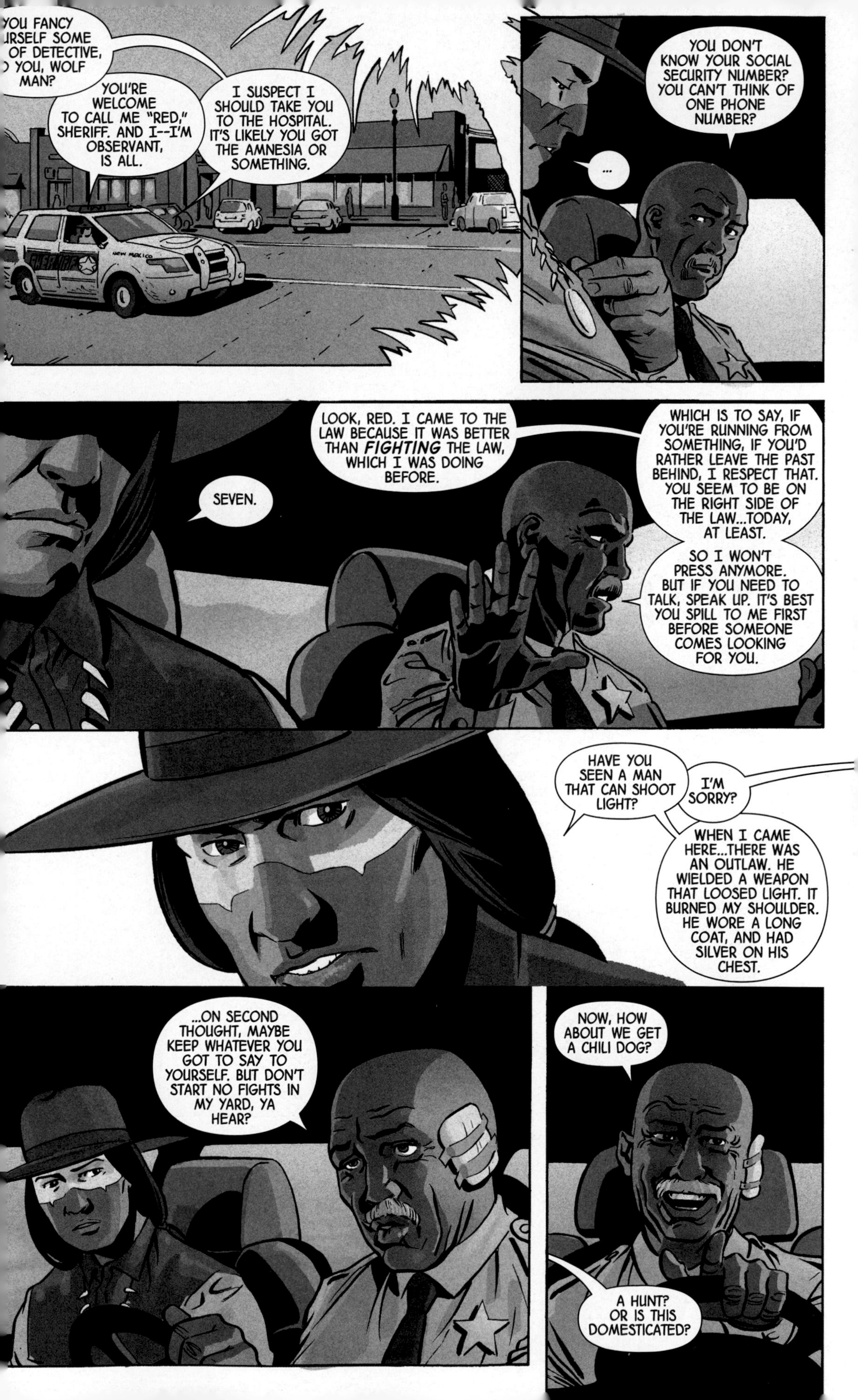
YOU FANCY
URSELF SOME
OF DETECTIVE,
D YOU, WOLF
MAN?
YOU'RE
WELCOME
TO CALL ME "RED,"
SHERIFF. AND I--I'M
OBSERVANT,
IS ALL.
I SUSPECT I
SHOULD TAKE YOU
TO THE HOSPITAL.
IT'S LIKELY YOU GOT
THE AMNESIA OR
SOMETHING.
SHERIFF
NEW MEXICO
YOU DON'T
KNOW YOUR SOCIAL
SECURITY NUMBER?
YOU CAN'T THINK OF
ONE PHONE
NUMBER?
...
SEVEN.
LOOK, RED. I CAME TO THE
LAW BECAUSE IT WAS BETTER
THAN *FIGHTING* THE LAW,
WHICH I WAS DOING
BEFORE.
WHICH IS TO SAY, IF
YOU'RE RUNNING FROM
SOMETHING, IF YOU'D
RATHER LEAVE THE PAST
BEHIND, I RESPECT THAT.
YOU SEEM TO BE ON
THE RIGHT SIDE OF
THE LAW...TODAY,
AT LEAST.
SO I WON'T
PRESS ANYMORE.
BUT IF YOU NEED TO
TALK, SPEAK UP. IT'S BEST
YOU SPILL TO ME FIRST
BEFORE SOMEONE
COMES LOOKING
FOR YOU.
HAVE YOU
SEEN A MAN
THAT CAN SHOOT
LIGHT?
I'M
SORRY?
WHEN I CAME
HERE...THERE WAS
AN OUTLAW. HE
WIELDED A WEAPON
THAT LOOSED LIGHT. IT
BURNED MY SHOULDER.
HE WORE A LONG
COAT, AND HAD
SILVER ON HIS
CHEST.
...ON SECOND
THOUGHT, MAYBE
KEEP WHATEVER YOU
GOT TO SAY TO
YOURSELF. BUT DON'T
START NO FIGHTS IN
MY YARD, YA
HEAR?
NOW, HOW
ABOUT WE GET
A CHILI DOG?
A HUNT?
OR IS THIS
DOMESTICATED?

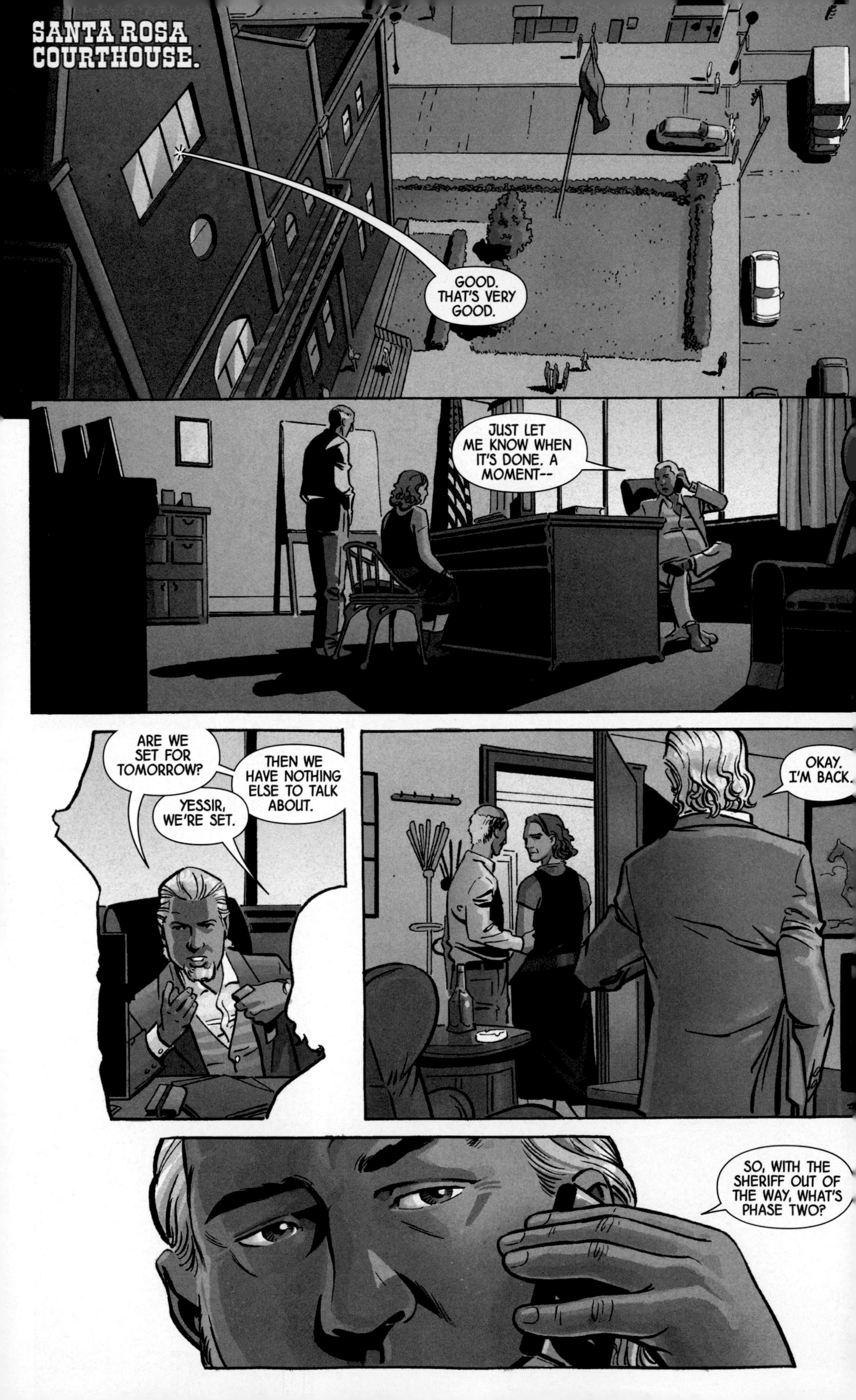
SANTA ROSA COURTHOUSE.
GOOD. THAT'S VERY GOOD.
JUST LET ME KNOW WHEN IT'S DONE. A MOMENT--
ARE WE SET FOR TOMORROW?
YESSIR, WE'RE SET.
THEN WE HAVE NOTHING ELSE TO TALK ABOUT.
OKAY. I'M BACK.
SO, WITH THE SHERIFF OUT OF THE WAY, WHAT'S PHASE TWO?

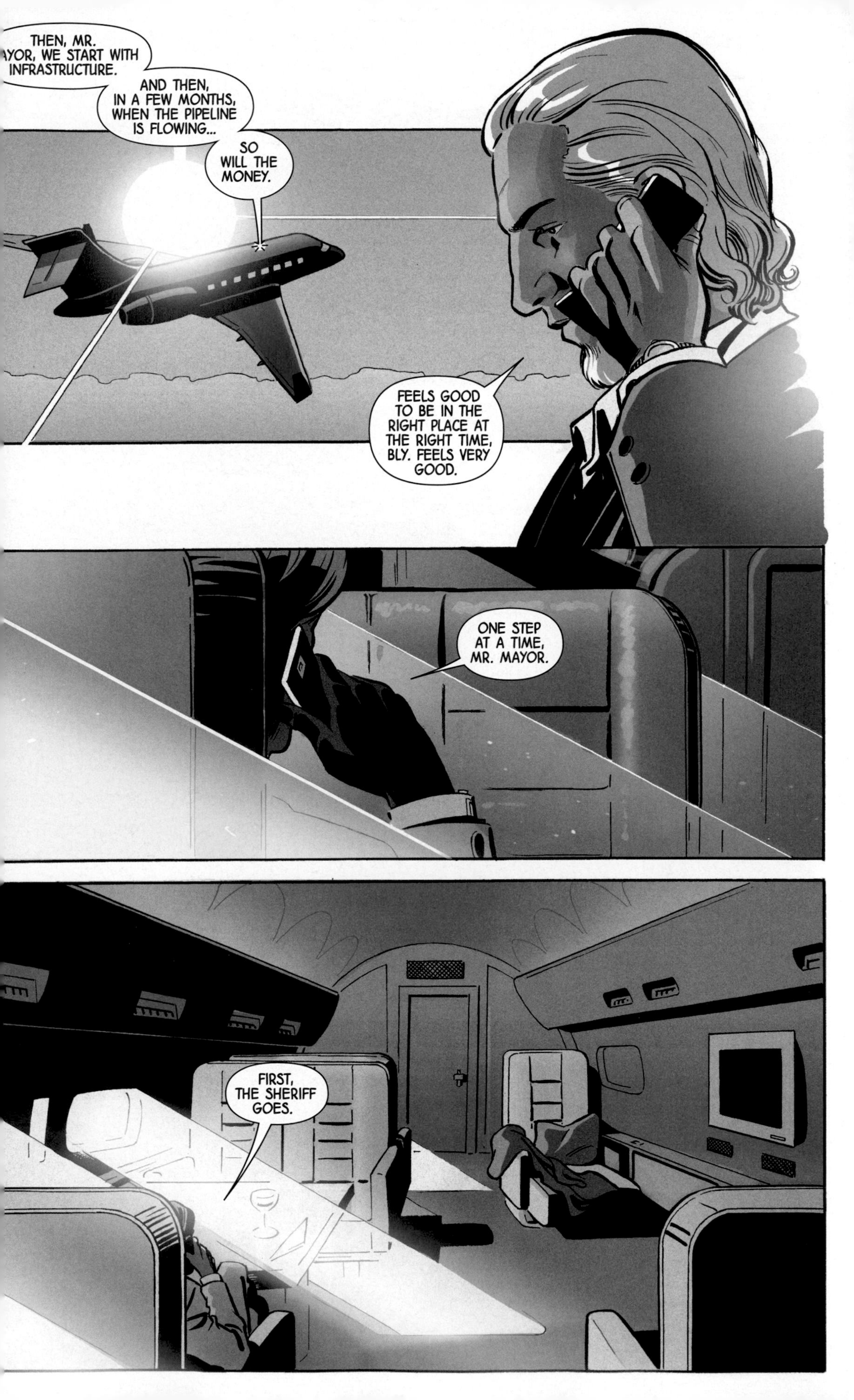
THEN, MR. MAYOR, WE START WITH INFRASTRUCTURE.
AND THEN, IN A FEW MONTHS, WHEN THE PIPELINE IS FLOWING...
SO WILL THE MONEY.
FEELS GOOD TO BE IN THE RIGHT PLACE AT THE RIGHT TIME, BLY. FEELS VERY GOOD.
ONE STEP AT A TIME, MR. MAYOR.
FIRST, THE SHERIFF GOES.

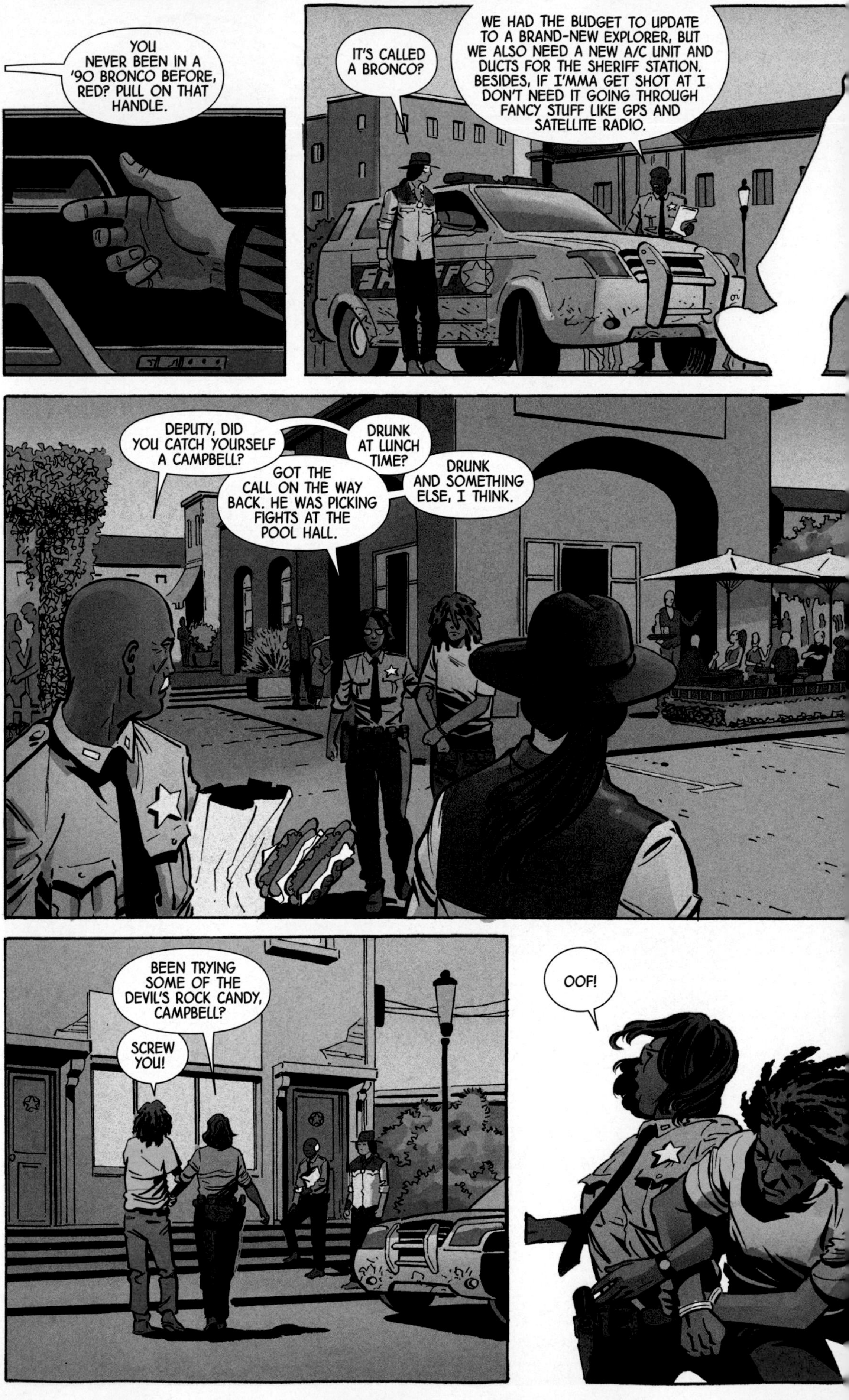
YOU NEVER BEEN IN A '90 BRONCO BEFORE, RED? PULL ON THAT HANDLE.
IT'S CALLED A BRONCO?
WE HAD THE BUDGET TO UPDATE TO A BRAND-NEW EXPLORER, BUT WE ALSO NEED A NEW A/C UNIT AND DUCTS FOR THE SHERIFF STATION. BESIDES, IF I'MMA GET SHOT AT I DON'T NEED IT GOING THROUGH FANCY STUFF LIKE GPS AND SATELLITE RADIO.
DEPUTY, DID YOU CATCH YOURSELF A CAMPBELL?
DRUNK AT LUNCH TIME?
GOT THE CALL ON THE WAY BACK. HE WAS PICKING FIGHTS AT THE POOL HALL.
DRUNK AND SOMETHING ELSE, I THINK.
BEEN TRYING SOME OF THE DEVIL'S ROCK CANDY, CAMPBELL?
SCREW YOU!
OOF!

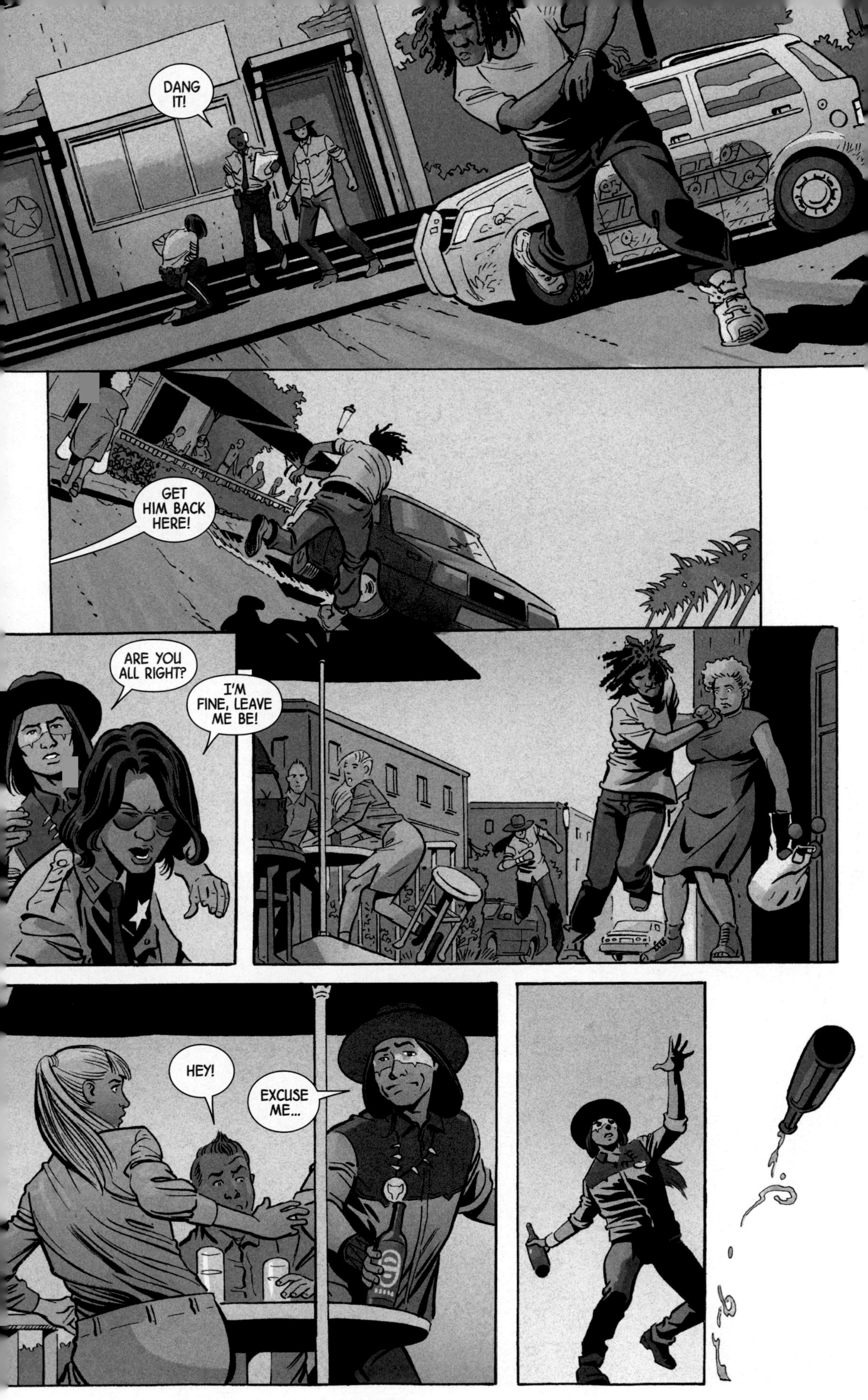
DANG IT!
GET HIM BACK HERE!
ARE YOU ALL RIGHT?
I'M FINE, LEAVE ME BE!
HEY!
EXCUSE ME...

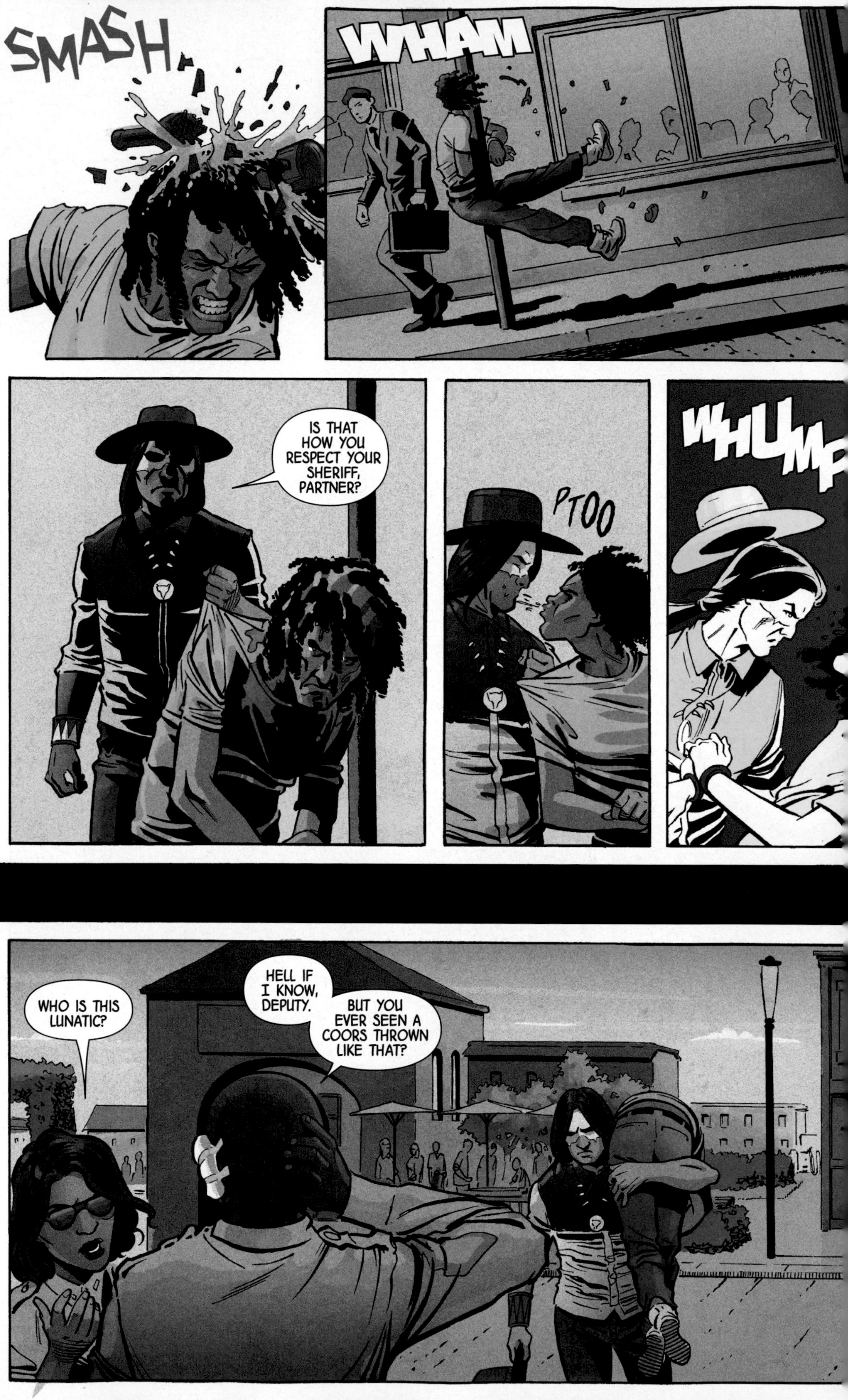
SMASH
WHAM
IS THAT HOW YOU RESPECT YOUR SHERIFF, PARTNER?
PTOO
WHUMP
WHO IS THIS LUNATIC?
HELL IF I KNOW, DEPUTY.
BUT YOU EVER SEEN A COORS THROWN LIKE THAT?

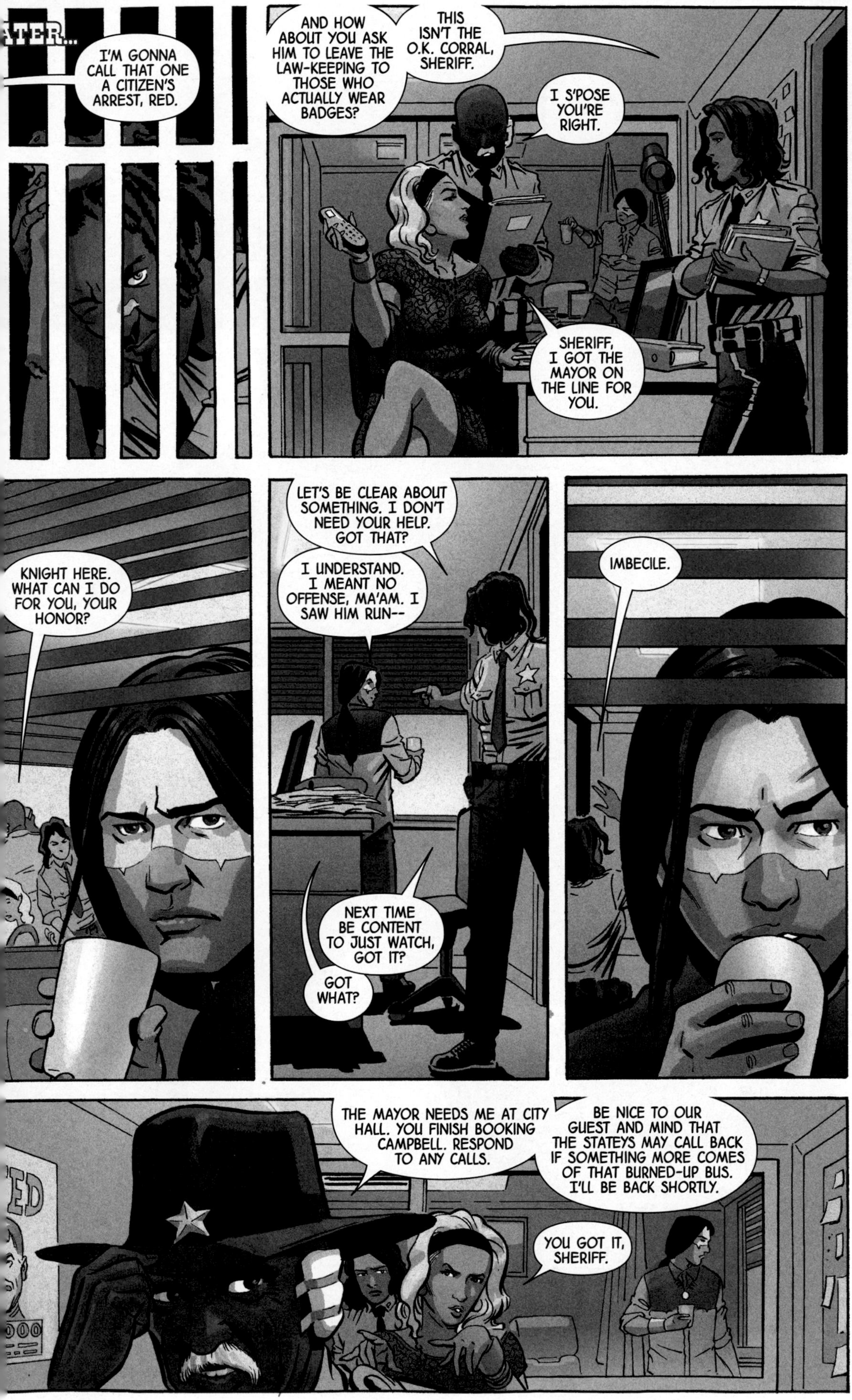
ATER...
I'M GONNA CALL THAT ONE A CITIZEN'S ARREST, RED.
AND HOW ABOUT YOU ASK HIM TO LEAVE THE LAW-KEEPING TO THOSE WHO ACTUALLY WEAR BADGES?
THIS ISN'T THE O.K. CORRAL, SHERIFF.
I S'POSE YOU'RE RIGHT.
SHERIFF, I GOT THE MAYOR ON THE LINE FOR YOU.
KNIGHT HERE. WHAT CAN I DO FOR YOU, YOUR HONOR?
LET'S BE CLEAR ABOUT SOMETHING. I DON'T NEED YOUR HELP. GOT THAT?
I UNDERSTAND. I MEANT NO OFFENSE, MA'AM. I SAW HIM RUN--
NEXT TIME BE CONTENT TO JUST WATCH, GOT IT?
GOT WHAT?
IMBECILE.
THE MAYOR NEEDS ME AT CITY HALL. YOU FINISH BOOKING CAMPBELL. RESPOND TO ANY CALLS.
BE NICE TO OUR GUEST AND MIND THAT THE STATEYS MAY CALL BACK IF SOMETHING MORE COMES OF THAT BURNED-UP BUS. I'LL BE BACK SHORTLY.
YOU GOT IT, SHERIFF.

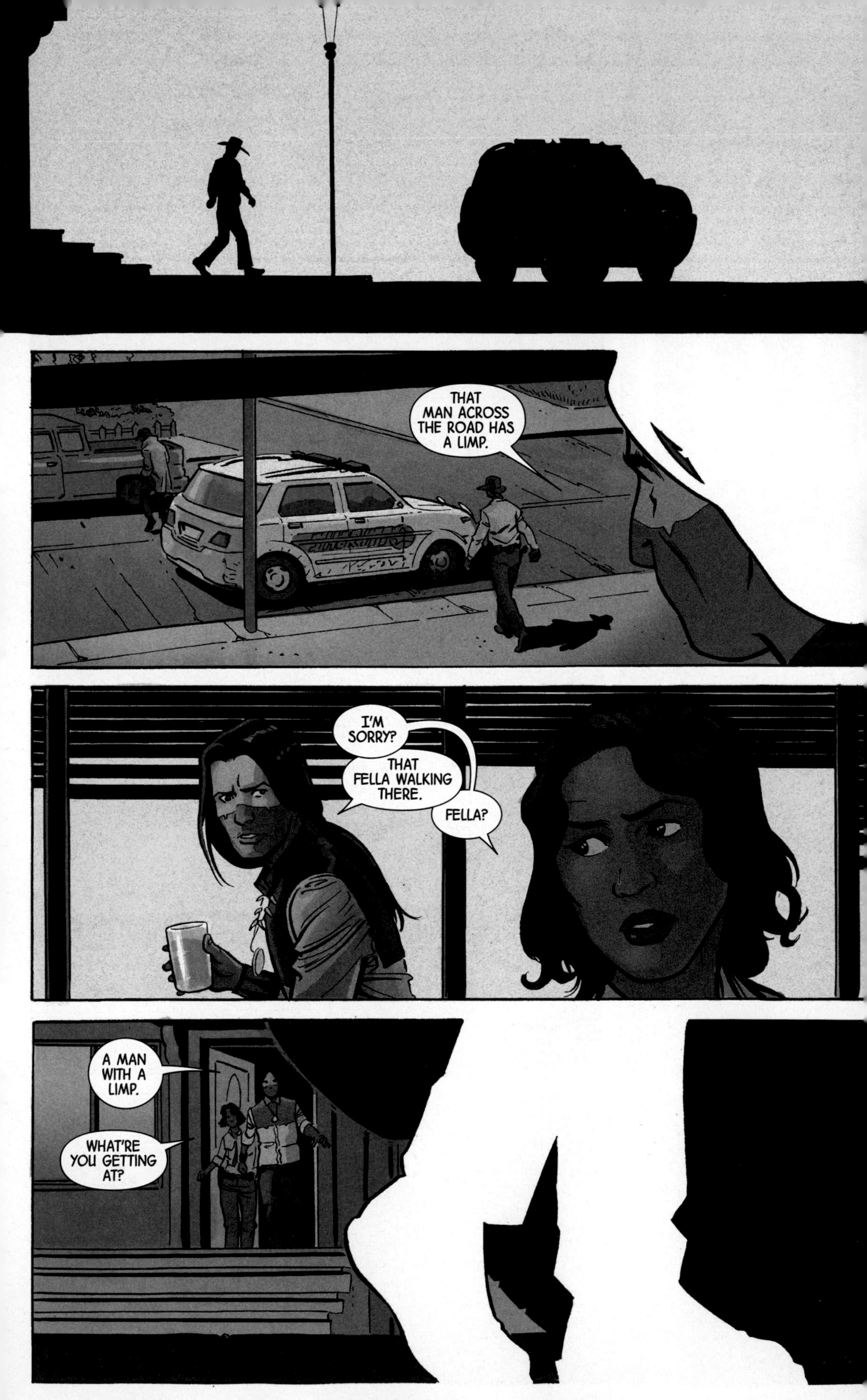
THAT MAN ACROSS THE ROAD HAS A LIMP.
I'M SORRY?
THAT FELLA WALKING THERE.
FELLA?
A MAN WITH A LIMP.
WHAT'RE YOU GETTING AT?

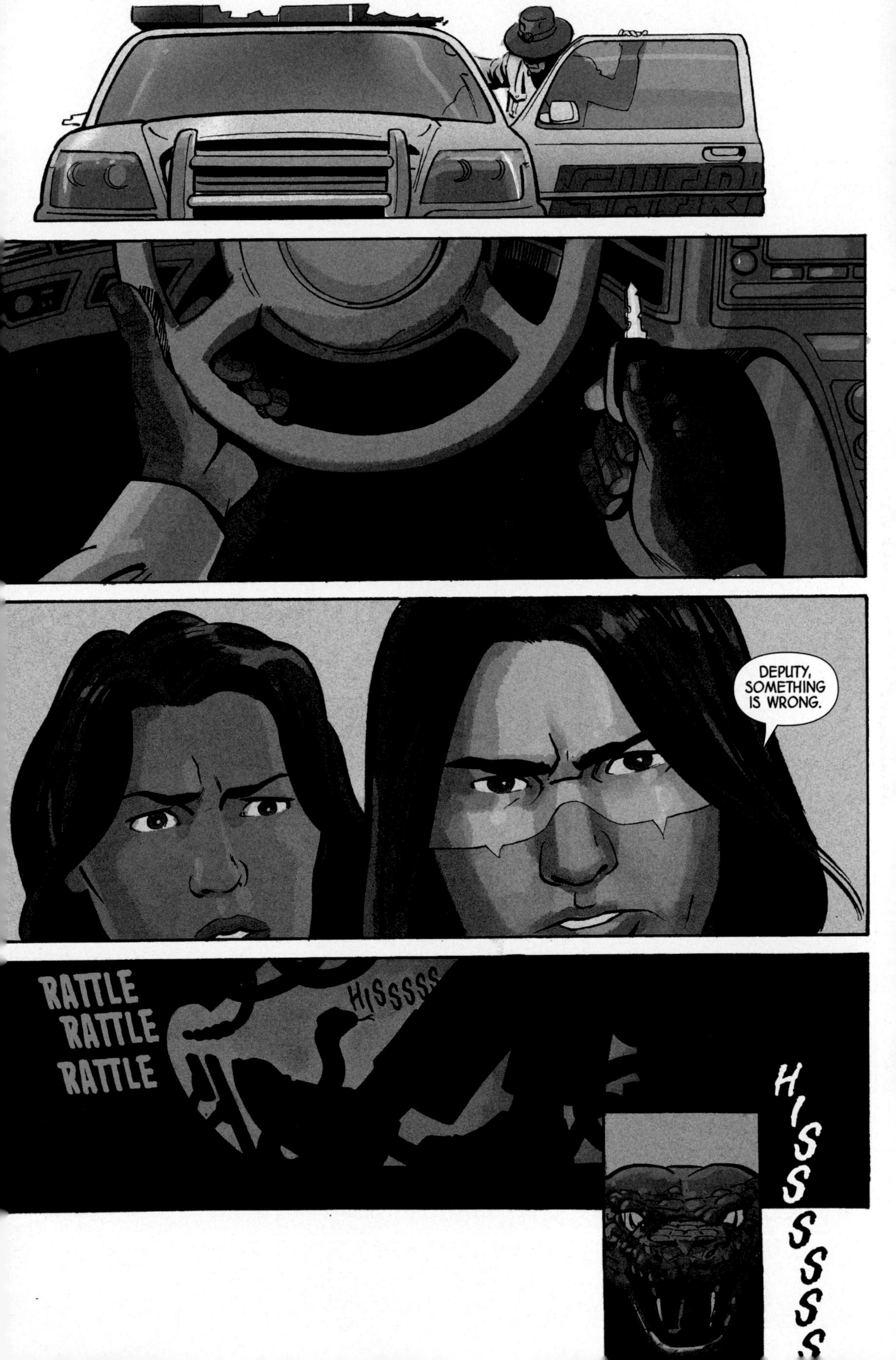
DEPUTY, SOMETHING IS WRONG.
RATTLE
RATTLE
RATTLE
HISSSSS
HISSSSS

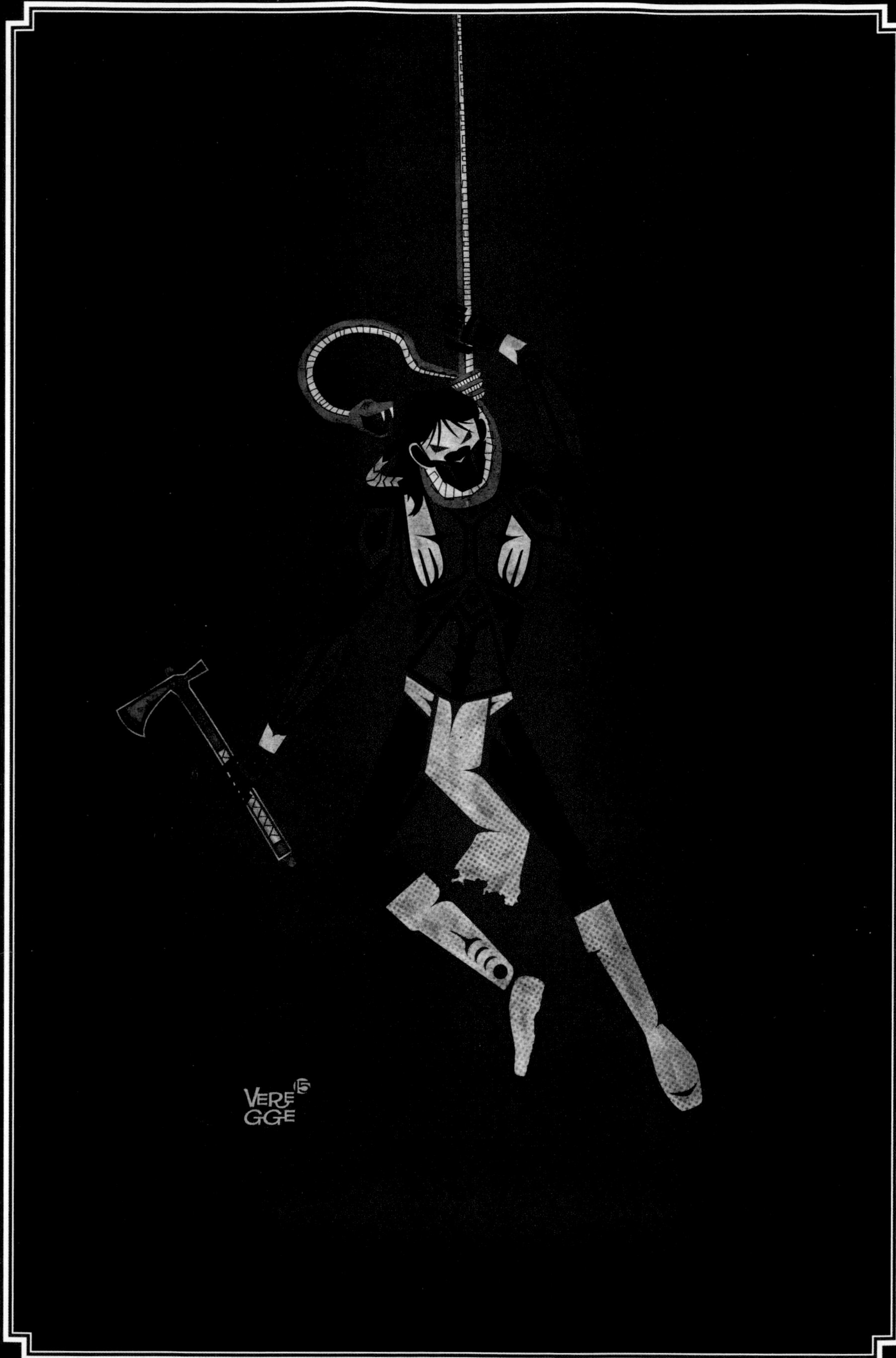
VERE
GGE
15

4

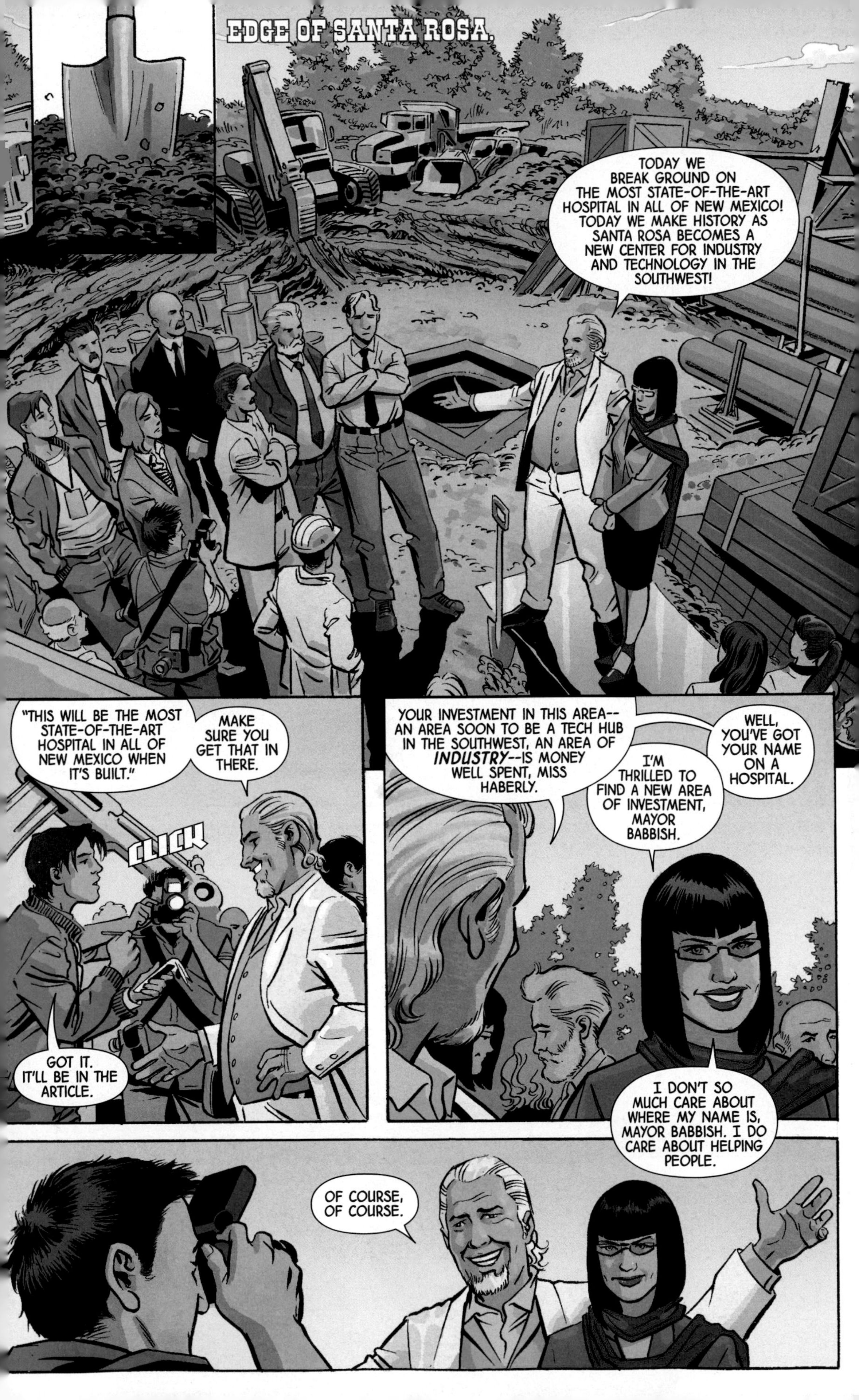
EDGE OF SANTA ROSA.
TODAY WE BREAK GROUND ON THE MOST STATE-OF-THE-ART HOSPITAL IN ALL OF NEW MEXICO! TODAY WE MAKE HISTORY AS SANTA ROSA BECOMES A NEW CENTER FOR INDUSTRY AND TECHNOLOGY IN THE SOUTHWEST!
"THIS WILL BE THE MOST STATE-OF-THE-ART HOSPITAL IN ALL OF NEW MEXICO WHEN IT'S BUILT."
MAKE SURE YOU GET THAT IN THERE.
CLICK
GOT IT. IT'LL BE IN THE ARTICLE.
YOUR INVESTMENT IN THIS AREA-- AN AREA SOON TO BE A TECH HUB IN THE SOUTHWEST, AN AREA OF *INDUSTRY*--IS MONEY WELL SPENT, MISS HABERLY.
I'M THRILLED TO FIND A NEW AREA OF INVESTMENT, MAYOR BABBISH.
WELL, YOU'VE GOT YOUR NAME ON A HOSPITAL.
I DON'T SO MUCH CARE ABOUT WHERE MY NAME IS, MAYOR BABBISH. I DO CARE ABOUT HELPING PEOPLE.
OF COURSE, OF COURSE.

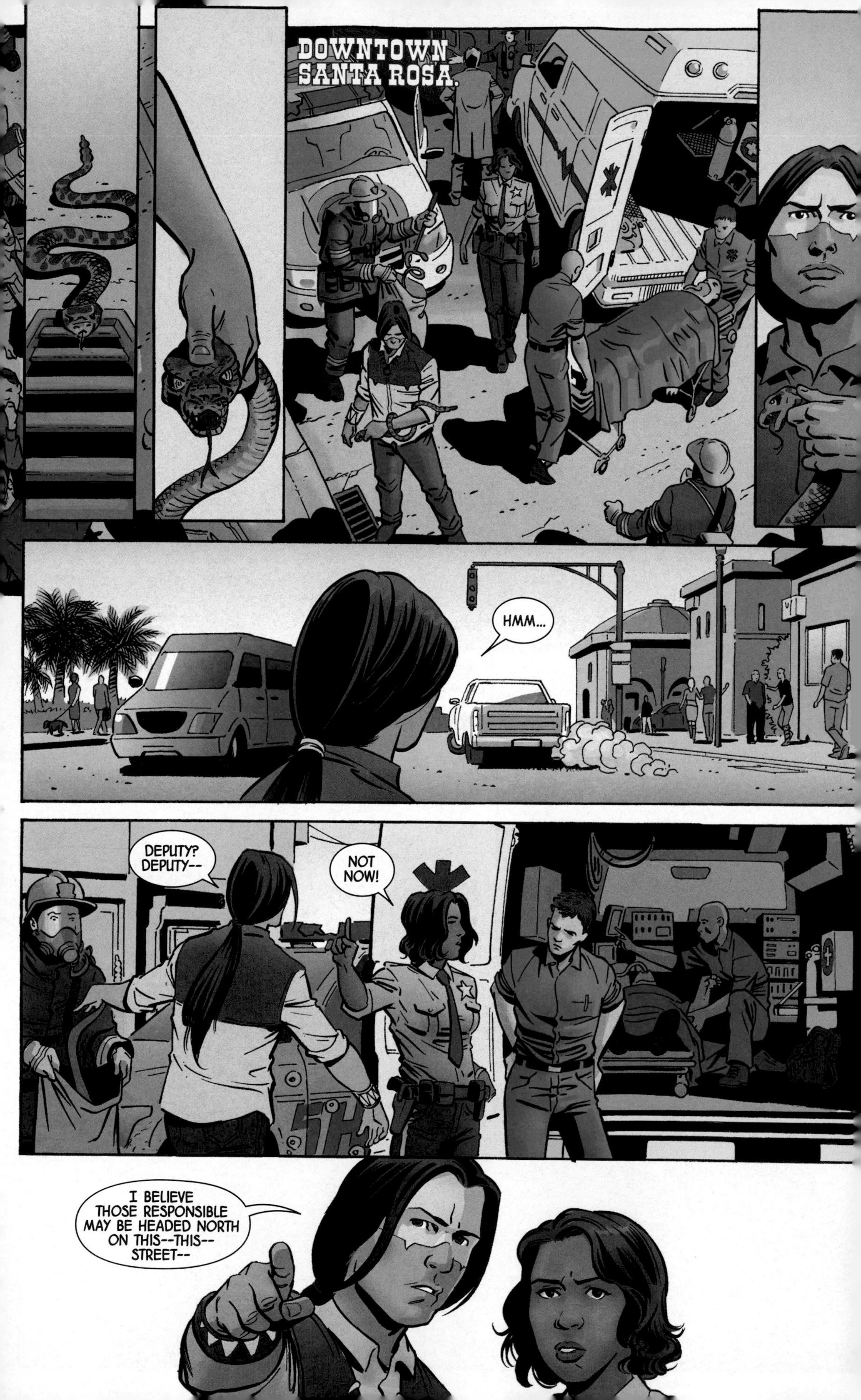
DOWNTOWN SANTA ROSA.
HMM...
DEPUTY? DEPUTY--
NOT NOW!
I BELIEVE THOSE RESPONSIBLE MAY BE HEADED NORTH ON THIS--THIS-- STREET--

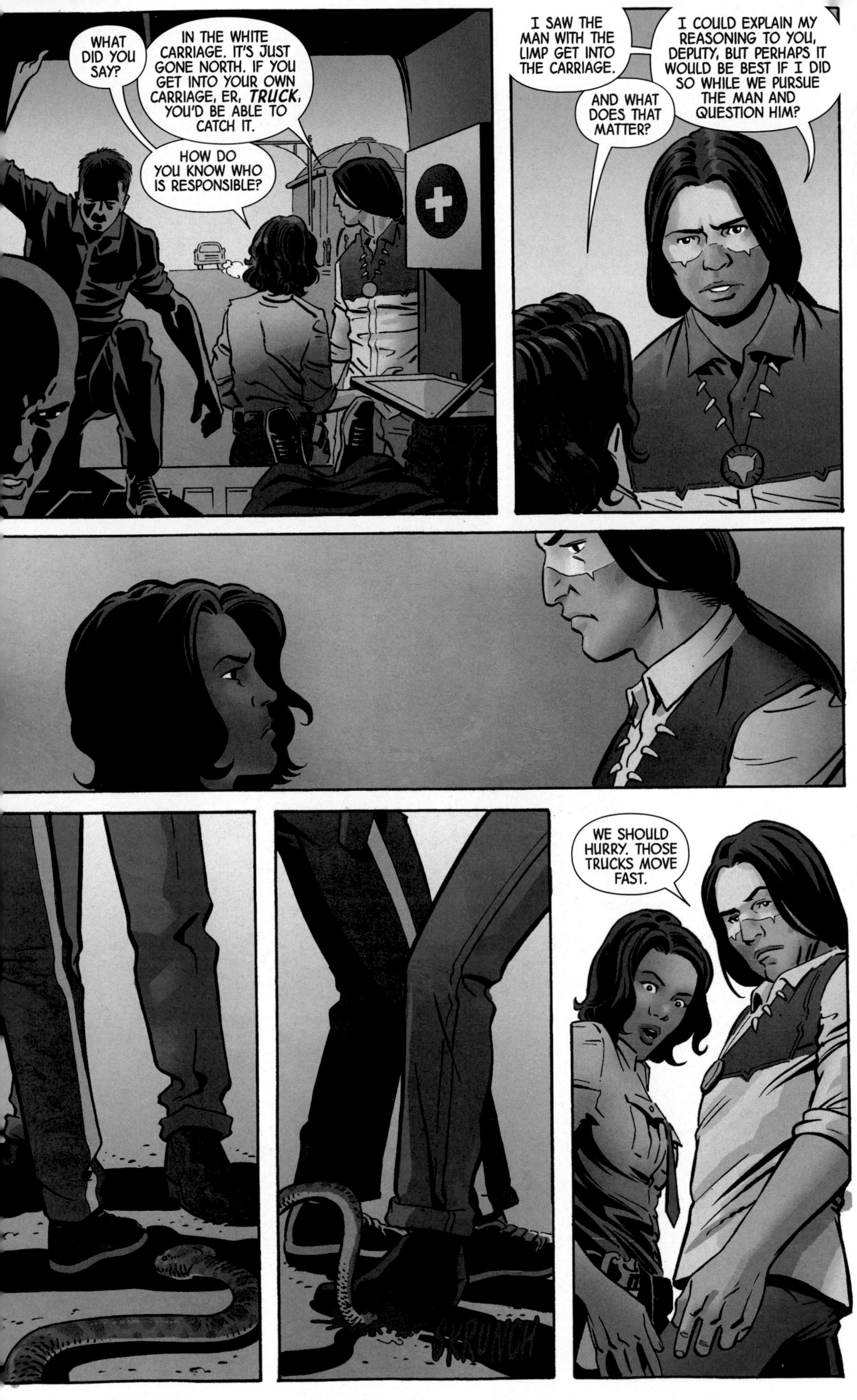
WHAT DID YOU SAY?
IN THE WHITE CARRIAGE. IT'S JUST GONE NORTH. IF YOU GET INTO YOUR OWN CARRIAGE, ER, TRUCK, YOU'D BE ABLE TO CATCH IT.
HOW DO YOU KNOW WHO IS RESPONSIBLE?
I SAW THE MAN WITH THE LIMP GET INTO THE CARRIAGE.
AND WHAT DOES THAT MATTER?
I COULD EXPLAIN MY REASONING TO YOU, DEPUTY, BUT PERHAPS IT WOULD BE BEST IF I DID SO WHILE WE PURSUE THE MAN AND QUESTION HIM?
SKRUNCH
WE SHOULD HURRY. THOSE TRUCKS MOVE FAST.

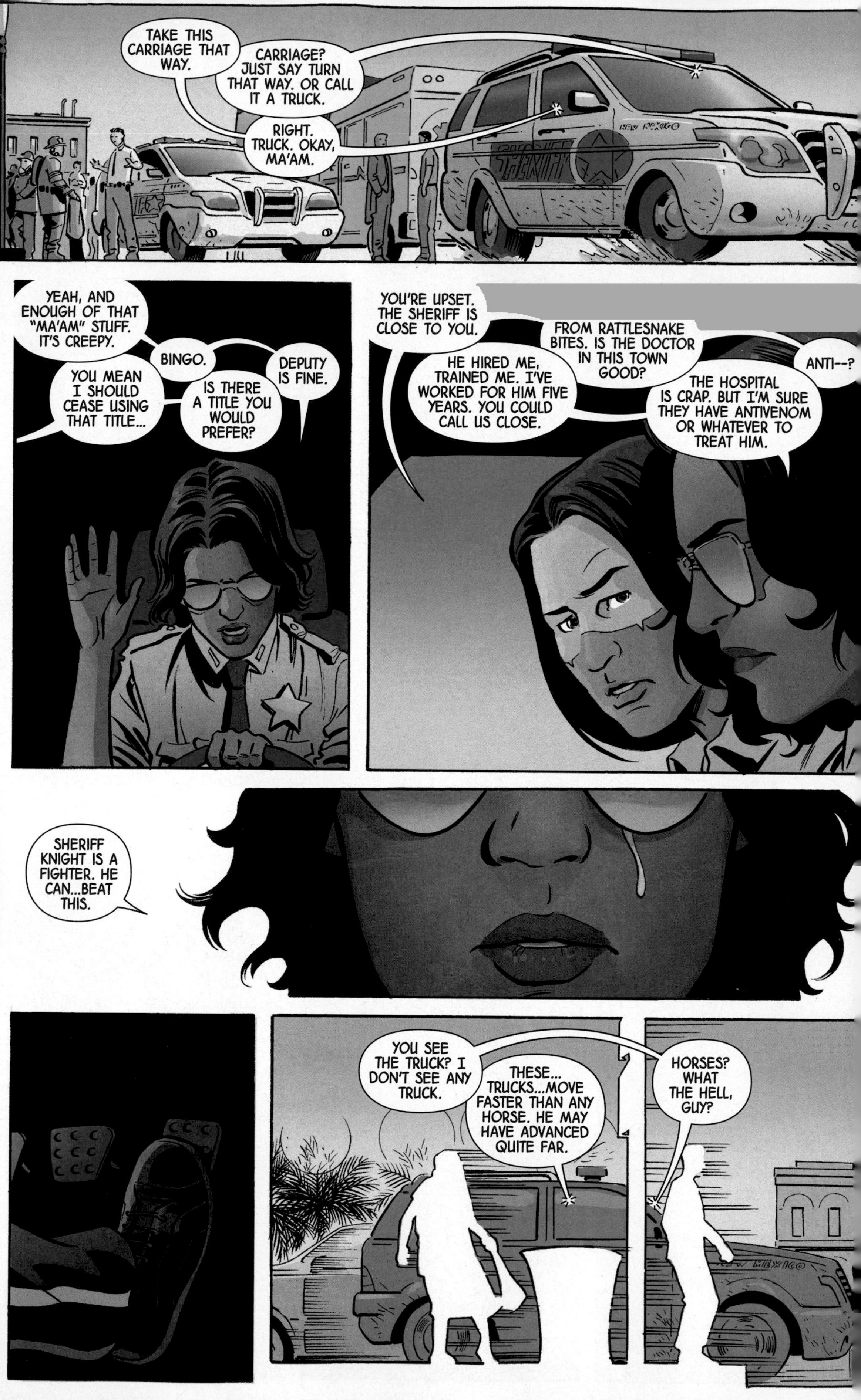
TAKE THIS CARRIAGE THAT WAY.
CARRIAGE? JUST SAY TURN THAT WAY. OR CALL IT A TRUCK.
RIGHT. TRUCK. OKAY, MA'AM.
YEAH, AND ENOUGH OF THAT "MA'AM" STUFF. IT'S CREEPY.
YOU MEAN I SHOULD CEASE USING THAT TITLE...
BINGO.
IS THERE A TITLE YOU WOULD PREFER?
DEPUTY IS FINE.
YOU'RE UPSET. THE SHERIFF IS CLOSE TO YOU.
HE HIRED ME, TRAINED ME. I'VE WORKED FOR HIM FIVE YEARS. YOU COULD CALL US CLOSE.
FROM RATTLESNAKE BITES. IS THE DOCTOR IN THIS TOWN GOOD?
THE HOSPITAL IS CRAP. BUT I'M SURE THEY HAVE ANTIVENOM OR WHATEVER TO TREAT HIM.
ANTI--?
SHERIFF KNIGHT IS A FIGHTER. HE CAN...BEAT THIS.
YOU SEE THE TRUCK? I DON'T SEE ANY TRUCK.
THESE... TRUCKS...MOVE FASTER THAN ANY HORSE. HE MAY HAVE ADVANCED QUITE FAR.
HORSES? WHAT THE HELL, GUY?

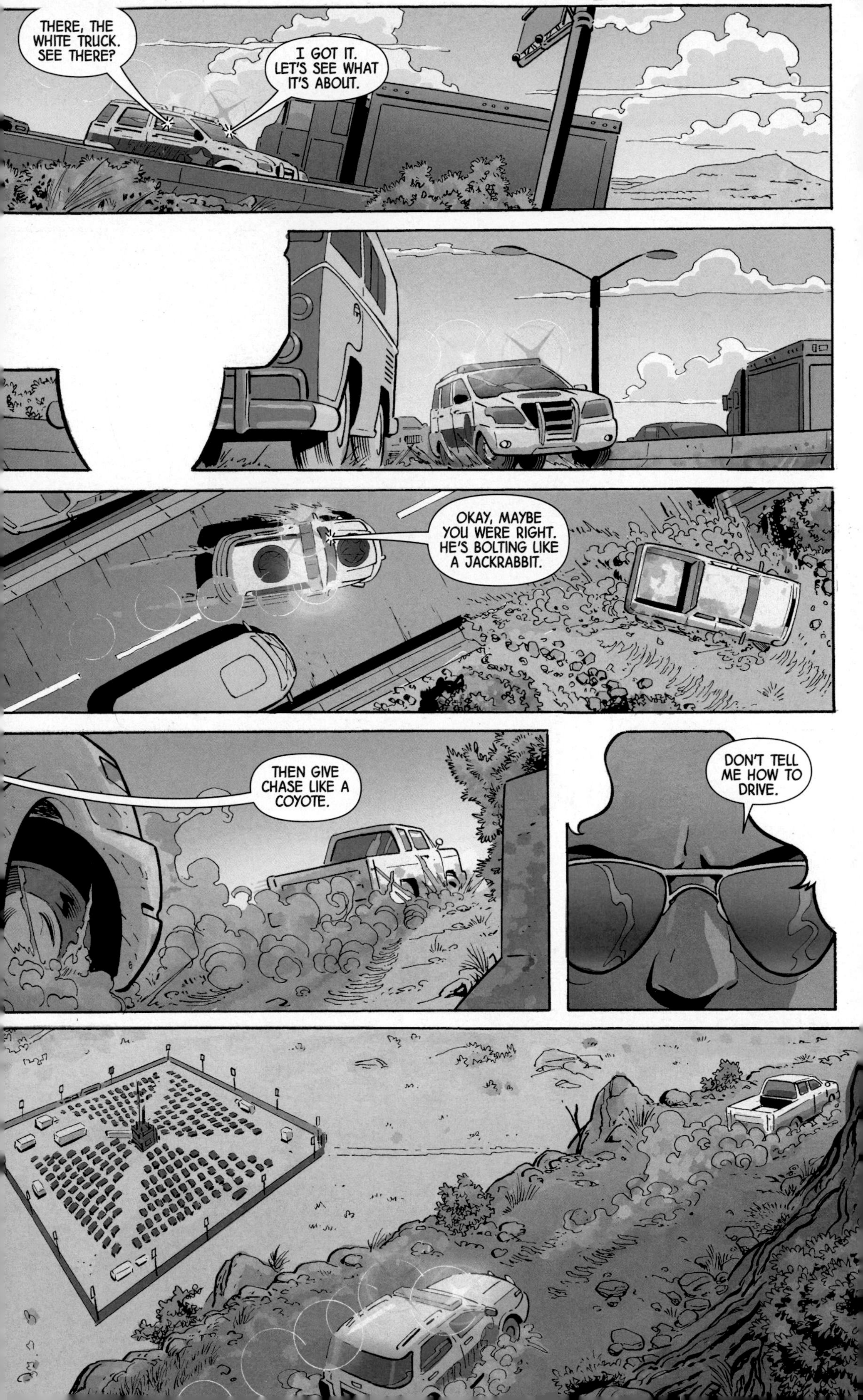
THERE, THE WHITE TRUCK. SEE THERE?
I GOT IT. LET'S SEE WHAT IT'S ABOUT.
OKAY, MAYBE YOU WERE RIGHT. HE'S BOLTING LIKE A JACKRABBIT.
THEN GIVE CHASE LIKE A COYOTE.
DON'T TELL ME HOW TO DRIVE.

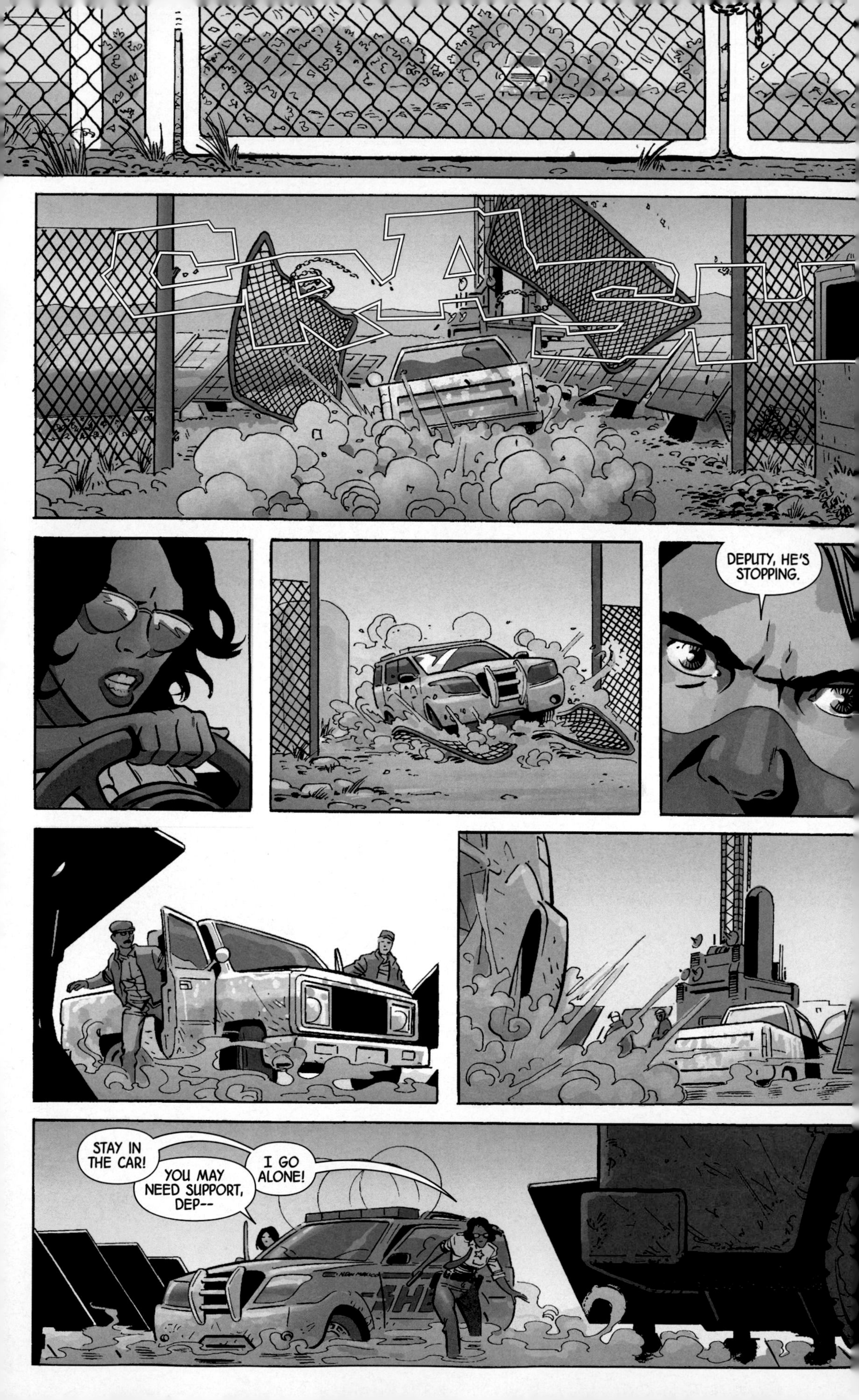
CRASH
DEPUTY, HE'S STOPPING.
STAY IN THE CAR!
YOU MAY NEED SUPPORT, DEP--
I GO ALONE!

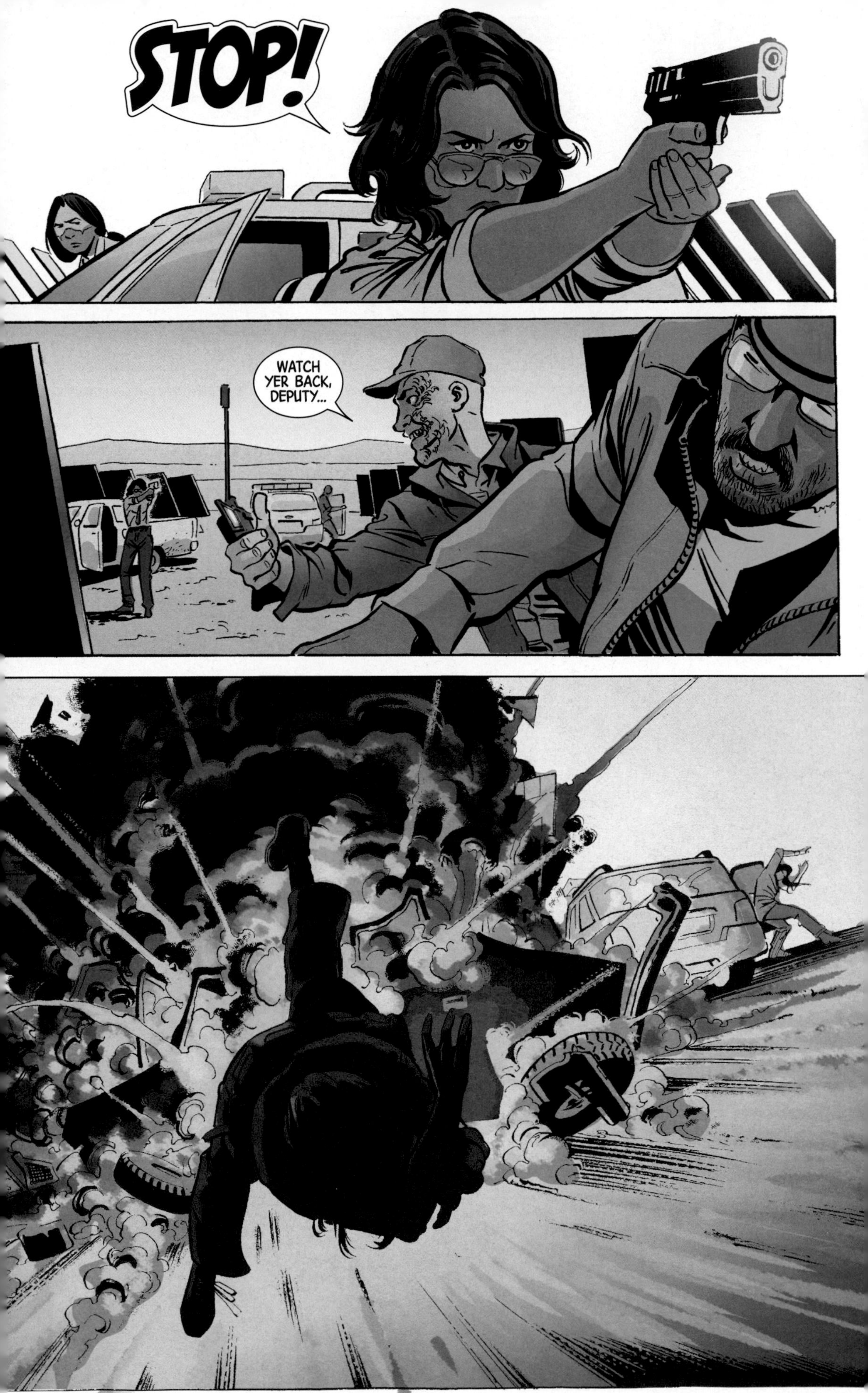
STOP!
WATCH YER BACK, DEPUTY...

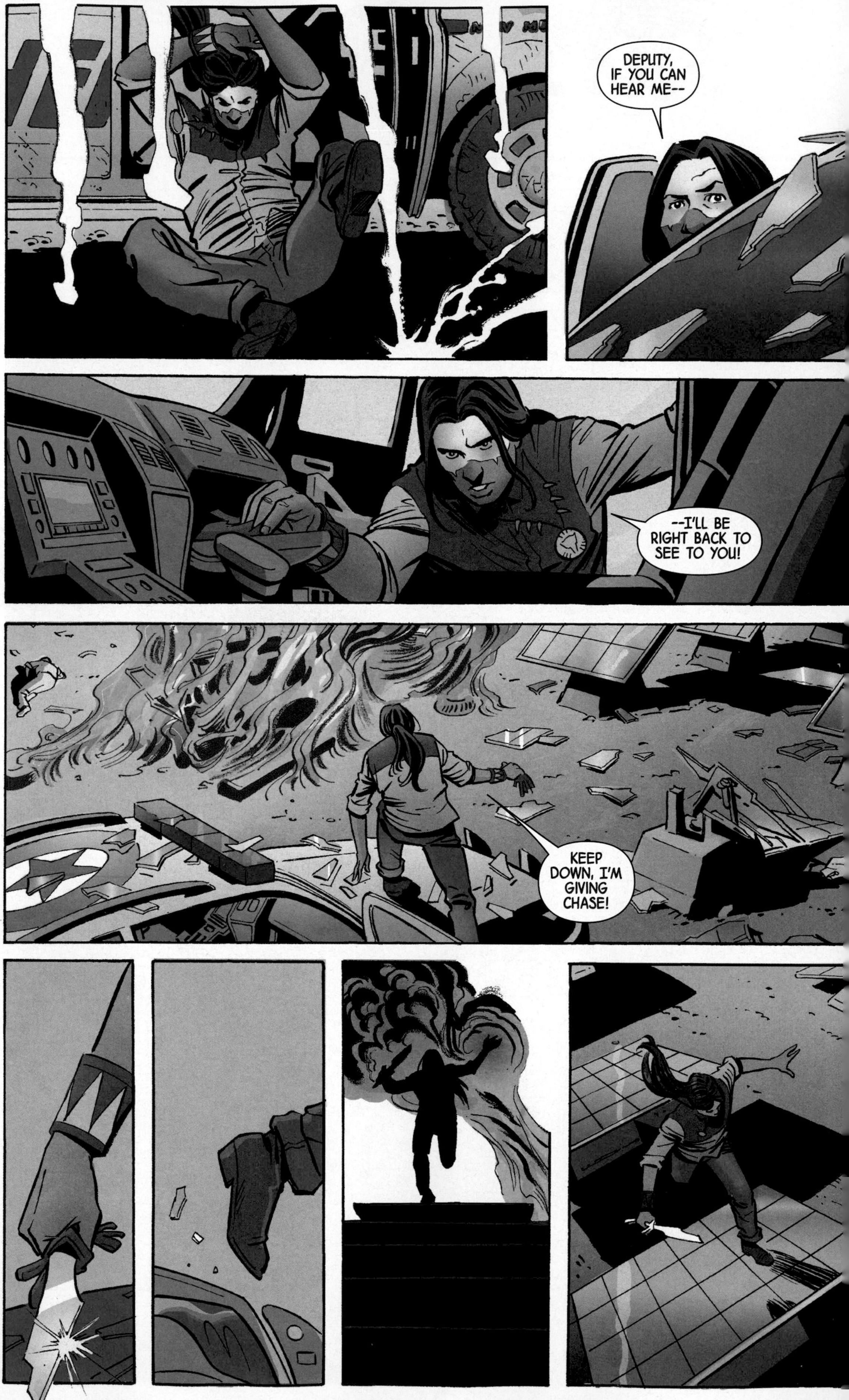
DEPUTY, IF YOU CAN HEAR ME--
--I'LL BE RIGHT BACK TO SEE TO YOU!
KEEP DOWN, I'M GIVING CHASE!

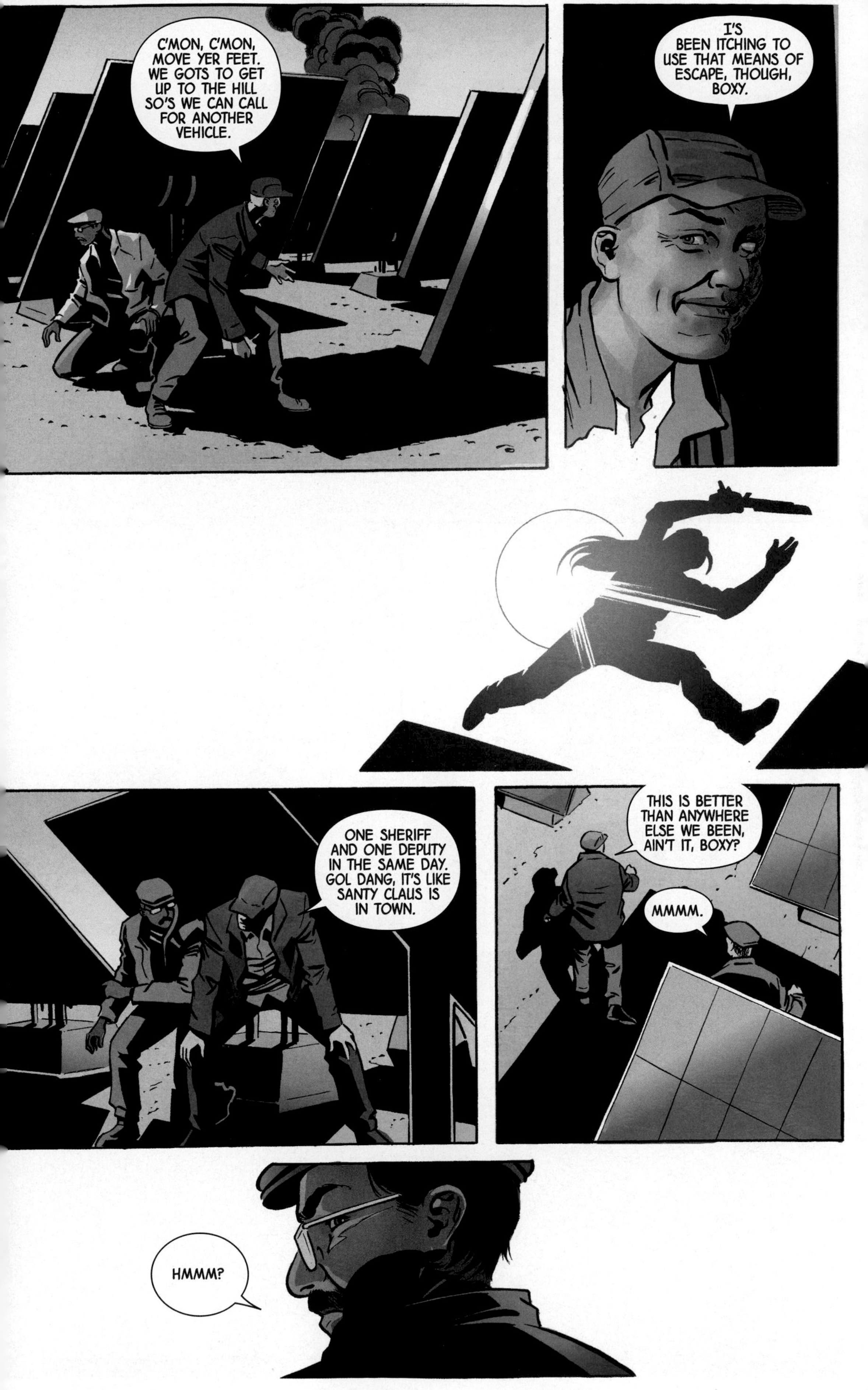
C'MON, C'MON, MOVE YER FEET. WE GOTS TO GET UP TO THE HILL SO'S WE CAN CALL FOR ANOTHER VEHICLE.
I'S BEEN ITCHING TO USE THAT MEANS OF ESCAPE, THOUGH, BOXY.
ONE SHERIFF AND ONE DEPUTY IN THE SAME DAY. GOL DANG, IT'S LIKE SANTY CLAUS IS IN TOWN.
THIS IS BETTER THAN ANYWHERE ELSE WE BEEN, AIN'T IT, BOXY?
MMMM.
HMMM?

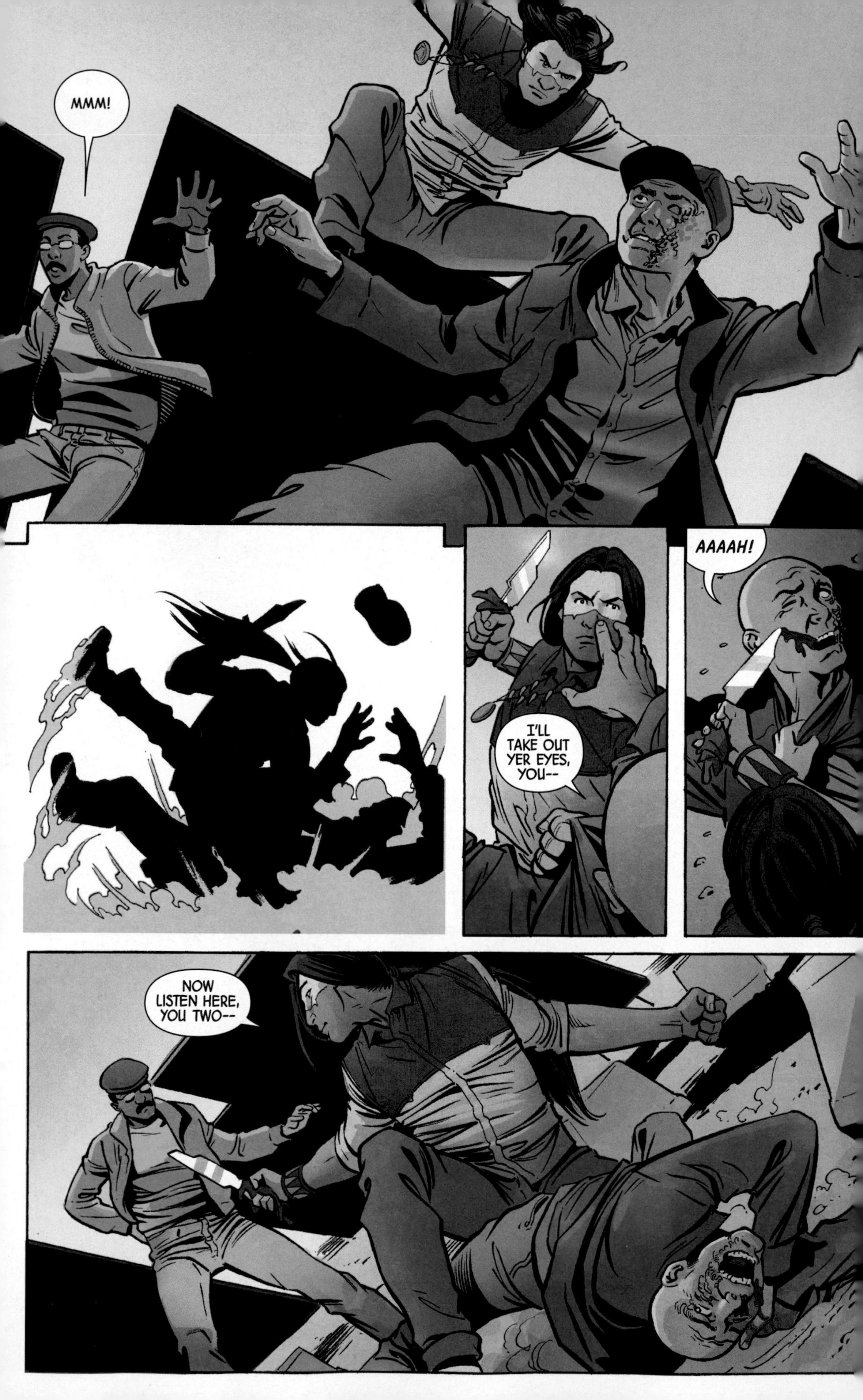
MMM!
I'LL TAKE OUT YER EYES, YOU--
AAAAH!
NOW LISTEN HERE, YOU TWO--

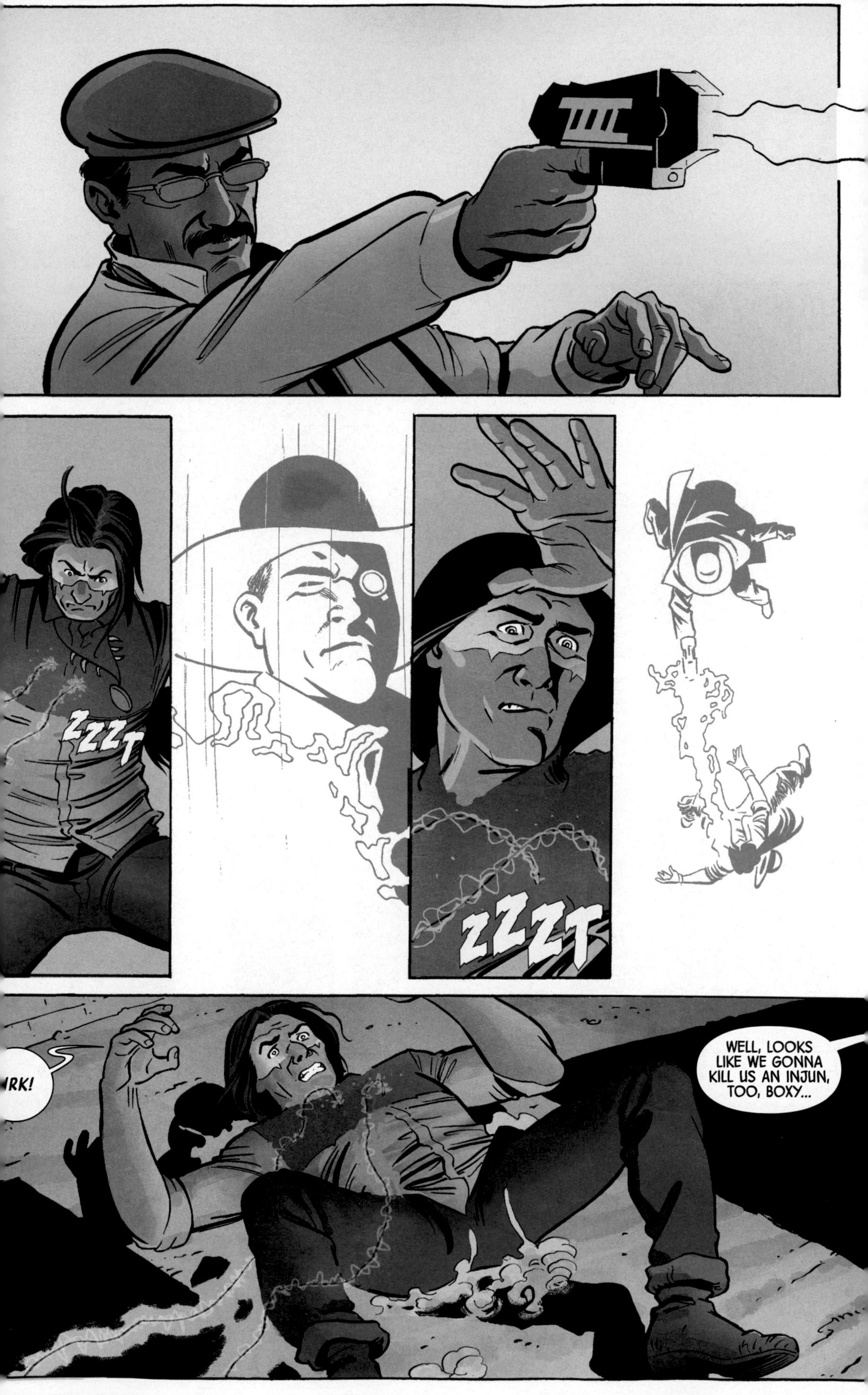
ZZZT
ZZZT
RK!
WELL, LOOKS LIKE WE GONNA KILL US AN INJUN, TOO, BOXY...

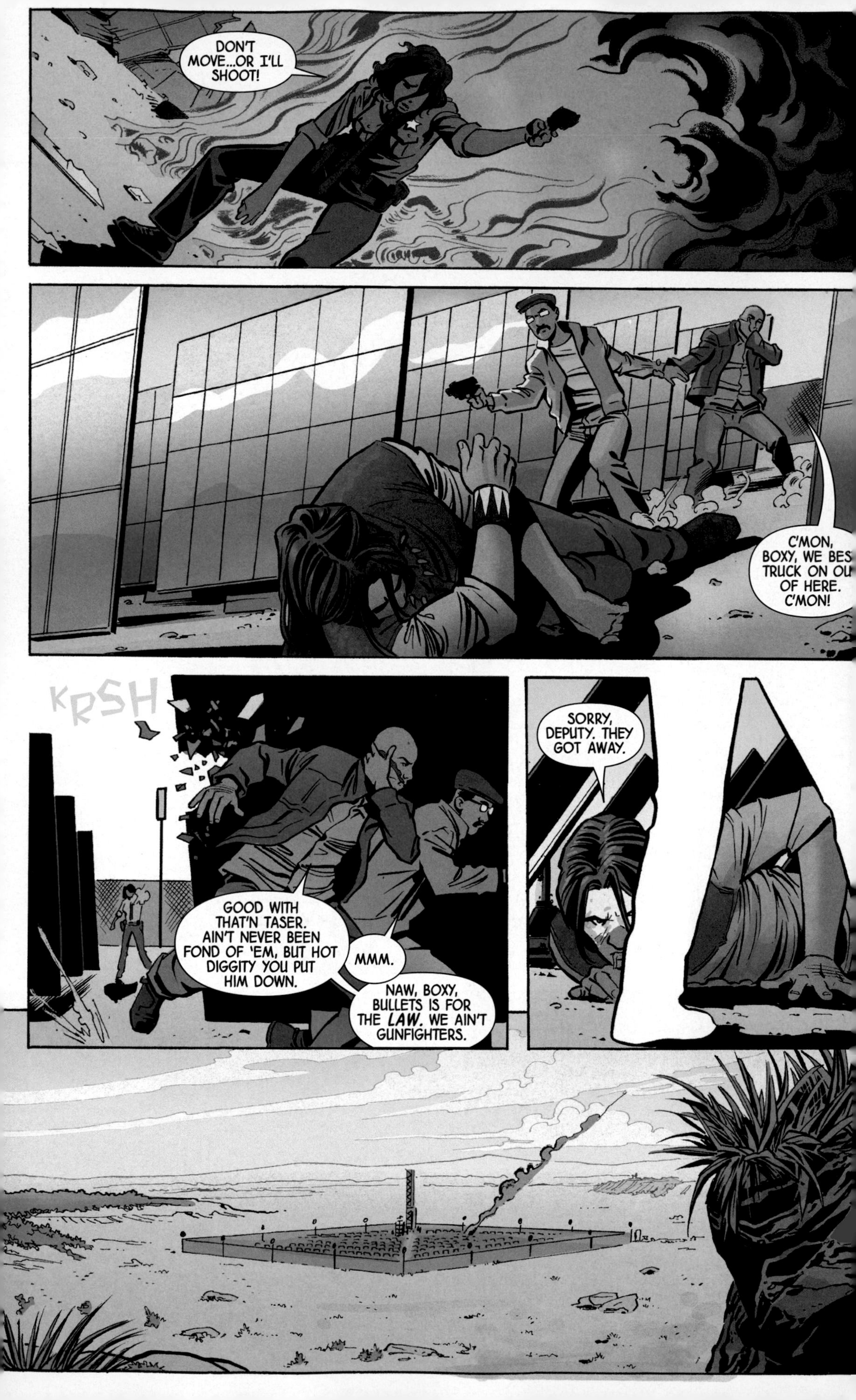
DON'T MOVE...OR I'LL SHOOT!
C'MON, BOXY, WE BES TRUCK ON OU OF HERE. C'MON!
KRSH
GOOD WITH THAT'N TASER. AIN'T NEVER BEEN FOND OF 'EM, BUT HOT DIGGITY YOU PUT HIM DOWN.
MMM.
NAW, BOXY, BULLETS IS FOR THE LAW. WE AIN'T GUNFIGHTERS.
SORRY, DEPUTY. THEY GOT AWAY.

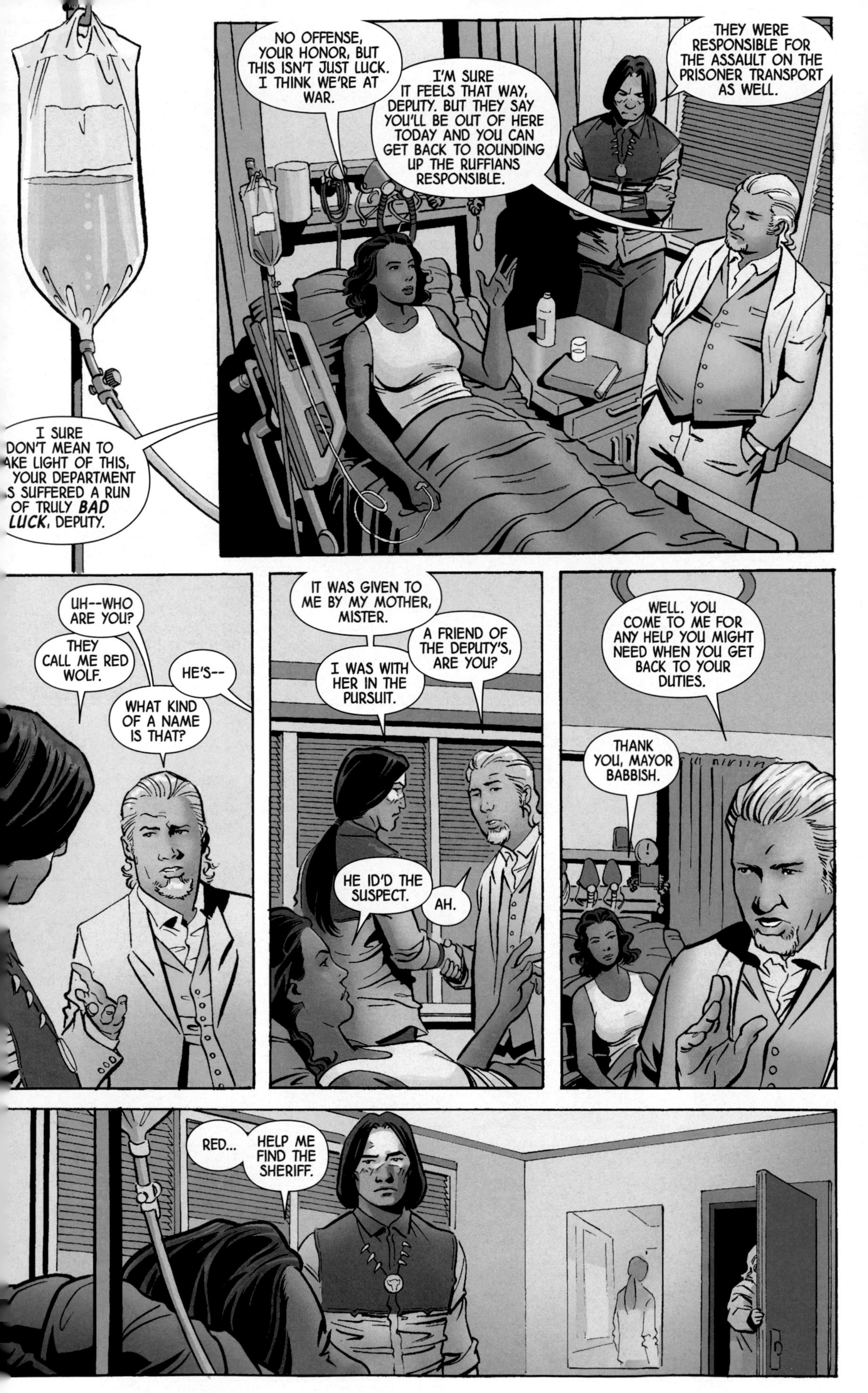
NO OFFENSE, YOUR HONOR, BUT THIS ISN'T JUST LUCK. I THINK WE'RE AT WAR.
I'M SURE IT FEELS THAT WAY, DEPUTY. BUT THEY SAY YOU'LL BE OUT OF HERE TODAY AND YOU CAN GET BACK TO ROUNDING UP THE RUFFIANS RESPONSIBLE.
THEY WERE RESPONSIBLE FOR THE ASSAULT ON THE PRISONER TRANSPORT AS WELL.
I SURE DON'T MEAN TO AKE LIGHT OF THIS, YOUR DEPARTMENT S SUFFERED A RUN OF TRULY **BAD LUCK**, DEPUTY.
UH--WHO ARE YOU?
THEY CALL ME RED WOLF.
HE'S--
WHAT KIND OF A NAME IS THAT?
IT WAS GIVEN TO ME BY MY MOTHER, MISTER.
A FRIEND OF THE DEPUTY'S, ARE YOU?
I WAS WITH HER IN THE PURSUIT.
HE ID'D THE SUSPECT.
AH.
WELL. YOU COME TO ME FOR ANY HELP YOU MIGHT NEED WHEN YOU GET BACK TO YOUR DUTIES.
THANK YOU, MAYOR BABBISH.
RED...
HELP ME FIND THE SHERIFF.

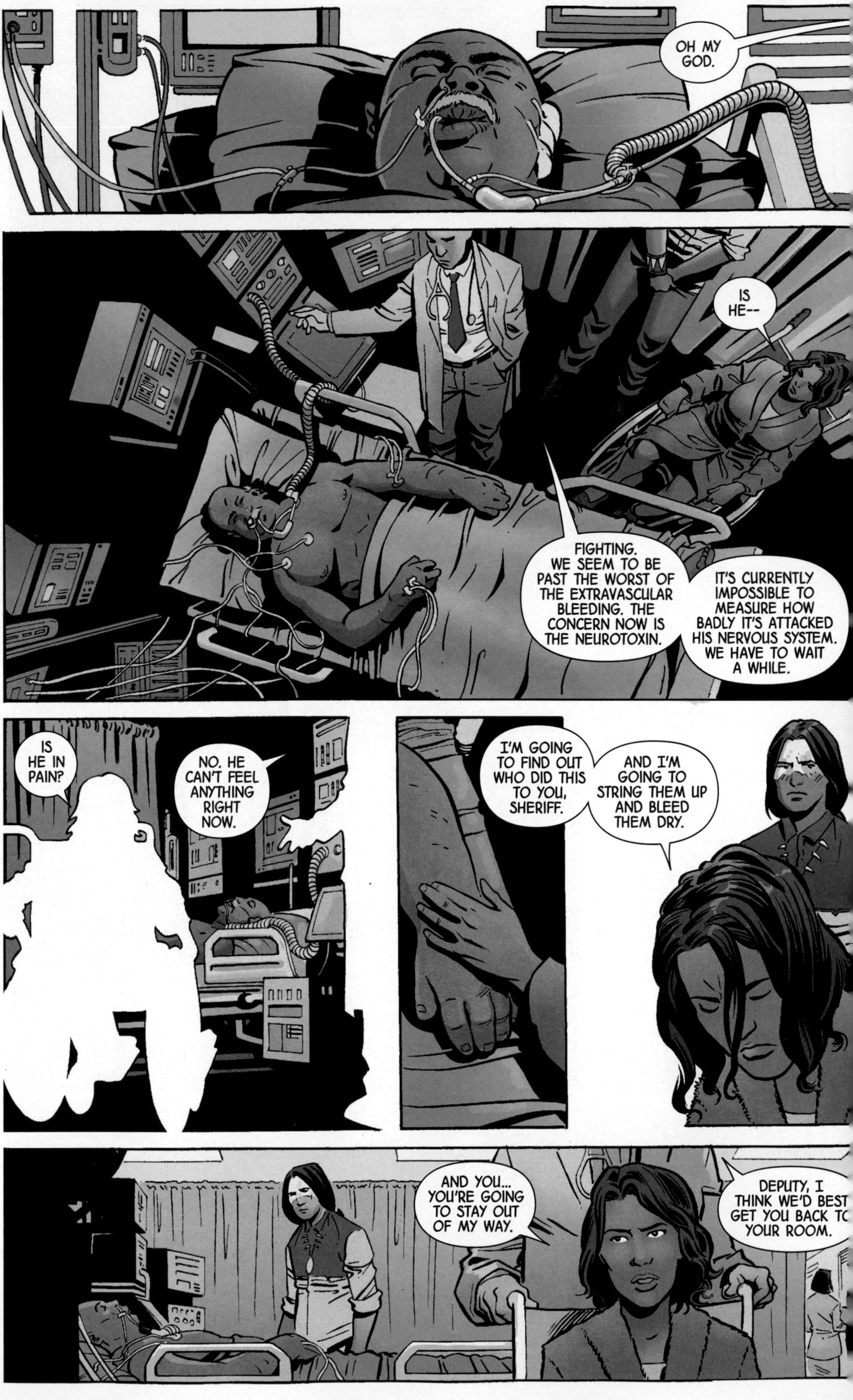
OH MY GOD.
IS HE--
FIGHTING. WE SEEM TO BE PAST THE WORST OF THE EXTRAVASCULAR BLEEDING. THE CONCERN NOW IS THE NEUROTOXIN.
IT'S CURRENTLY IMPOSSIBLE TO MEASURE HOW BADLY IT'S ATTACKED HIS NERVOUS SYSTEM. WE HAVE TO WAIT A WHILE.
IS HE IN PAIN?
NO. HE CAN'T FEEL ANYTHING RIGHT NOW.
I'M GOING TO FIND OUT WHO DID THIS TO YOU, SHERIFF.
AND I'M GOING TO STRING THEM UP AND BLEED THEM DRY.
AND YOU... YOU'RE GOING TO STAY OUT OF MY WAY.
DEPUTY, I THINK WE'D BEST GET YOU BACK TO YOUR ROOM.

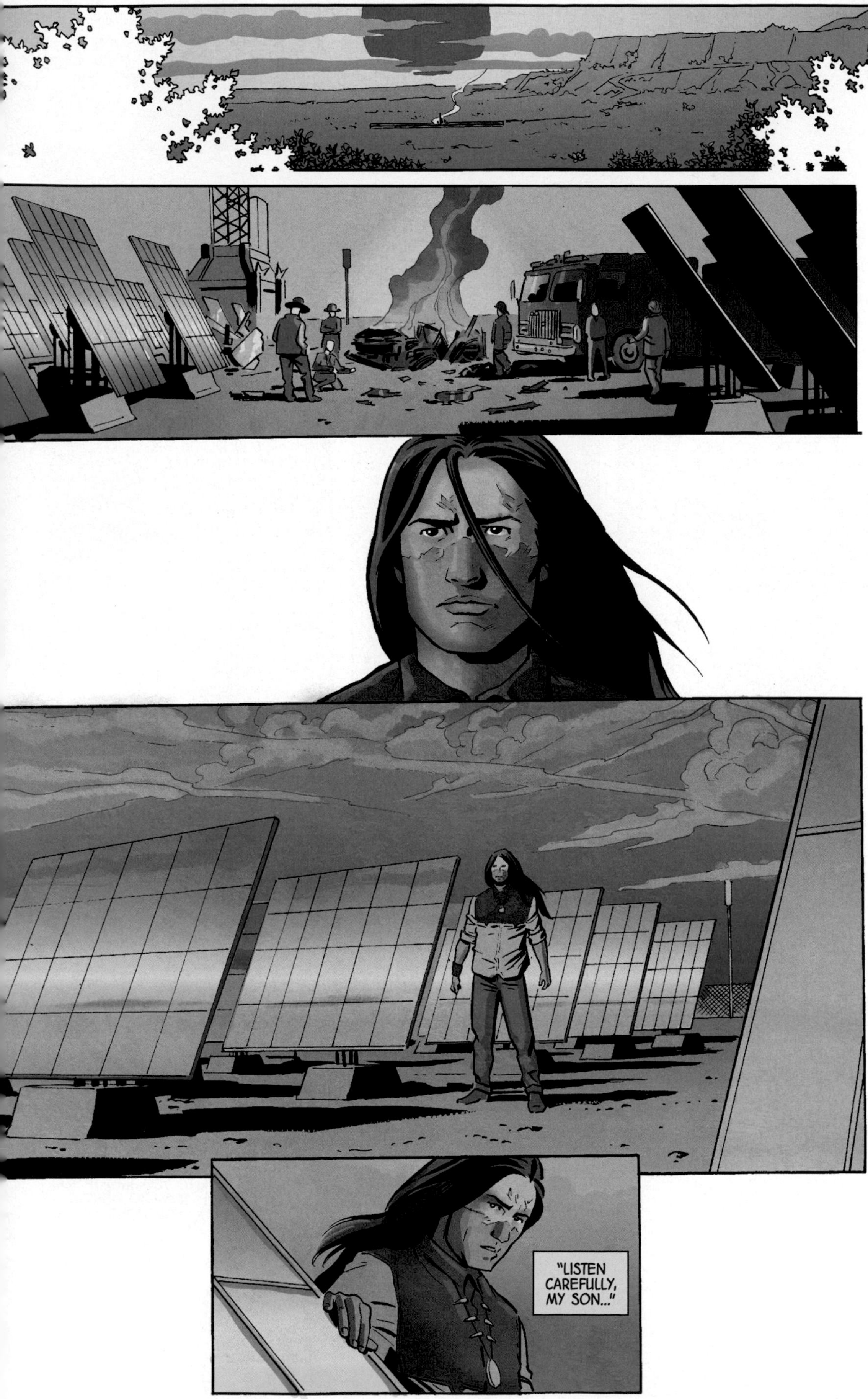
"LISTEN CAREFULLY, MY SON..."

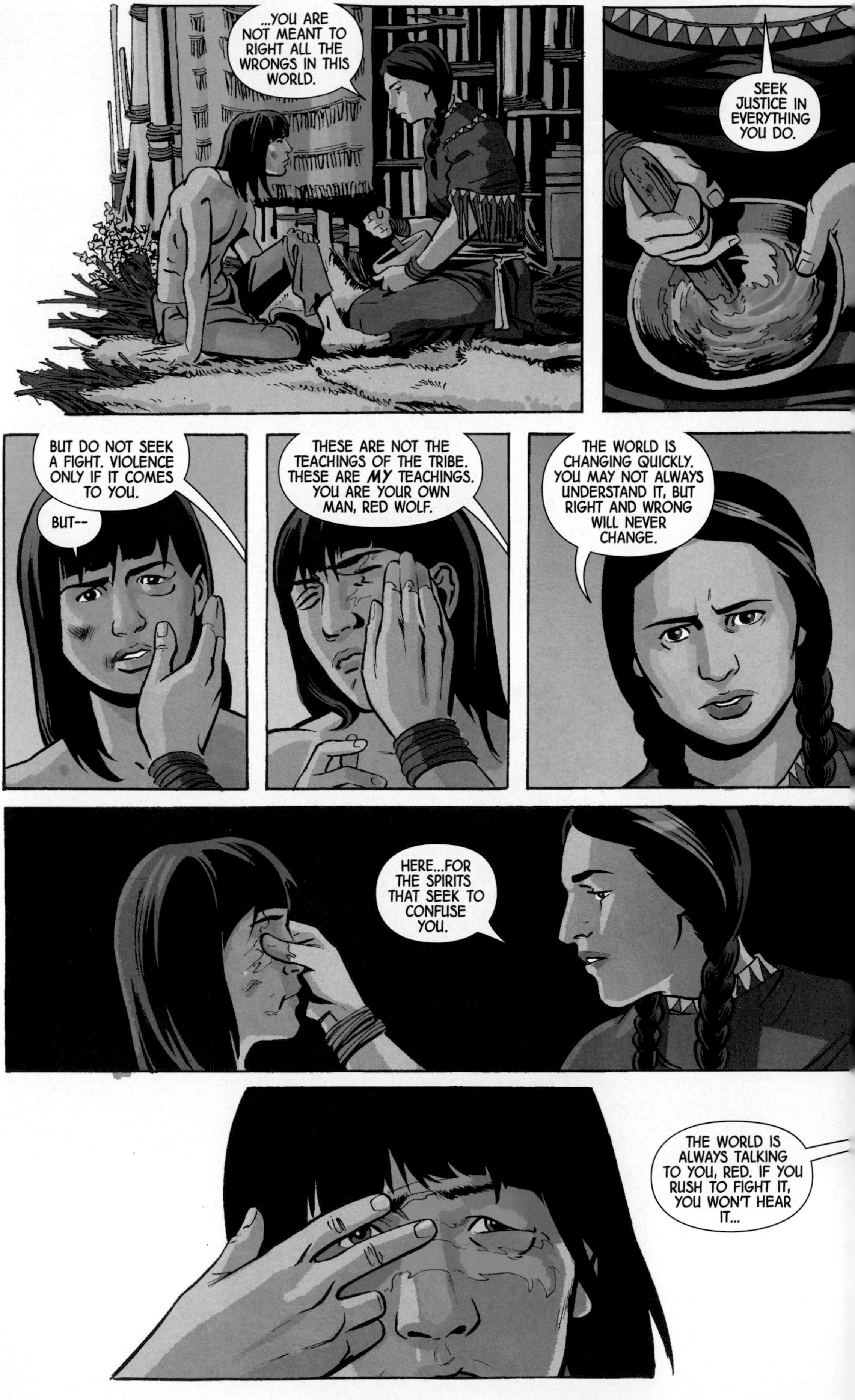
...YOU ARE NOT MEANT TO RIGHT ALL THE WRONGS IN THIS WORLD.
SEEK JUSTICE IN EVERYTHING YOU DO.
BUT DO NOT SEEK A FIGHT. VIOLENCE ONLY IF IT COMES TO YOU.
BUT--
THESE ARE NOT THE TEACHINGS OF THE TRIBE. THESE ARE *MY* TEACHINGS. YOU ARE YOUR OWN MAN, RED WOLF.
THE WORLD IS CHANGING QUICKLY. YOU MAY NOT ALWAYS UNDERSTAND IT, BUT RIGHT AND WRONG WILL NEVER CHANGE.
HERE...FOR THE SPIRITS THAT SEEK TO CONFUSE YOU.
THE WORLD IS ALWAYS TALKING TO YOU, RED. IF YOU RUSH TO FIGHT IT, YOU WON'T HEAR IT...

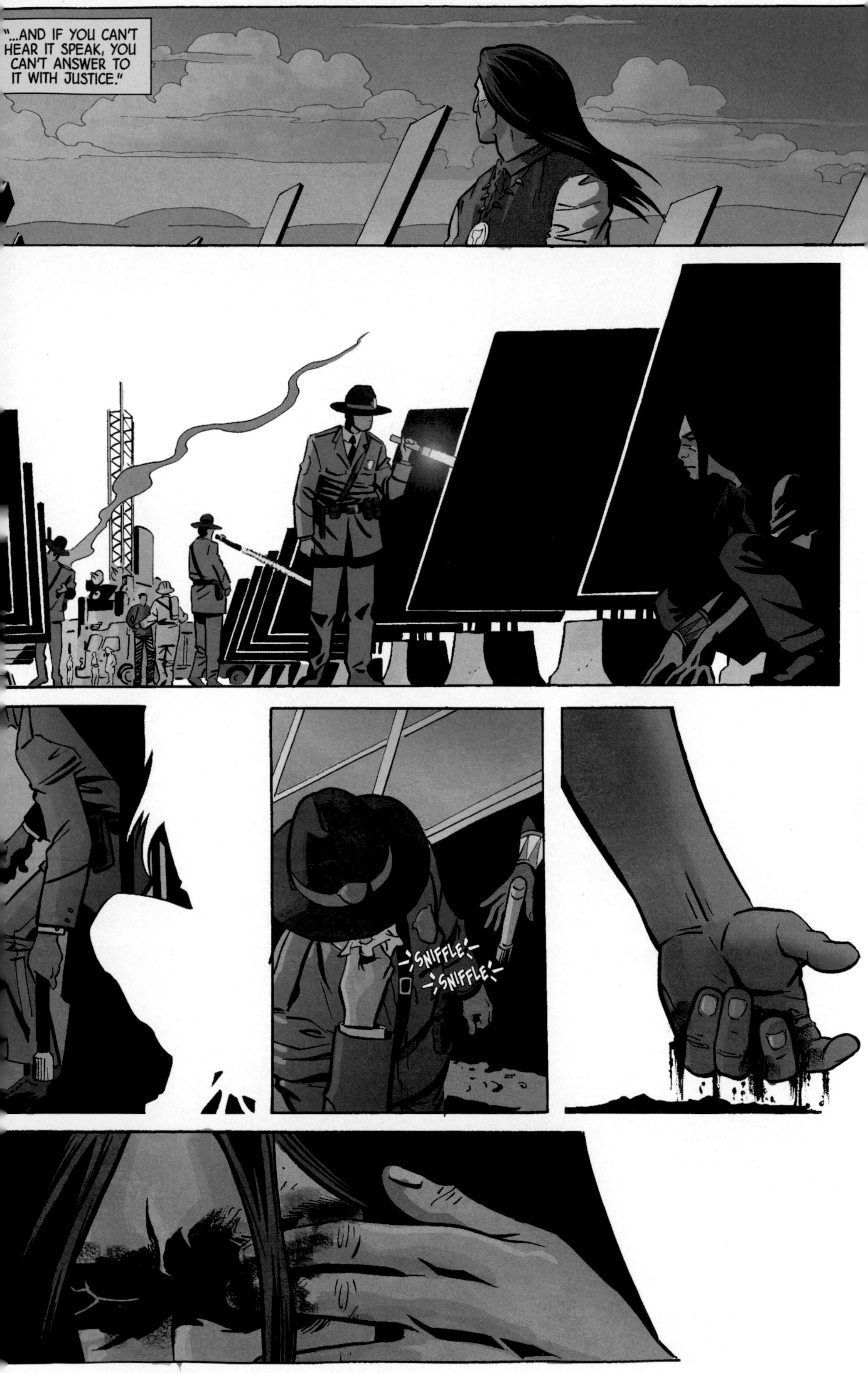
"...AND IF YOU CAN'T HEAR IT SPEAK, YOU CAN'T ANSWER TO IT WITH JUSTICE."
SNIFFLE
SNIFFLE

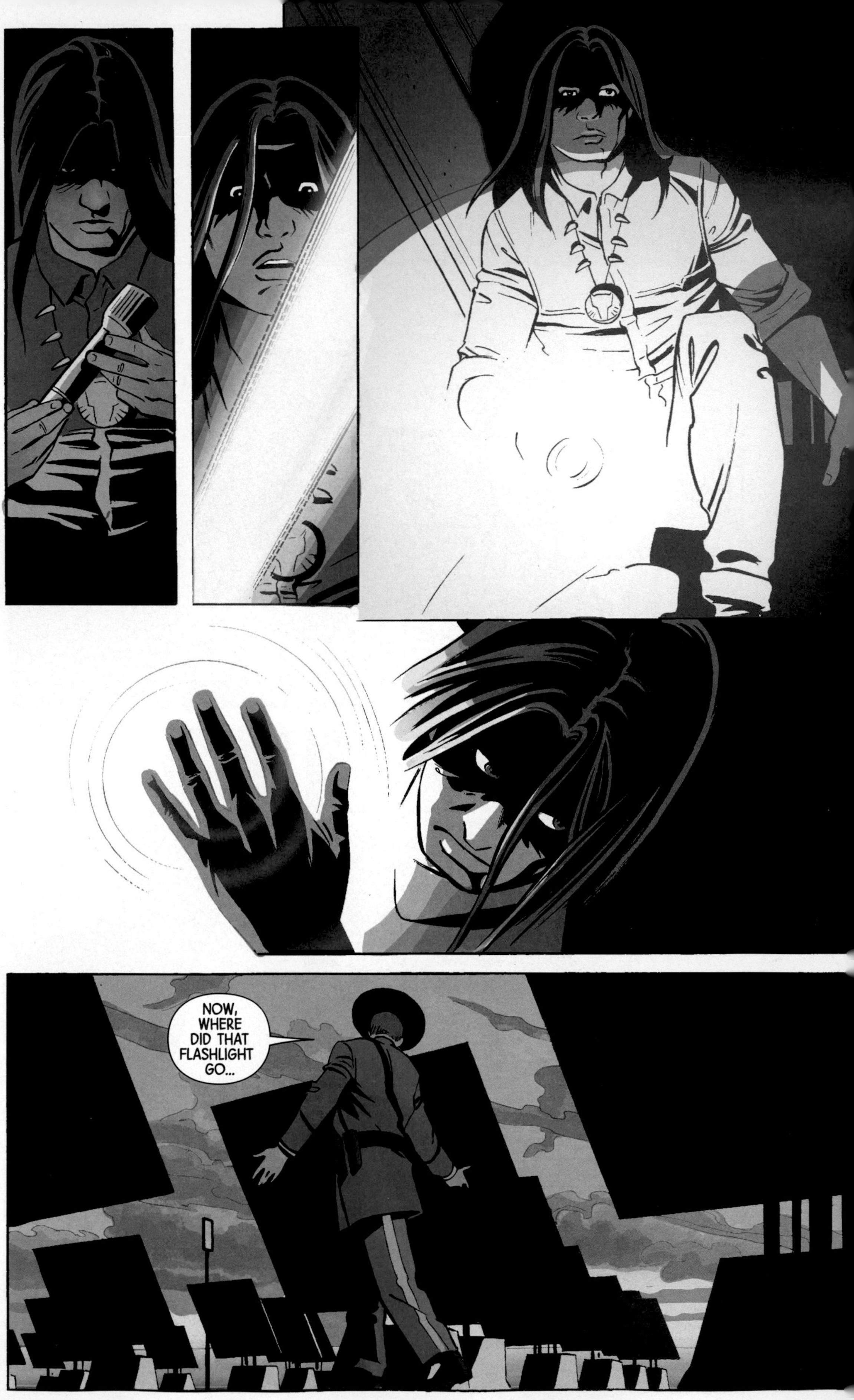
NOW, WHERE DID THAT FLASHLIGHT GO...

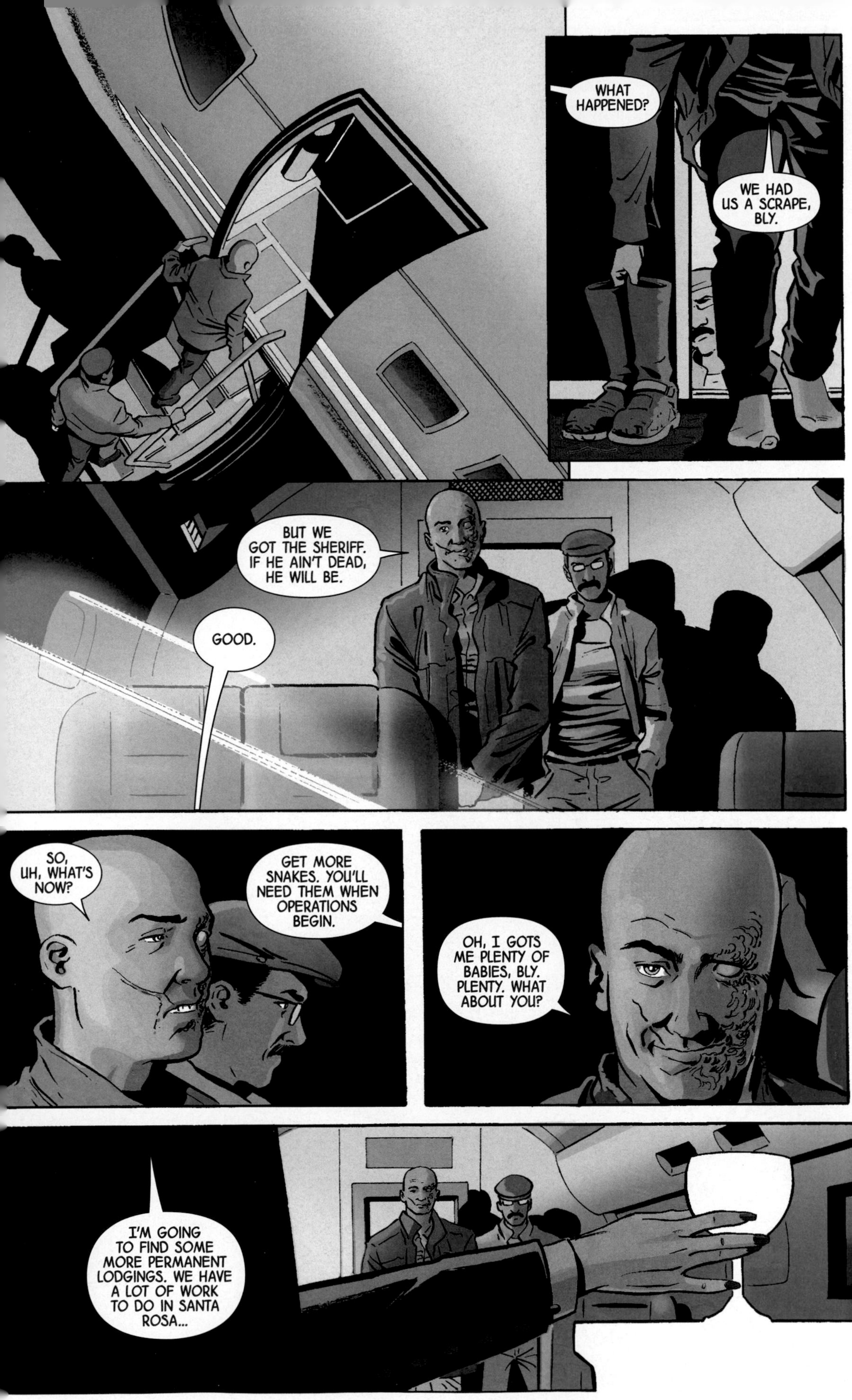
WHAT HAPPENED?
WE HAD US A SCRAPE, BLY.
BUT WE GOT THE SHERIFF. IF HE AIN'T DEAD, HE WILL BE.
GOOD.
SO, UH, WHAT'S NOW?
GET MORE SNAKES. YOU'LL NEED THEM WHEN OPERATIONS BEGIN.
OH, I GOTS ME PLENTY OF BABIES, BLY. PLENTY. WHAT ABOUT YOU?
I'M GOING TO FIND SOME MORE PERMANENT LODGINGS. WE HAVE A LOT OF WORK TO DO IN SANTA ROSA...

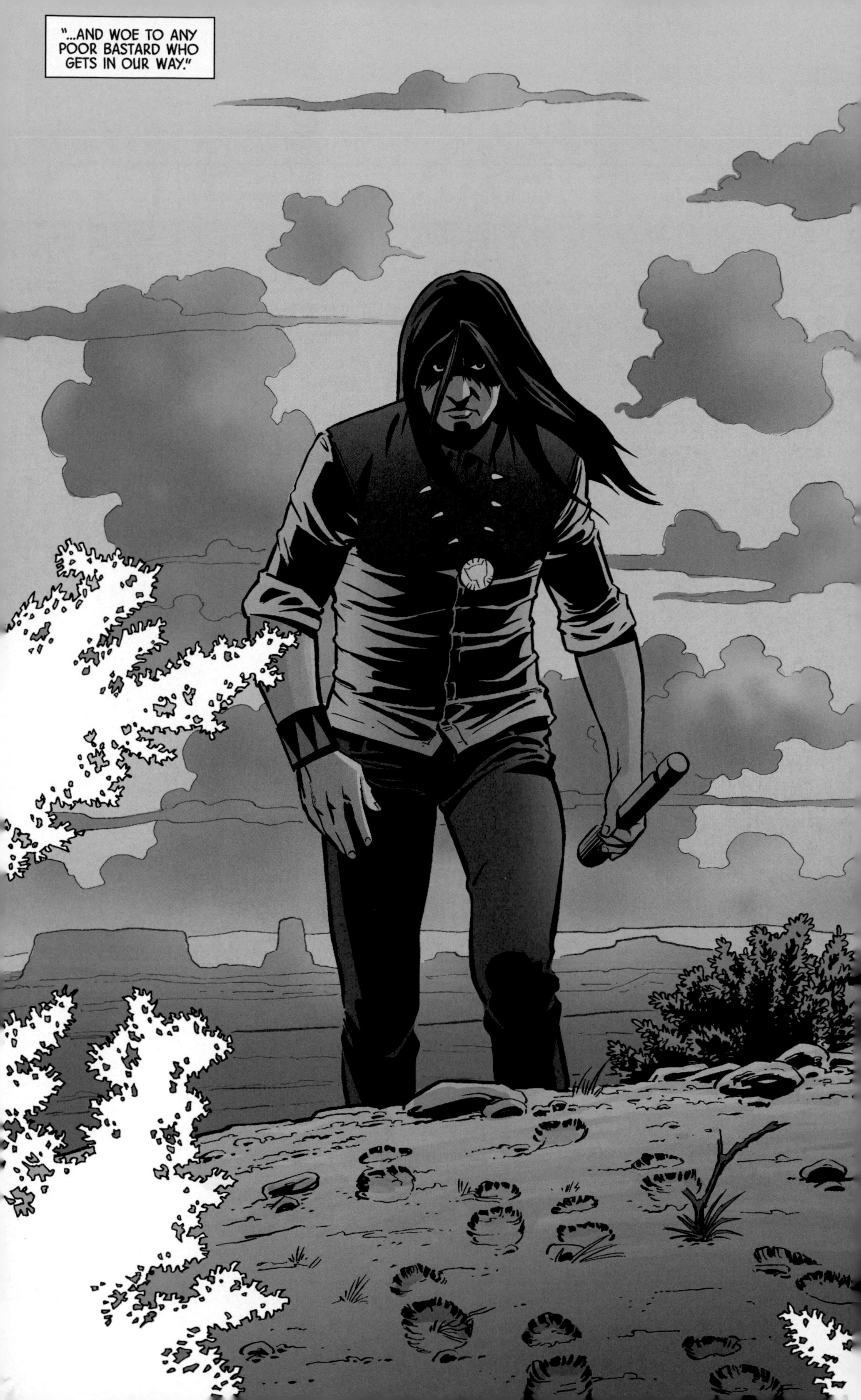
"...AND WOE TO ANY POOR BASTARD WHO GETS IN OUR WAY."

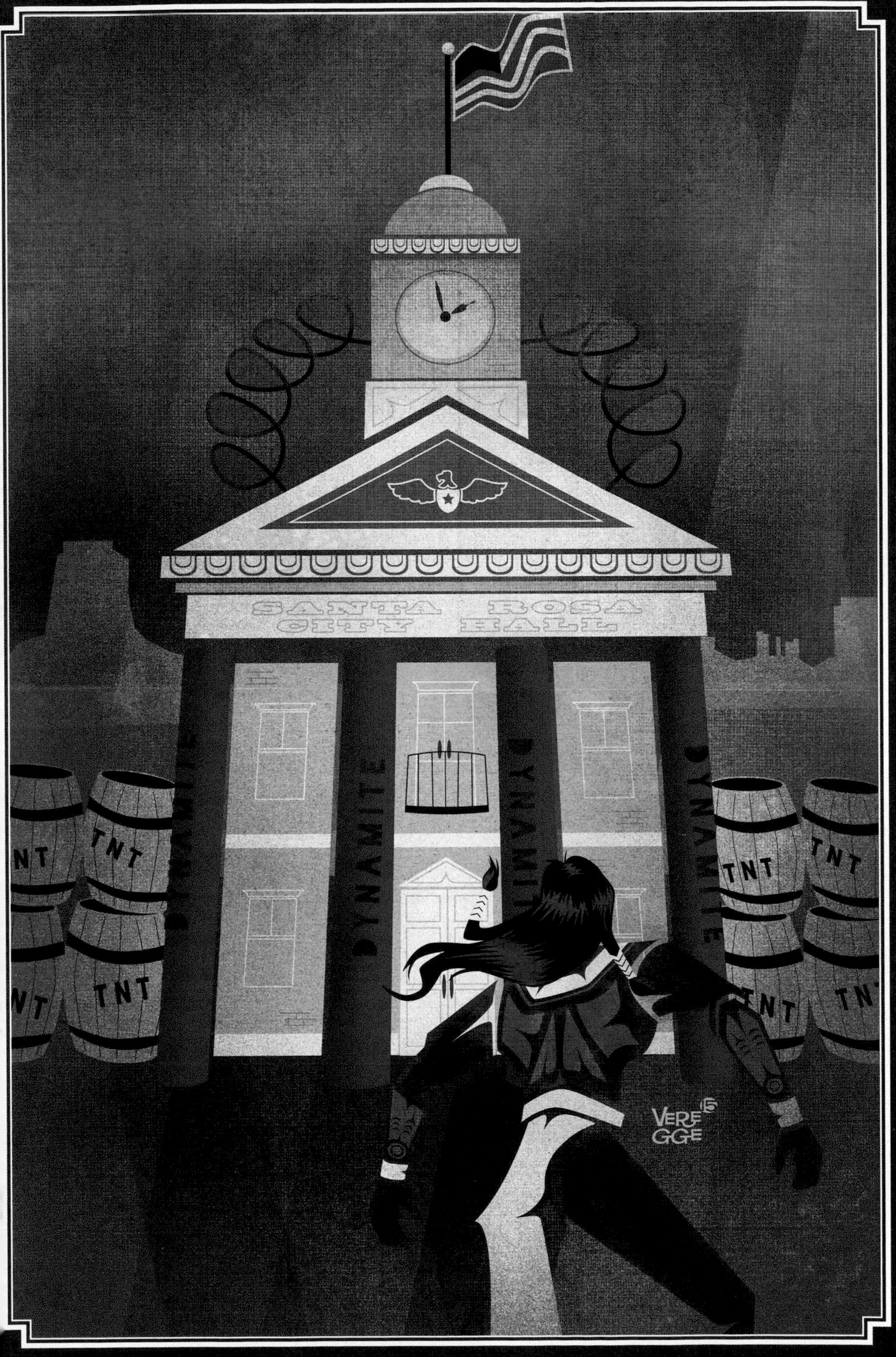
SANTA ROSA
CITY HALL
DYNAMITE
DYNAMITE
DYNAMITE
DYNAMITE
TNT
TNT
TNT
TNT
TNT
TNT
TNT
TNT
VEREGGE 15

OUTSIDE SANTA ROSA
NEW MEXICO.

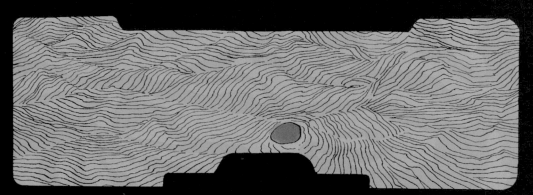

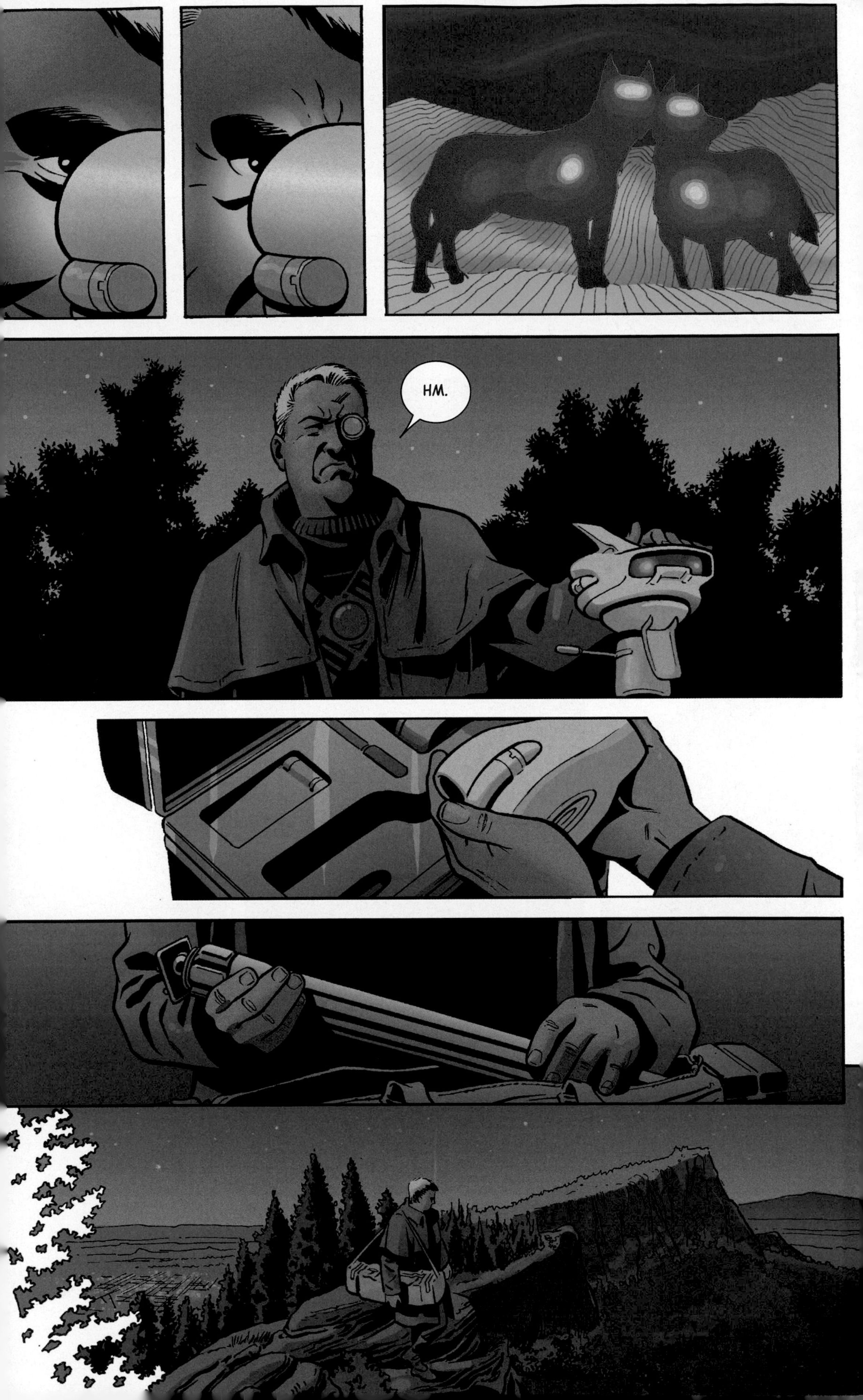
HM.

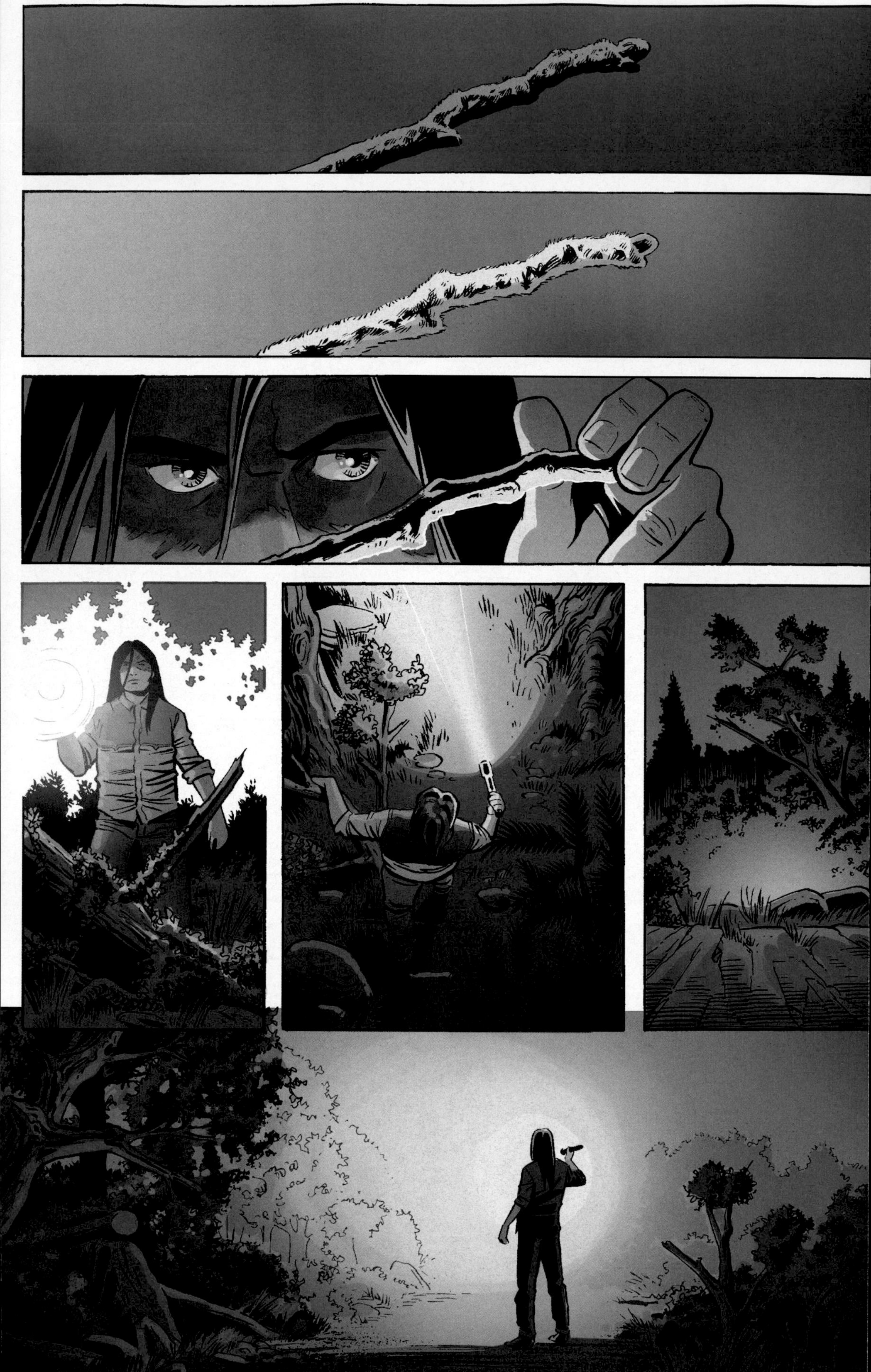

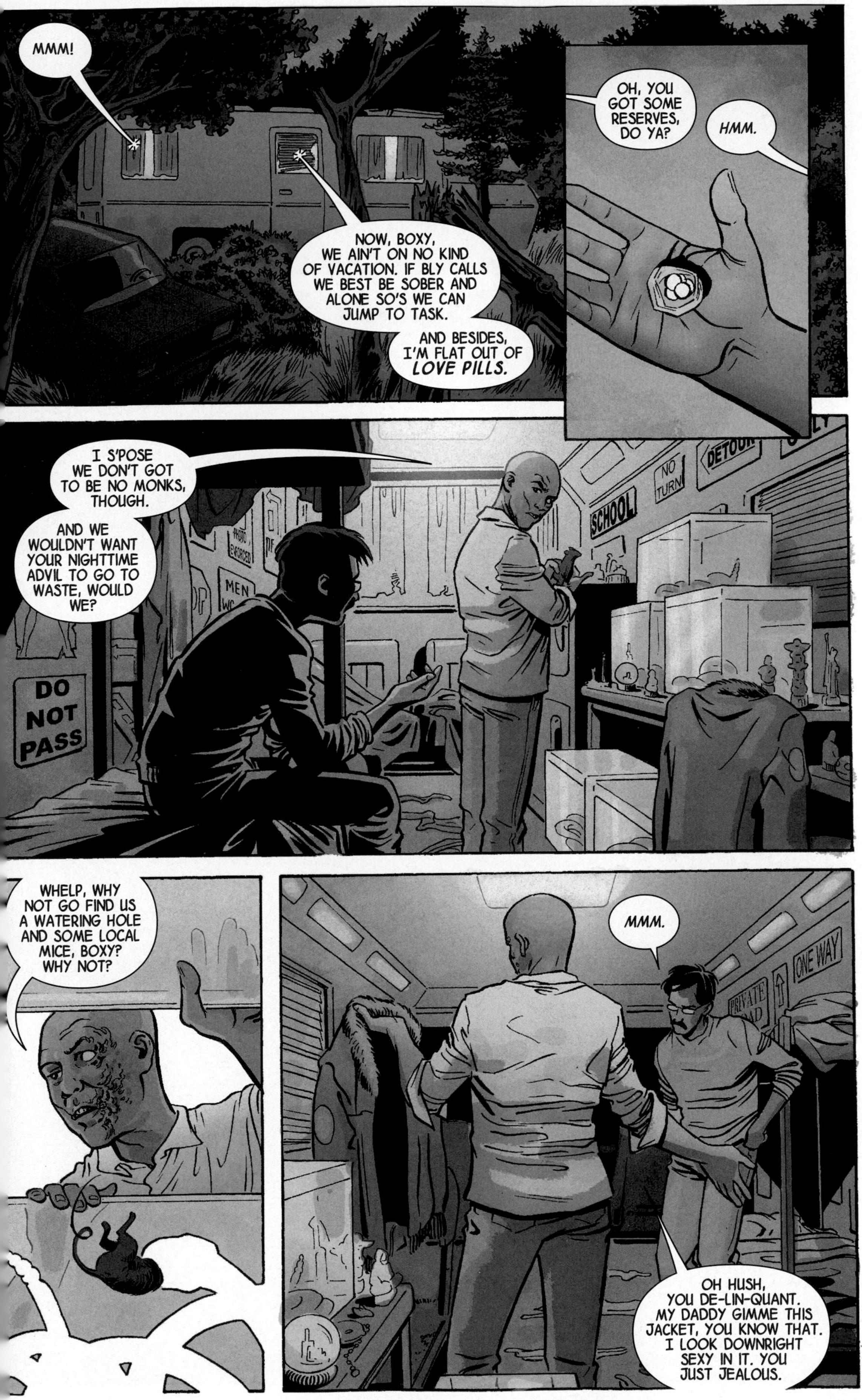
MMM!
NOW, BOXY, WE AIN'T ON NO KIND OF VACATION. IF BLY CALLS WE BEST BE SOBER AND ALONE SO'S WE CAN JUMP TO TASK.
AND BESIDES, I'M FLAT OUT OF *LOVE PILLS.*
OH, YOU GOT SOME RESERVES, DO YA?
HMM.
I S'POSE WE DON'T GOT TO BE NO MONKS, THOUGH.
AND WE WOULDN'T WANT YOUR NIGHTTIME ADVIL TO GO TO WASTE, WOULD WE?
SCHOOL
NO TURN
DETOUR
MEN WC
DO NOT PASS
WHELP, WHY NOT GO FIND US A WATERING HOLE AND SOME LOCAL MICE, BOXY? WHY NOT?
MMM.
ONE WAY
OH HUSH, YOU DE-LIN-QUANT. MY DADDY GIMME THIS JACKET, YOU KNOW THAT. I LOOK DOWNRIGHT SEXY IN IT. YOU JUST JEALOUS.

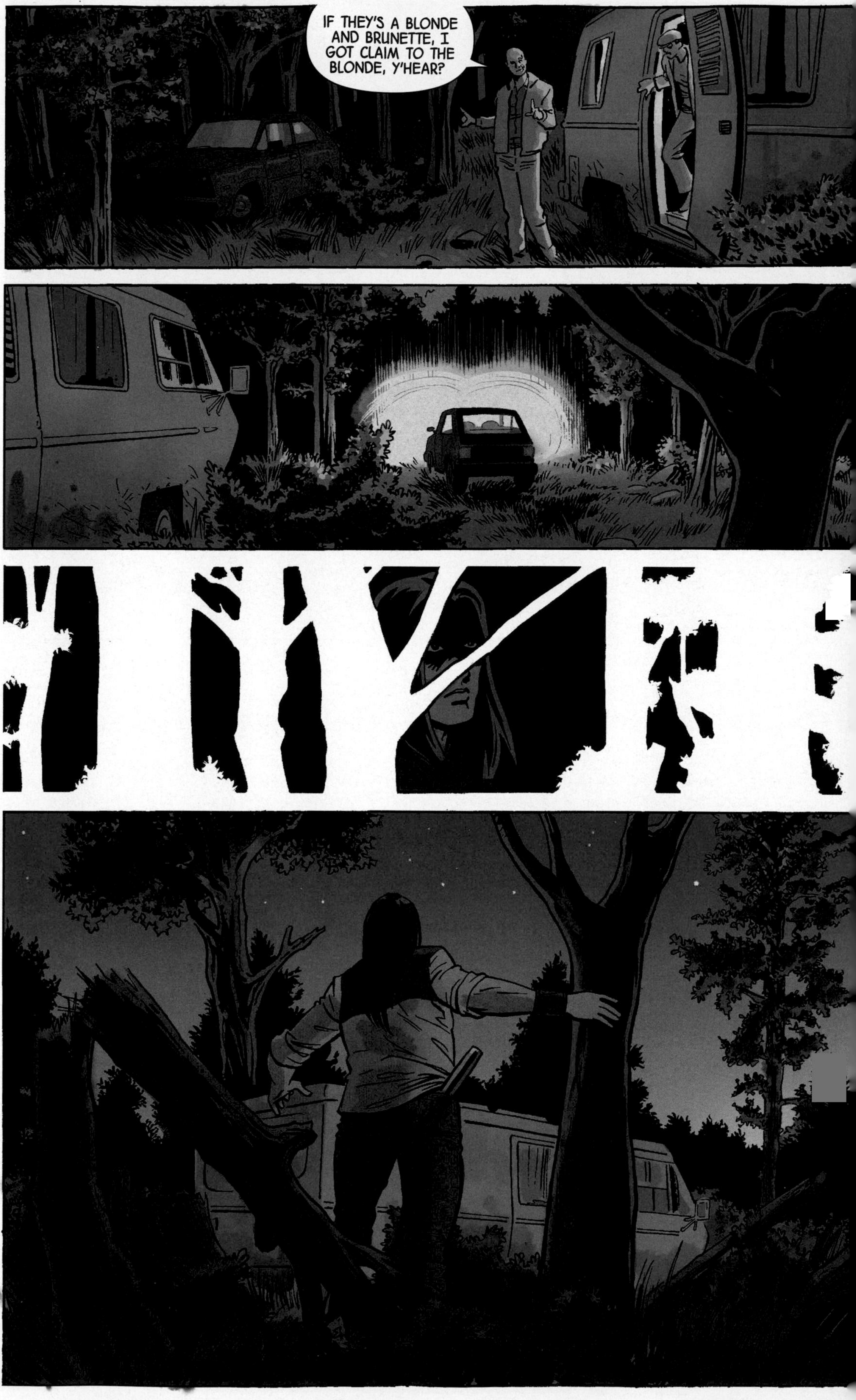
IF THEY'S A BLONDE AND BRUNETTE, I GOT CLAIM TO THE BLONDE, Y'HEAR?

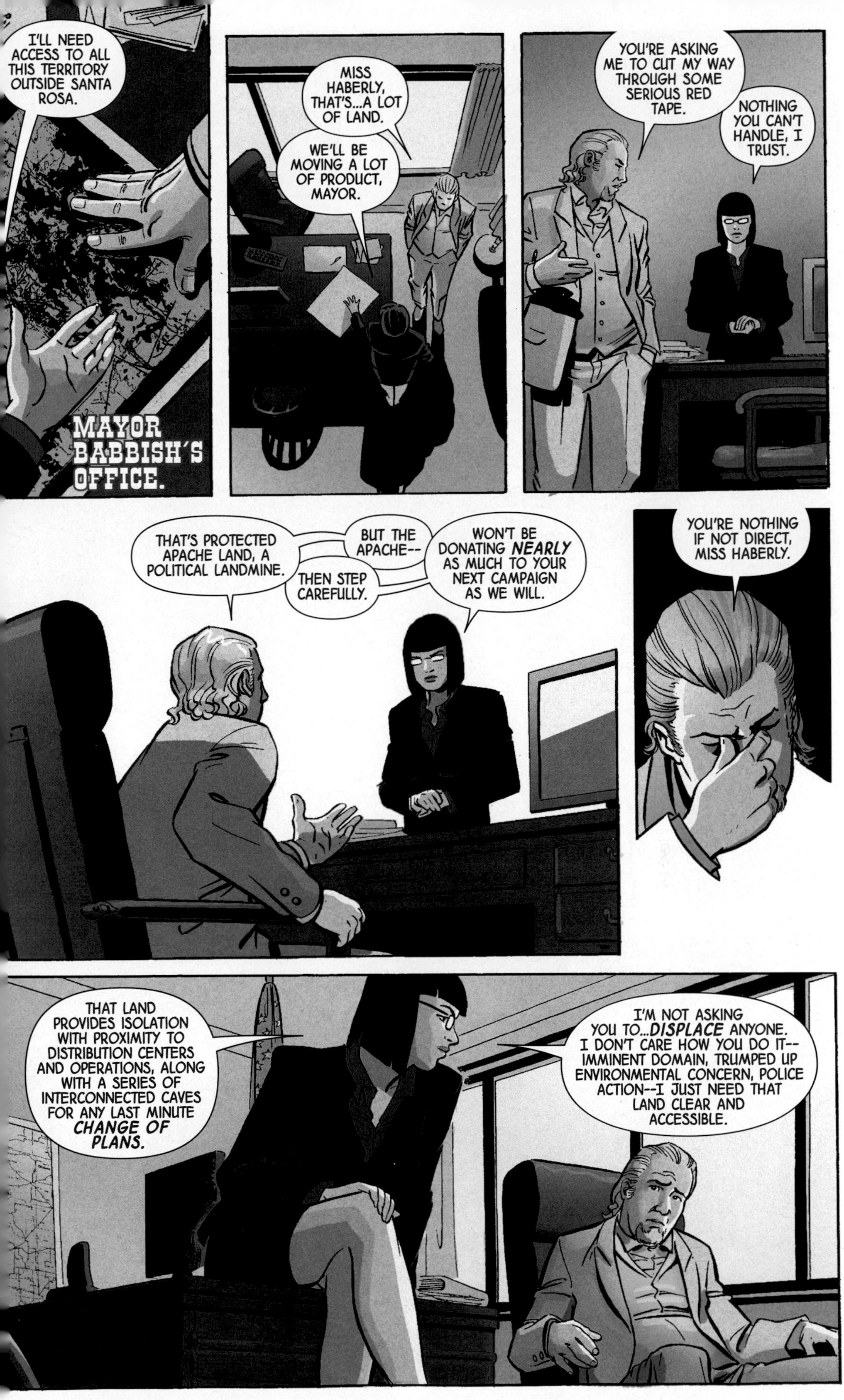
I'LL NEED ACCESS TO ALL THIS TERRITORY OUTSIDE SANTA ROSA.
MAYOR BABBISH'S OFFICE.
MISS HABERLY, THAT'S...A LOT OF LAND.
WE'LL BE MOVING A LOT OF PRODUCT, MAYOR.
YOU'RE ASKING ME TO CUT MY WAY THROUGH SOME SERIOUS RED TAPE.
NOTHING YOU CAN'T HANDLE, I TRUST.
THAT'S PROTECTED APACHE LAND, A POLITICAL LANDMINE.
THEN STEP CAREFULLY.
BUT THE APACHE--
WON'T BE DONATING *NEARLY* AS MUCH TO YOUR NEXT CAMPAIGN AS WE WILL.
YOU'RE NOTHING IF NOT DIRECT, MISS HABERLY.
THAT LAND PROVIDES ISOLATION WITH PROXIMITY TO DISTRIBUTION CENTERS AND OPERATIONS, ALONG WITH A SERIES OF INTERCONNECTED CAVES FOR ANY LAST MINUTE *CHANGE OF PLANS.*
I'M NOT ASKING YOU TO...*DISPLACE* ANYONE. I DON'T CARE HOW YOU DO IT--IMMINENT DOMAIN, TRUMPED UP ENVIRONMENTAL CONCERN, POLICE ACTION--I JUST NEED THAT LAND CLEAR AND ACCESSIBLE.

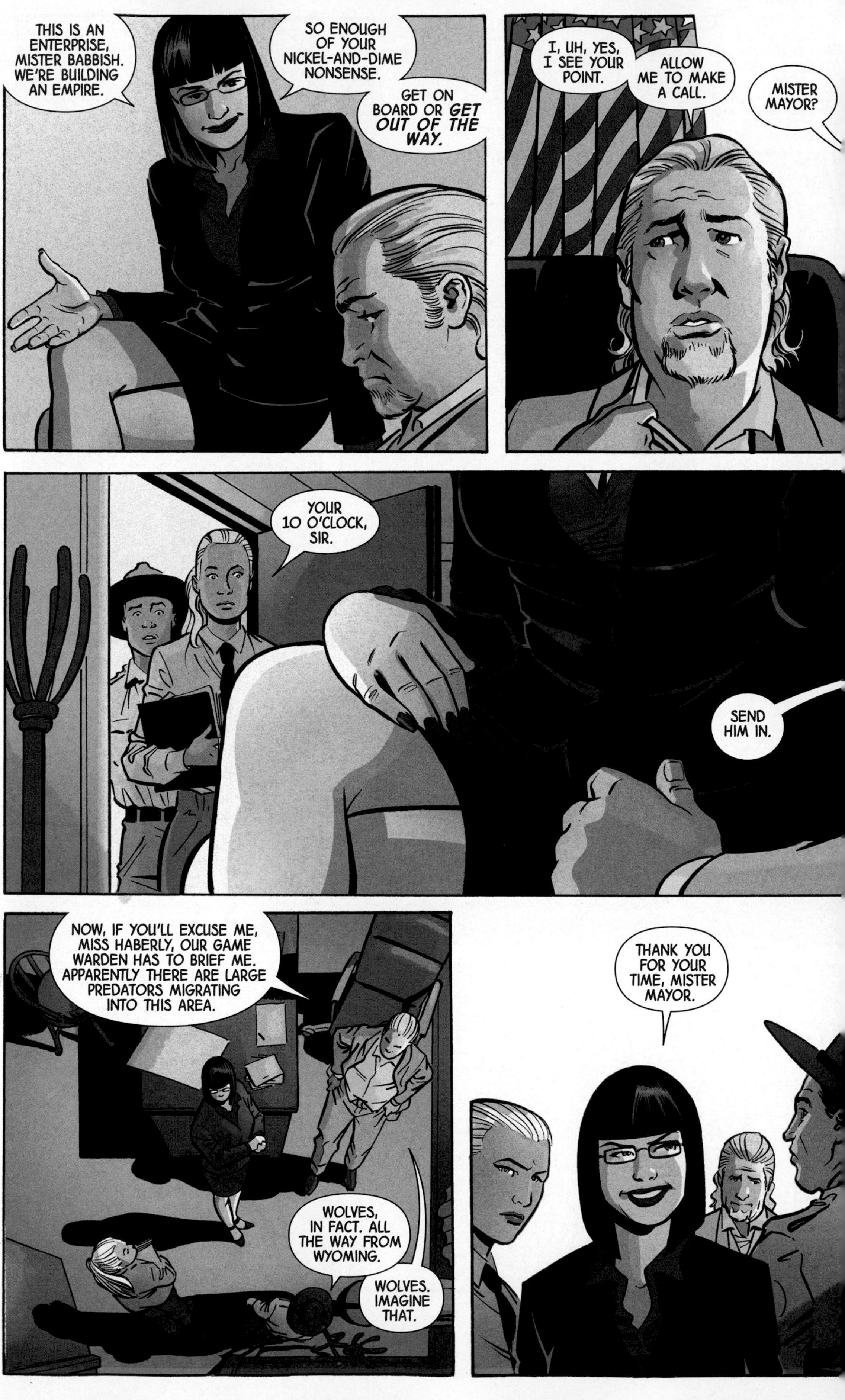
THIS IS AN ENTERPRISE, MISTER BABBISH. WE'RE BUILDING AN EMPIRE.
SO ENOUGH OF YOUR NICKEL-AND-DIME NONSENSE.
GET ON BOARD OR GET OUT OF THE WAY.
I, UH, YES, I SEE YOUR POINT.
ALLOW ME TO MAKE A CALL.
MISTER MAYOR?
YOUR 10 O'CLOCK, SIR.
SEND HIM IN.
NOW, IF YOU'LL EXCUSE ME, MISS HABERLY, OUR GAME WARDEN HAS TO BRIEF ME. APPARENTLY THERE ARE LARGE PREDATORS MIGRATING INTO THIS AREA.
WOLVES, IN FACT. ALL THE WAY FROM WYOMING.
WOLVES. IMAGINE THAT.
THANK YOU FOR YOUR TIME, MISTER MAYOR.

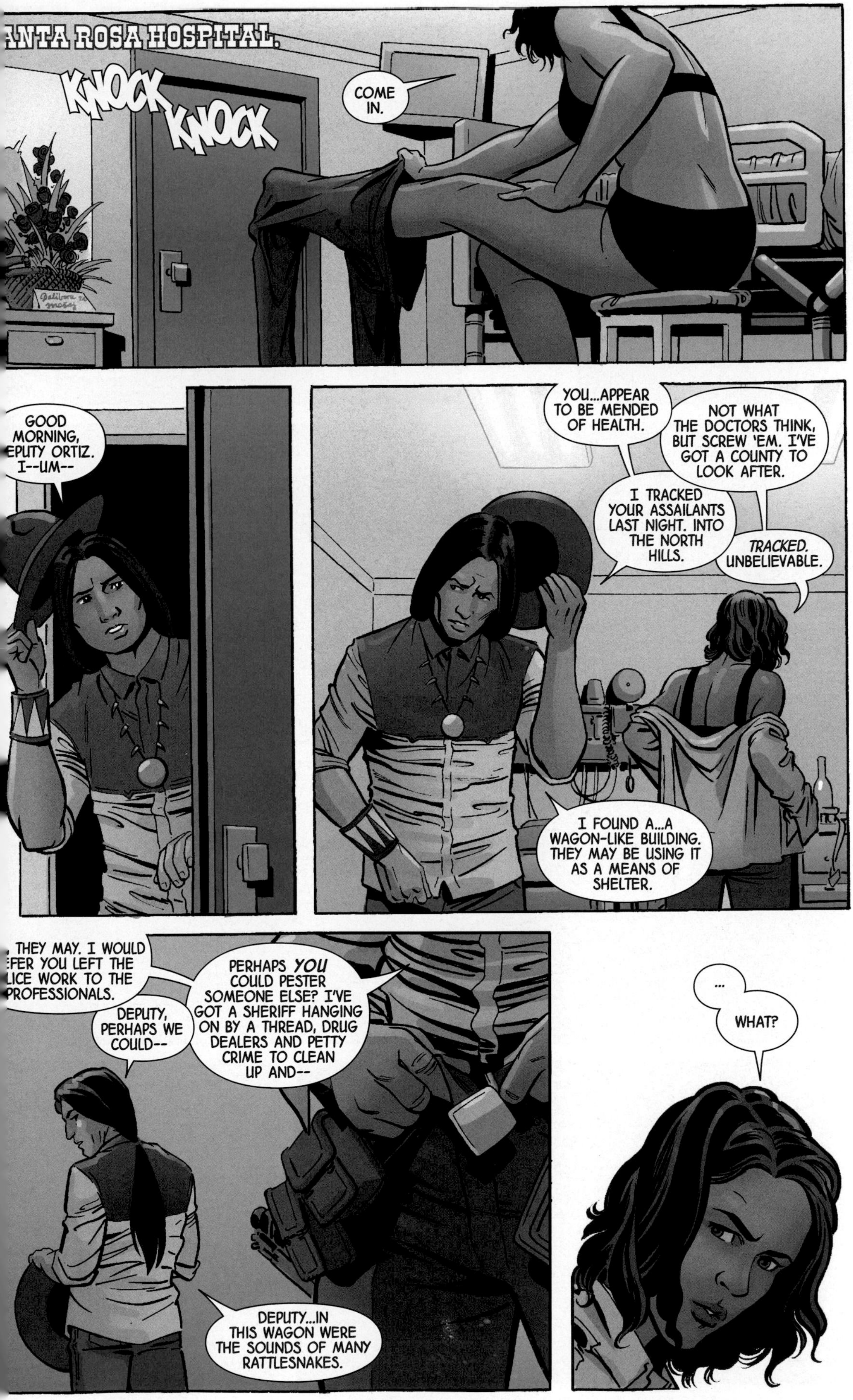
ANTA ROSA HOSPITAL.
KNOCK KNOCK
COME IN.
GOOD MORNING, EPUTY ORTIZ. I--UM--
YOU...APPEAR TO BE MENDED OF HEALTH.
NOT WHAT THE DOCTORS THINK, BUT SCREW 'EM. I'VE GOT A COUNTY TO LOOK AFTER.
I TRACKED YOUR ASSAILANTS LAST NIGHT. INTO THE NORTH HILLS.
TRACKED. UNBELIEVABLE.
I FOUND A...A WAGON-LIKE BUILDING. THEY MAY BE USING IT AS A MEANS OF SHELTER.
, THEY MAY. I WOULD EFER YOU LEFT THE LICE WORK TO THE PROFESSIONALS.
DEPUTY, PERHAPS WE COULD--
PERHAPS YOU COULD PESTER SOMEONE ELSE? I'VE GOT A SHERIFF HANGING ON BY A THREAD, DRUG DEALERS AND PETTY CRIME TO CLEAN UP AND--
DEPUTY...IN THIS WAGON WERE THE SOUNDS OF MANY RATTLESNAKES.
...
WHAT?

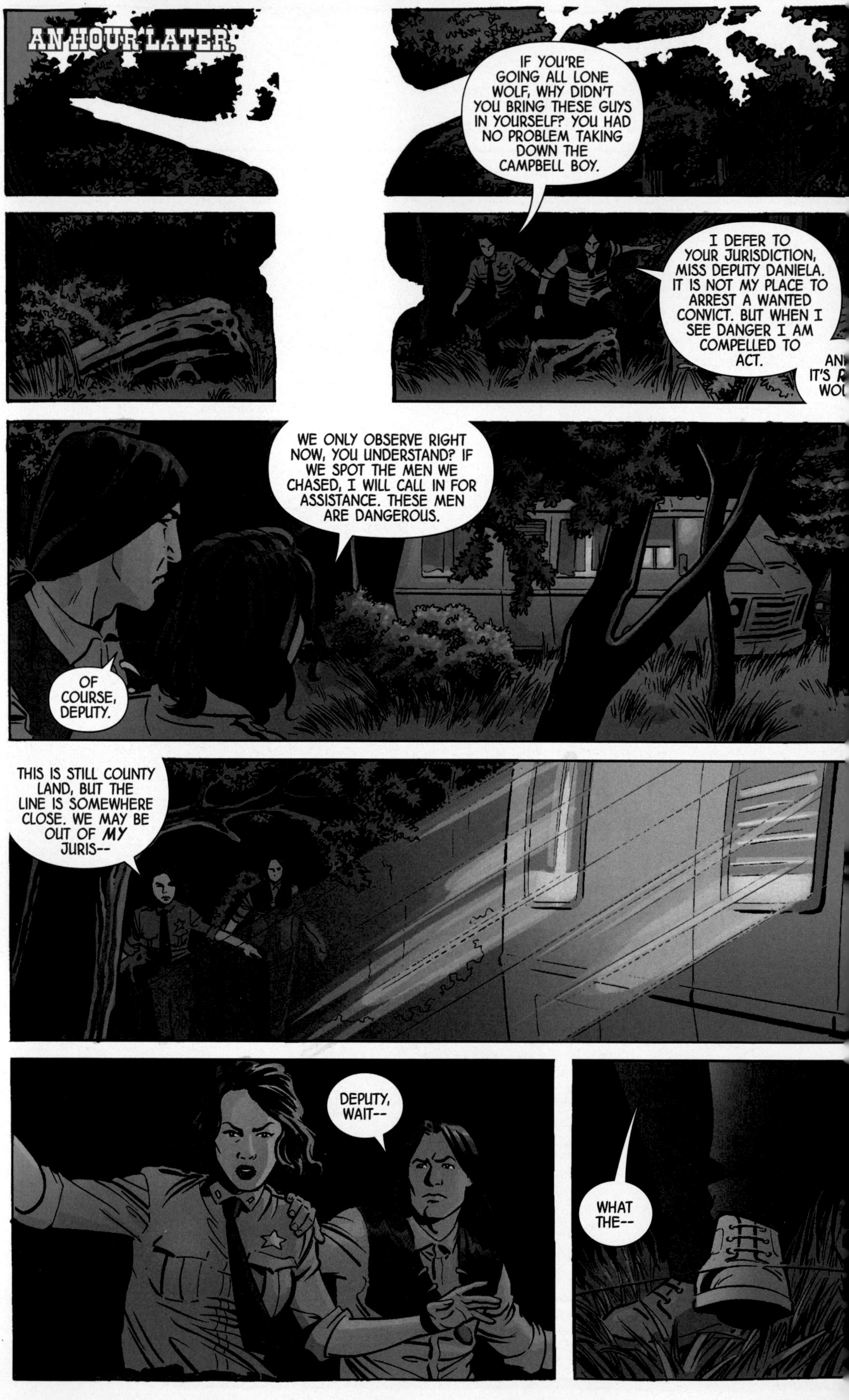
AN HOUR LATER.
IF YOU'RE GOING ALL LONE WOLF, WHY DIDN'T YOU BRING THESE GUYS IN YOURSELF? YOU HAD NO PROBLEM TAKING DOWN THE CAMPBELL BOY.
I DEFER TO YOUR JURISDICTION, MISS DEPUTY DANIELA. IT IS NOT MY PLACE TO ARREST A WANTED CONVICT. BUT WHEN I SEE DANGER I AM COMPELLED TO ACT.
WE ONLY OBSERVE RIGHT NOW, YOU UNDERSTAND? IF WE SPOT THE MEN WE CHASED, I WILL CALL IN FOR ASSISTANCE. THESE MEN ARE DANGEROUS.
OF COURSE, DEPUTY.
THIS IS STILL COUNTY LAND, BUT THE LINE IS SOMEWHERE CLOSE. WE MAY BE OUT OF *MY* JURIS--
DEPUTY, WAIT--
WHAT THE--

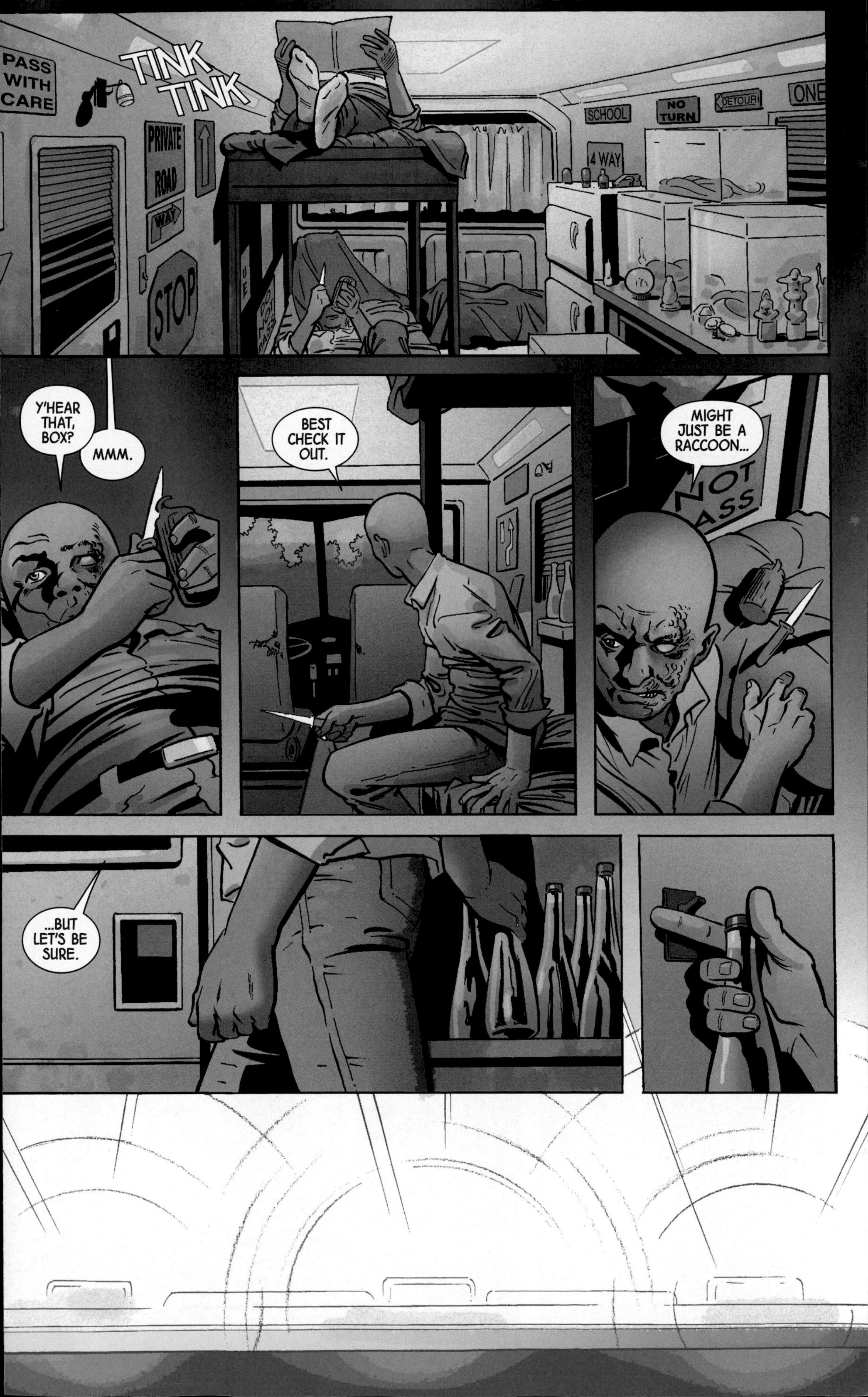
TINK TINK
PASS WITH CARE
PRIVATE ROAD
STOP
SCHOOL
NO TURN
DETOUR
4 WAY
Y'HEAR THAT, BOX?
MMM.
BEST CHECK IT OUT.
MIGHT JUST BE A RACCOON...
...BUT LET'S BE SURE.

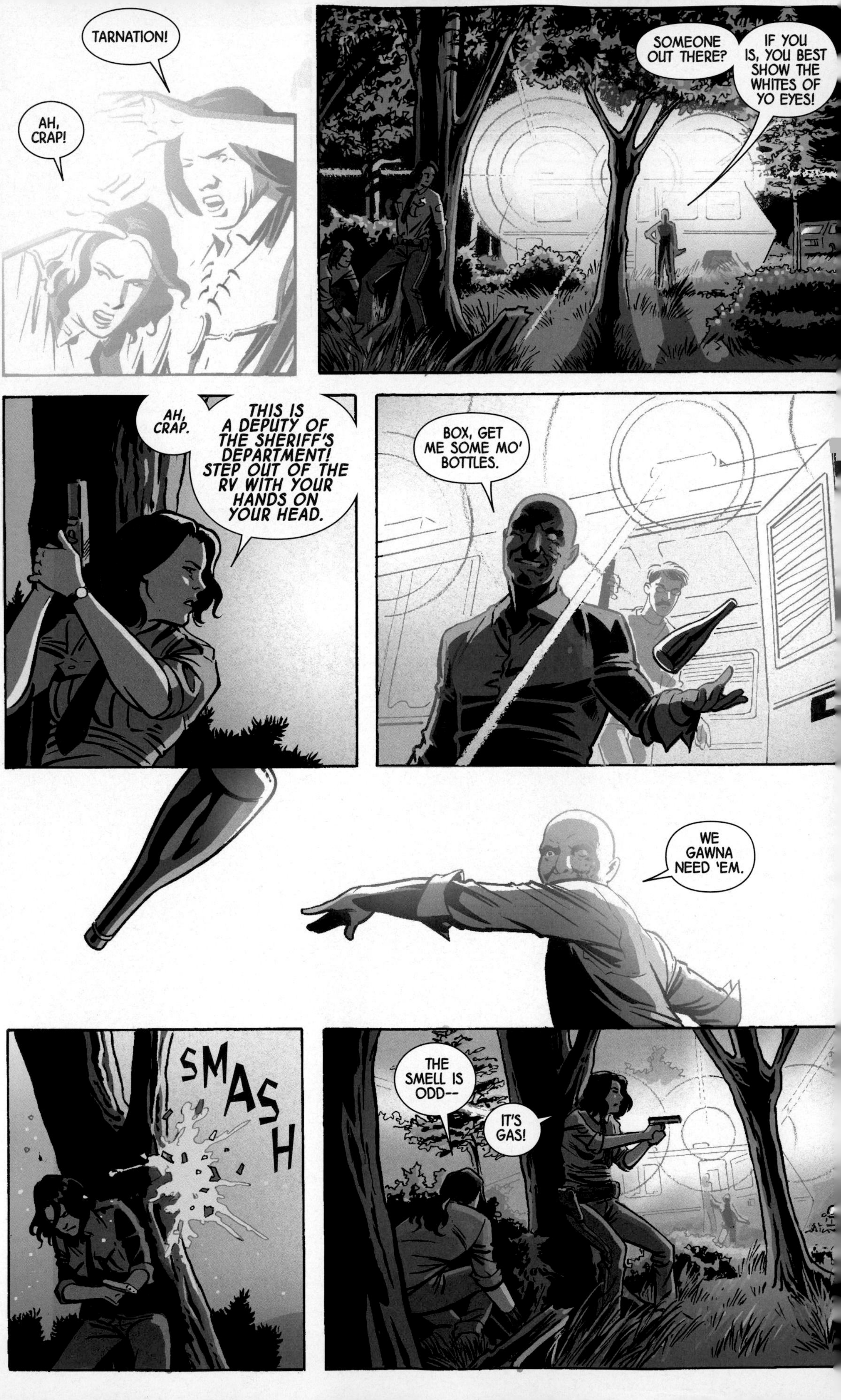
TARNATION!
AH, CRAP!
SOMEONE OUT THERE?
IF YOU IS, YOU BEST SHOW THE WHITES OF YO EYES!
AH, CRAP.
THIS IS A DEPUTY OF THE SHERIFF'S DEPARTMENT! STEP OUT OF THE RV WITH YOUR HANDS ON YOUR HEAD.
BOX, GET ME SOME MO' BOTTLES.
WE GAWNA NEED 'EM.
SMASH
THE SMELL IS ODD--
IT'S GAS!

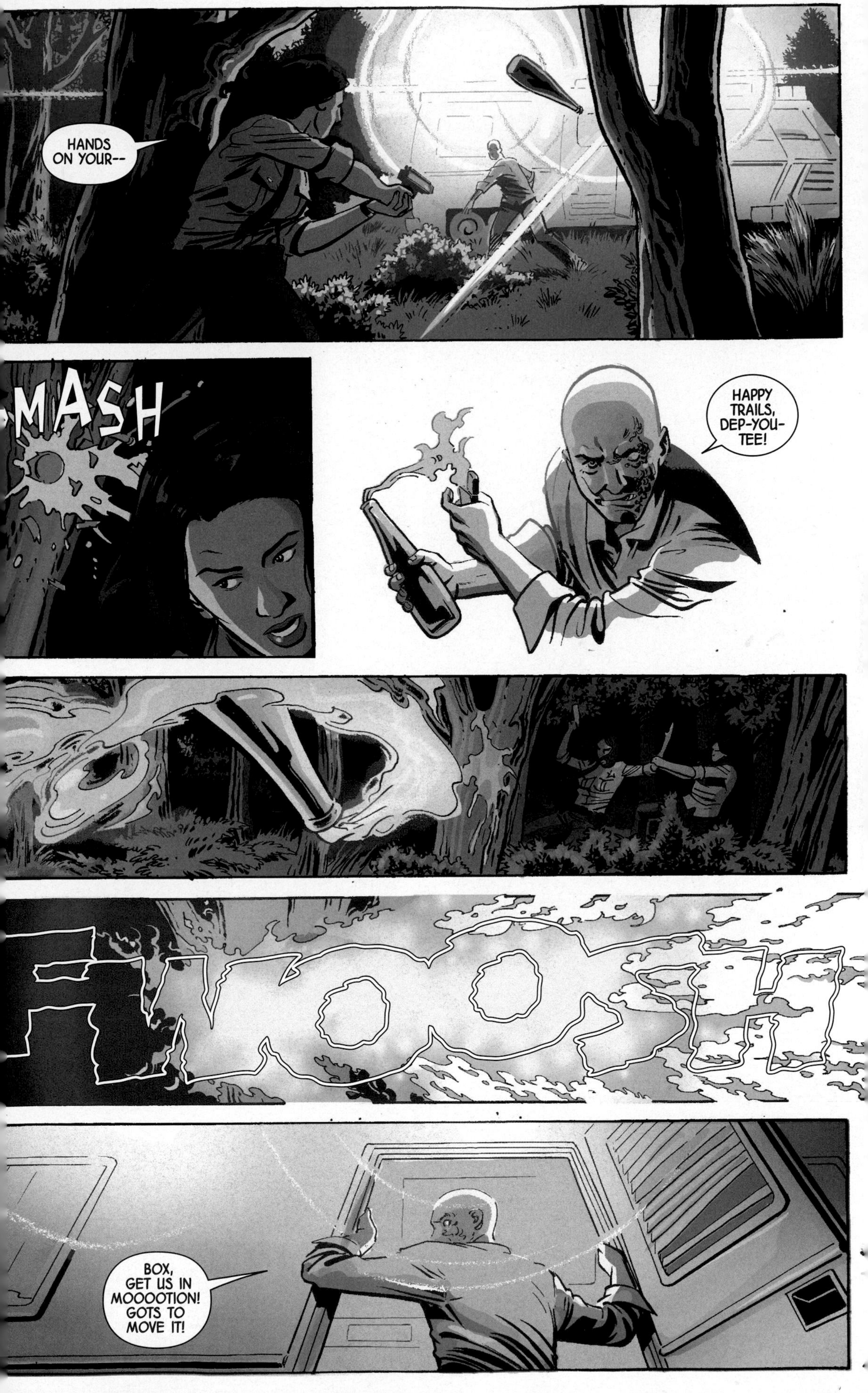
HANDS ON YOUR--
MASH
HAPPY TRAILS, DEP-YOU-TEE!
FWOOOSH
BOX, GET US IN MOOOOTION! GOTS TO MOVE IT!

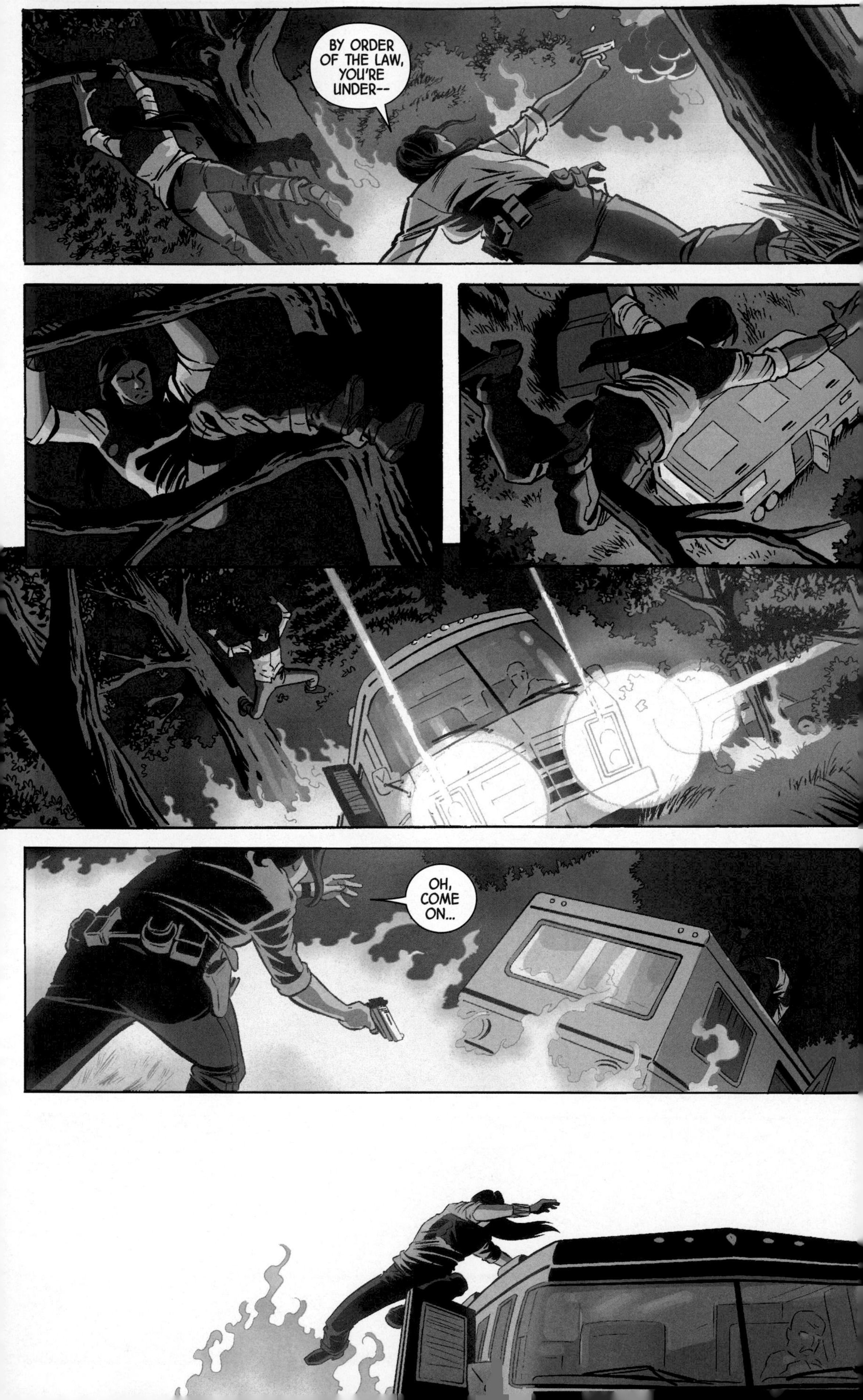
BY ORDER OF THE LAW, YOU'RE UNDER--
OH, COME ON...

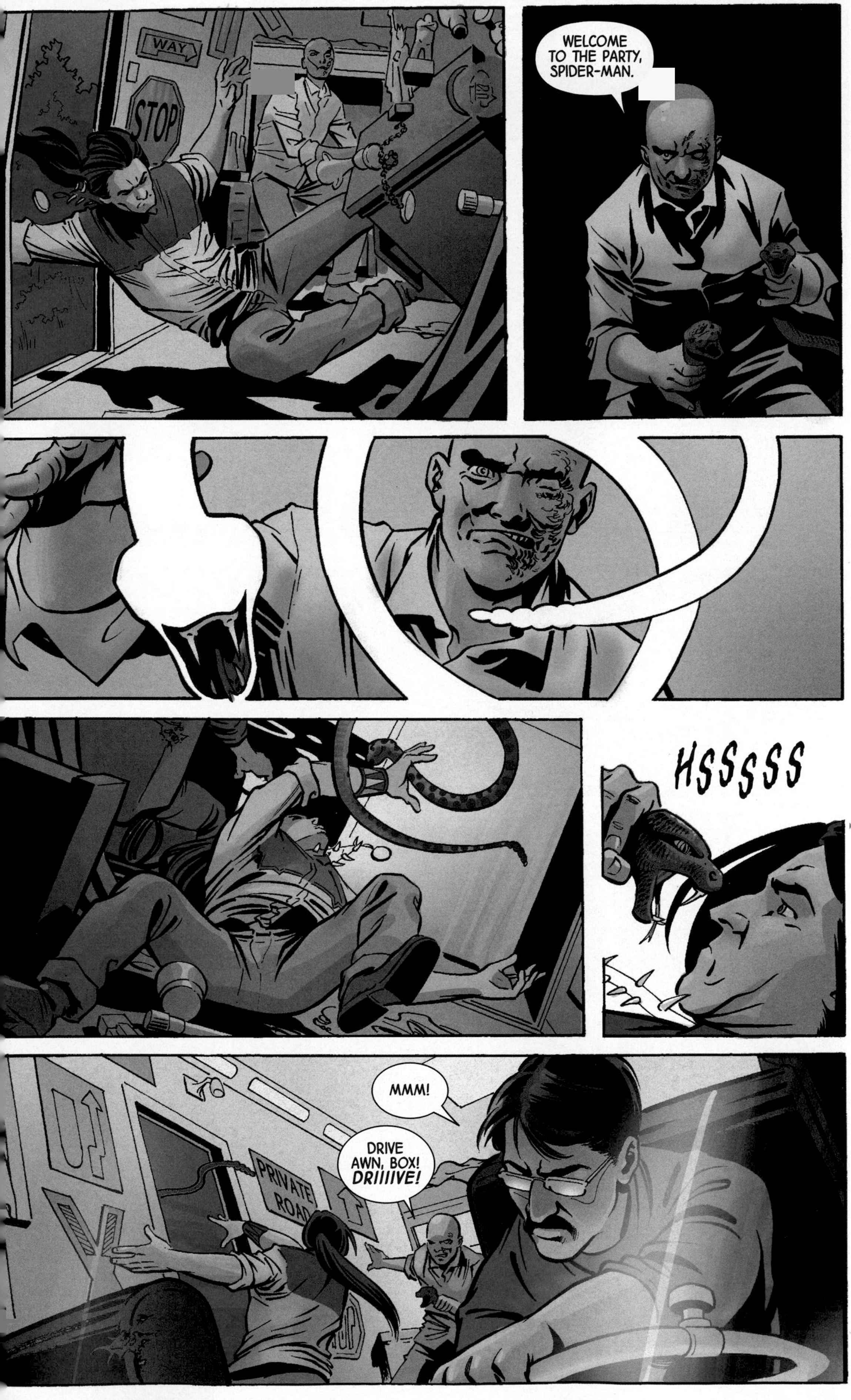
WELCOME TO THE PARTY, SPIDER-MAN.
HSSSSS
MMM!
DRIVE AWN, BOX! DRIIIIVE!

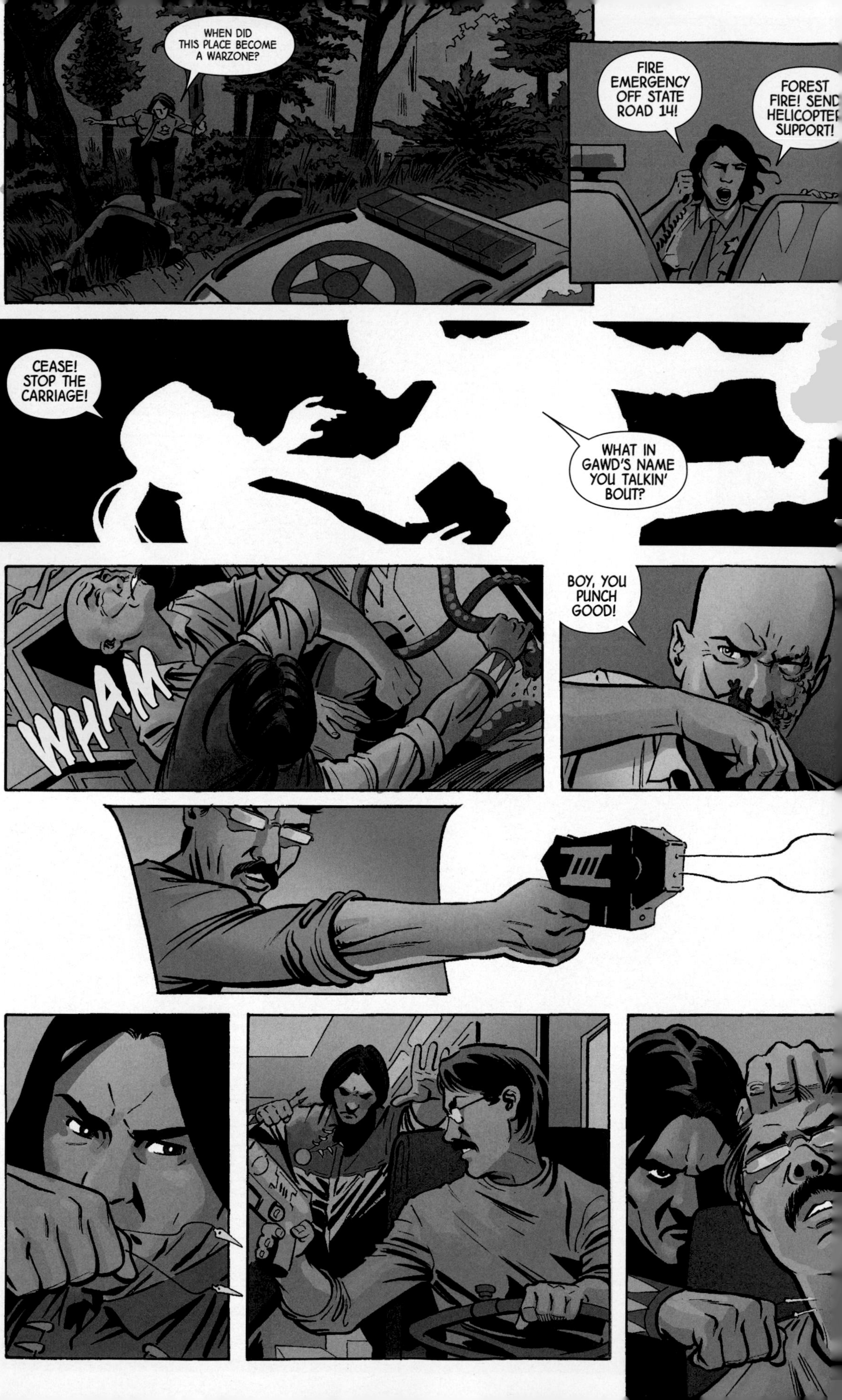
WHEN DID THIS PLACE BECOME A WARZONE?
FIRE EMERGENCY OFF STATE ROAD 14!
FOREST FIRE! SEND HELICOPTER SUPPORT!
CEASE! STOP THE CARRIAGE!
WHAT IN GAWD'S NAME YOU TALKIN' BOUT?
WHAM
BOY, YOU PUNCH GOOD!

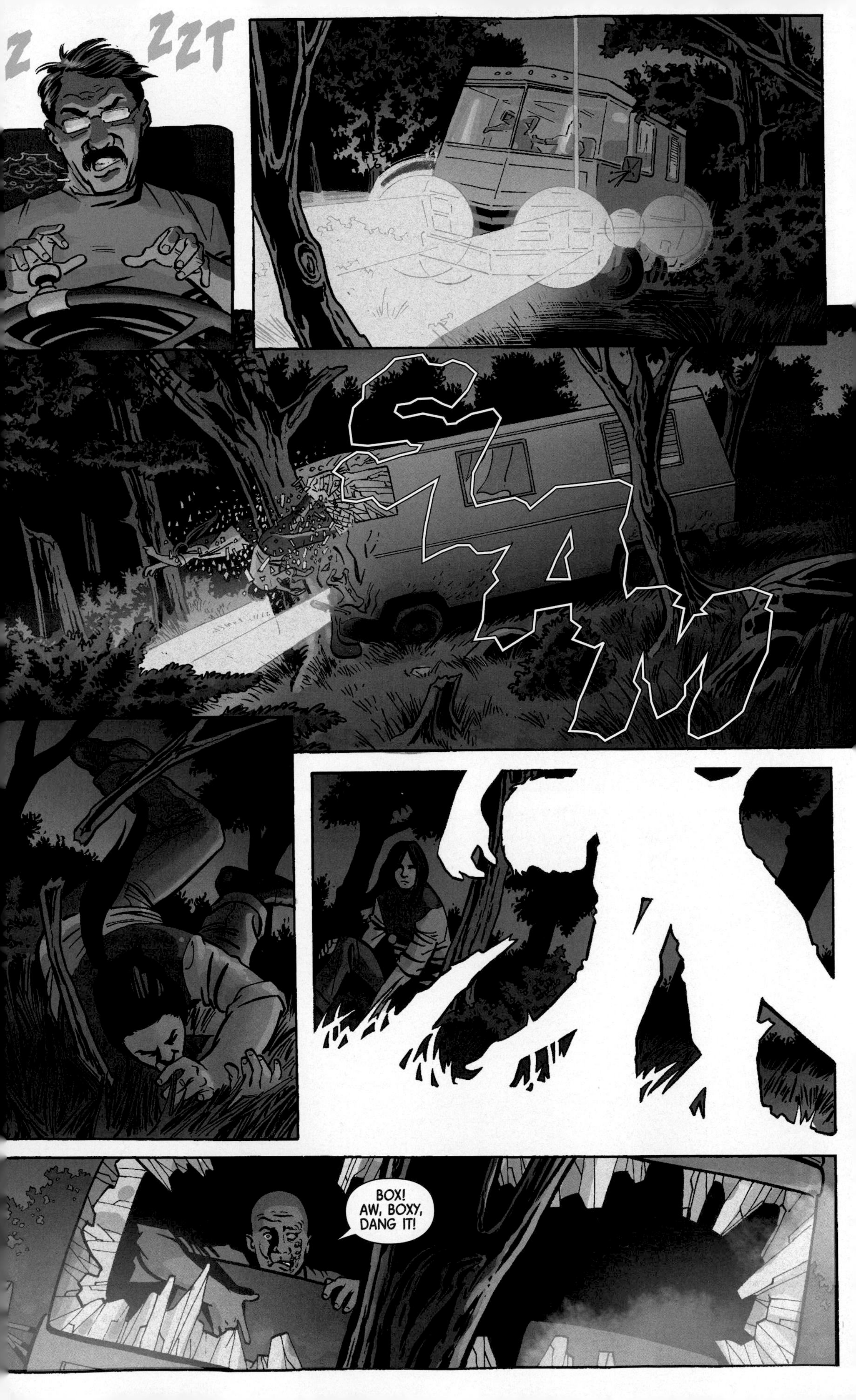
Z
ZZT
SLAM
BOX!
AW, BOXY,
DANG IT!

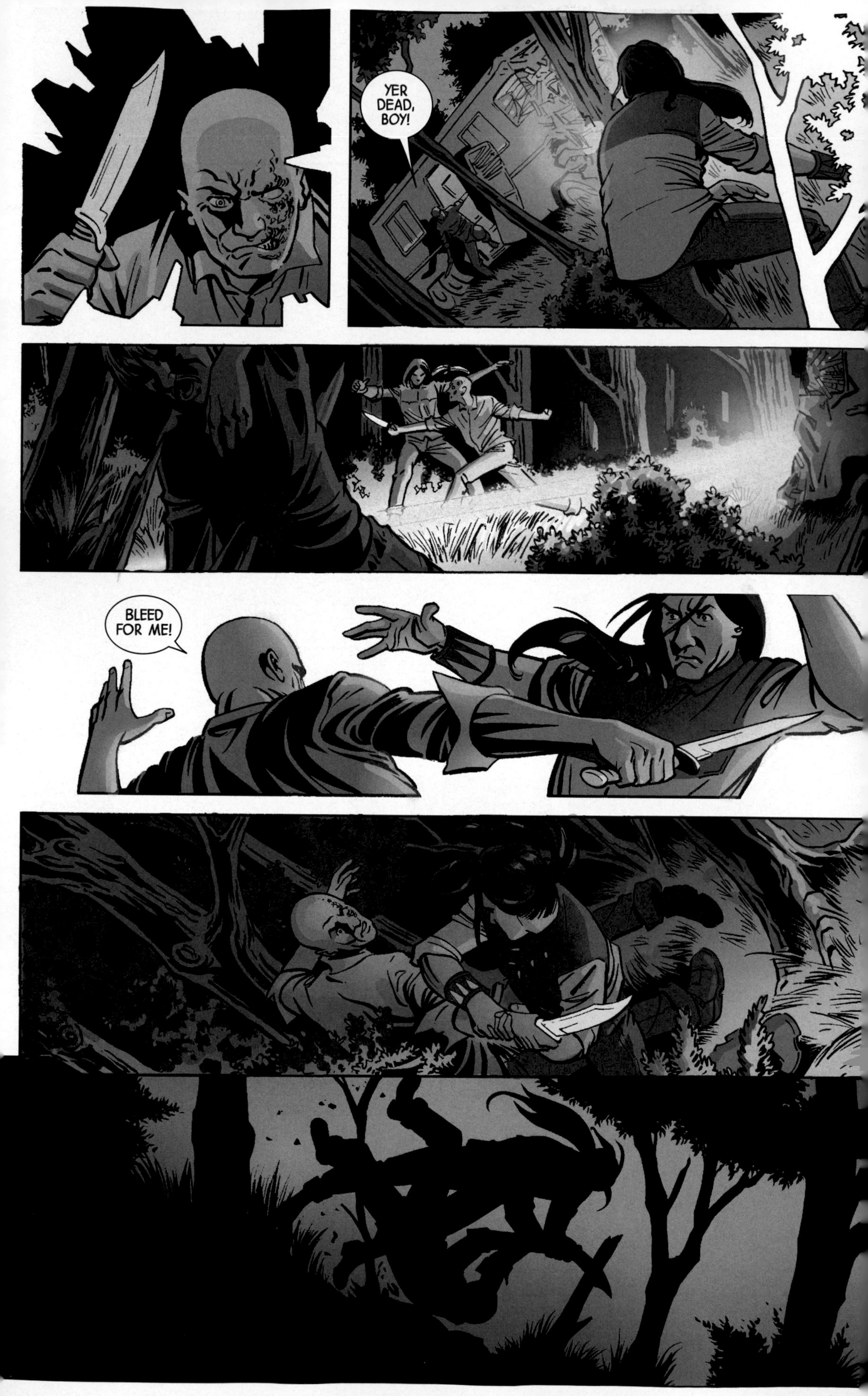
YER DEAD, BOY!
BLEED FOR ME!

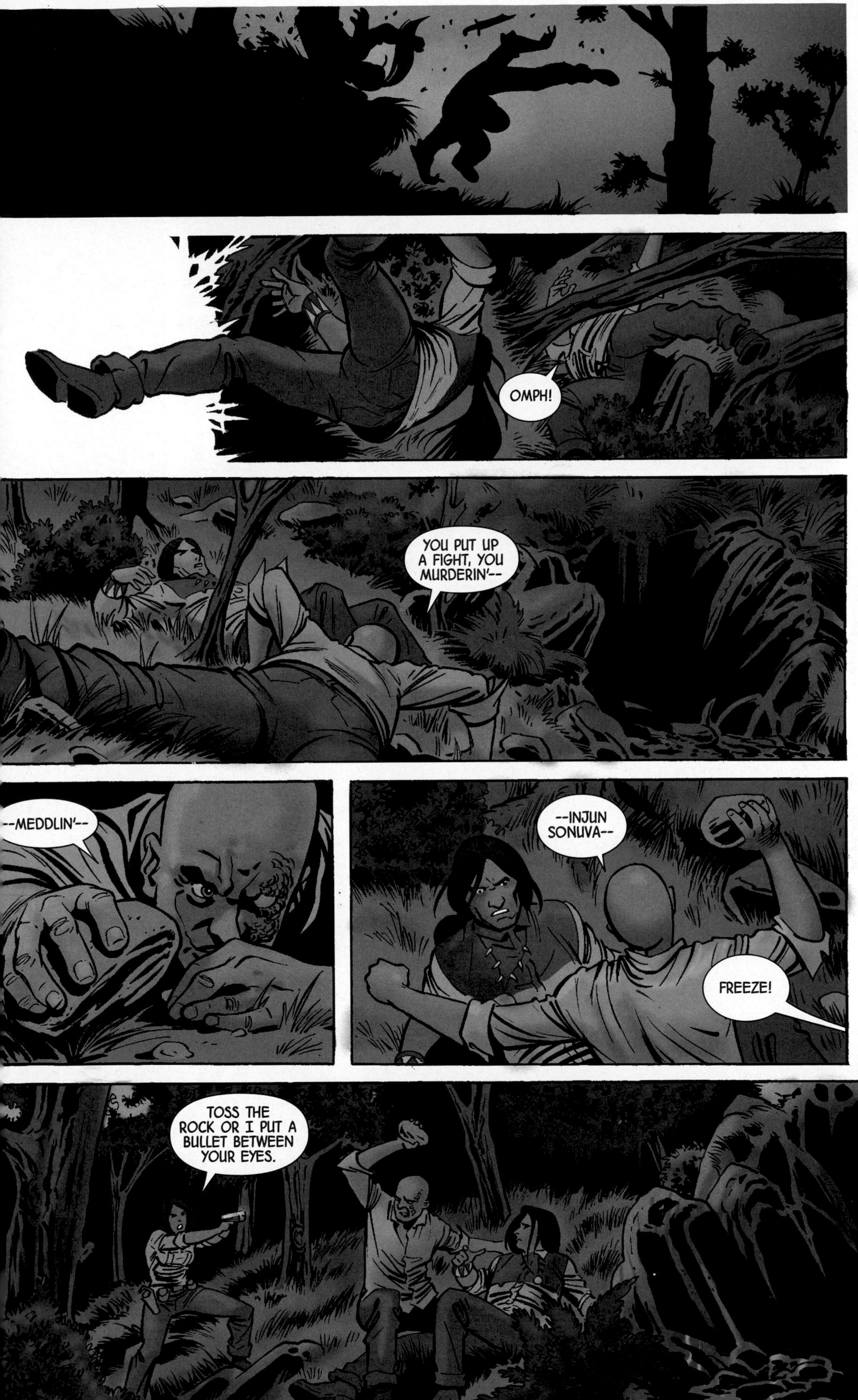
OMPH!
YOU PUT UP A FIGHT, YOU MURDERIN'--
--MEDDLIN'--
--INJUN SONUVA--
FREEZE!
TOSS THE ROCK OR I PUT A BULLET BETWEEN YOUR EYES.

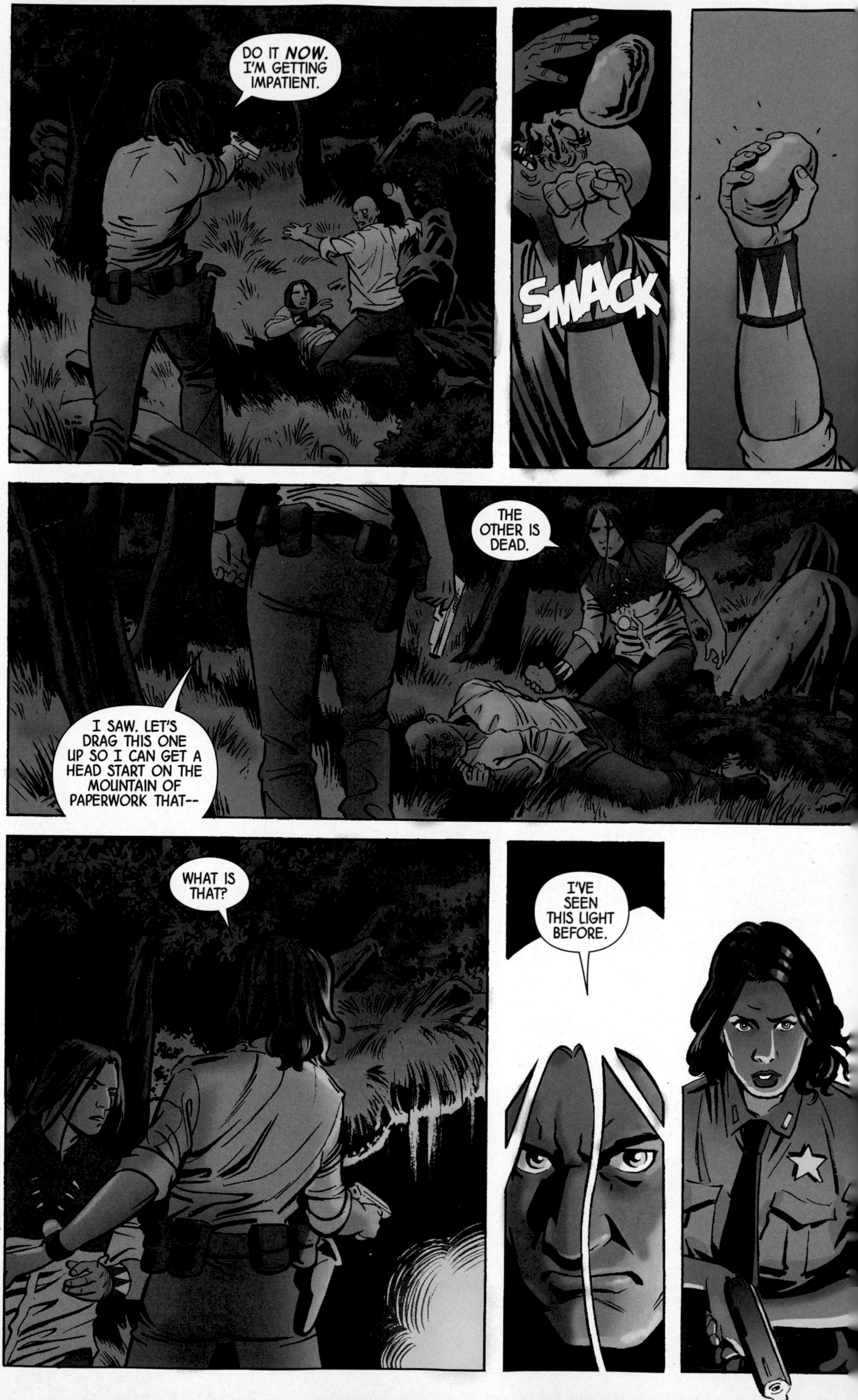
DO IT *NOW.* I'M GETTING IMPATIENT.
SMACK
THE OTHER IS DEAD.
I SAW. LET'S DRAG THIS ONE UP SO I CAN GET A HEAD START ON THE MOUNTAIN OF PAPERWORK THAT--
WHAT IS THAT?
I'VE SEEN THIS LIGHT BEFORE.

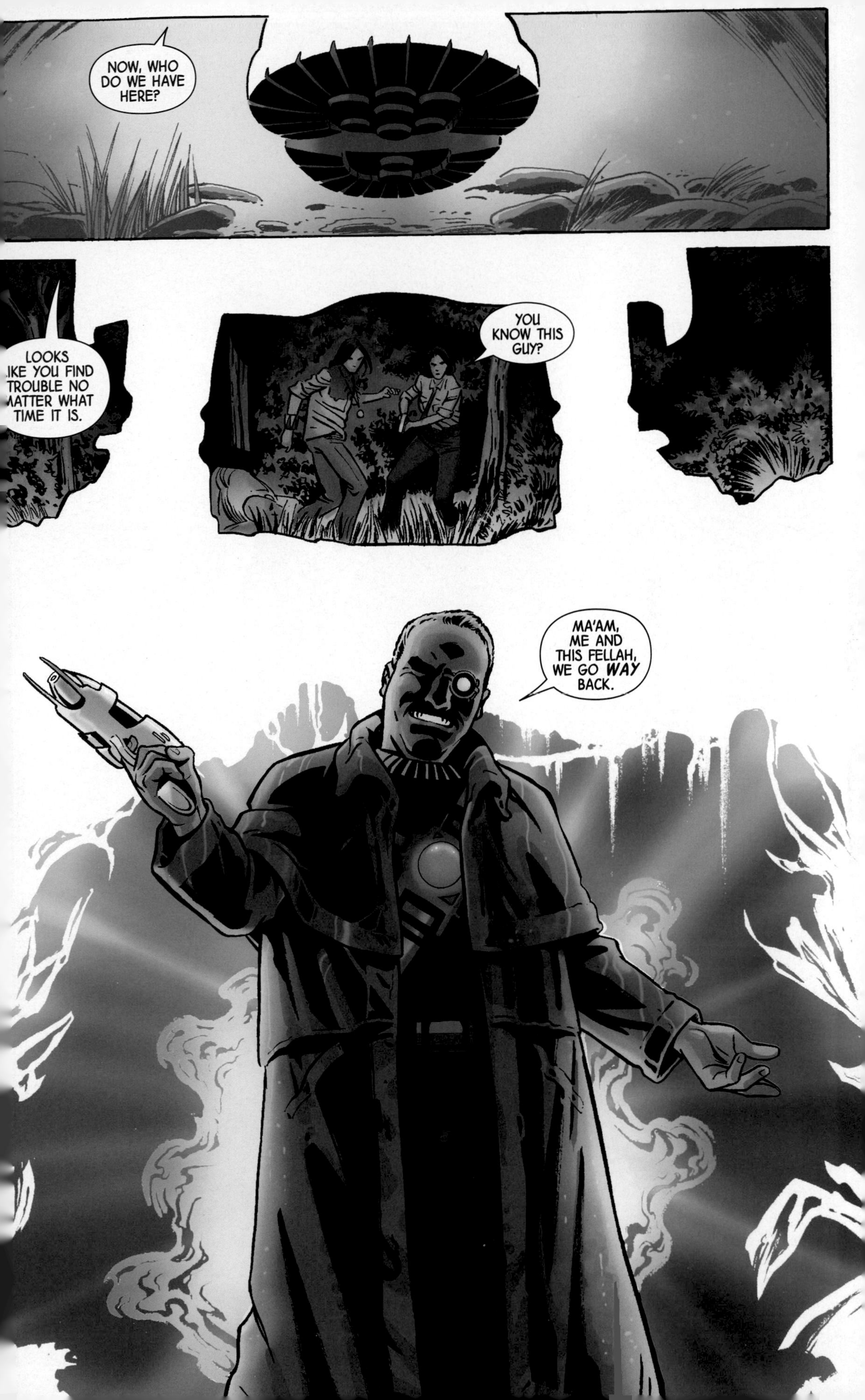
NOW, WHO DO WE HAVE HERE?
LOOKS LIKE YOU FIND TROUBLE NO MATTER WHAT TIME IT IS.
YOU KNOW THIS GUY?
MA'AM, ME AND THIS FELLAH, WE GO WAY BACK.

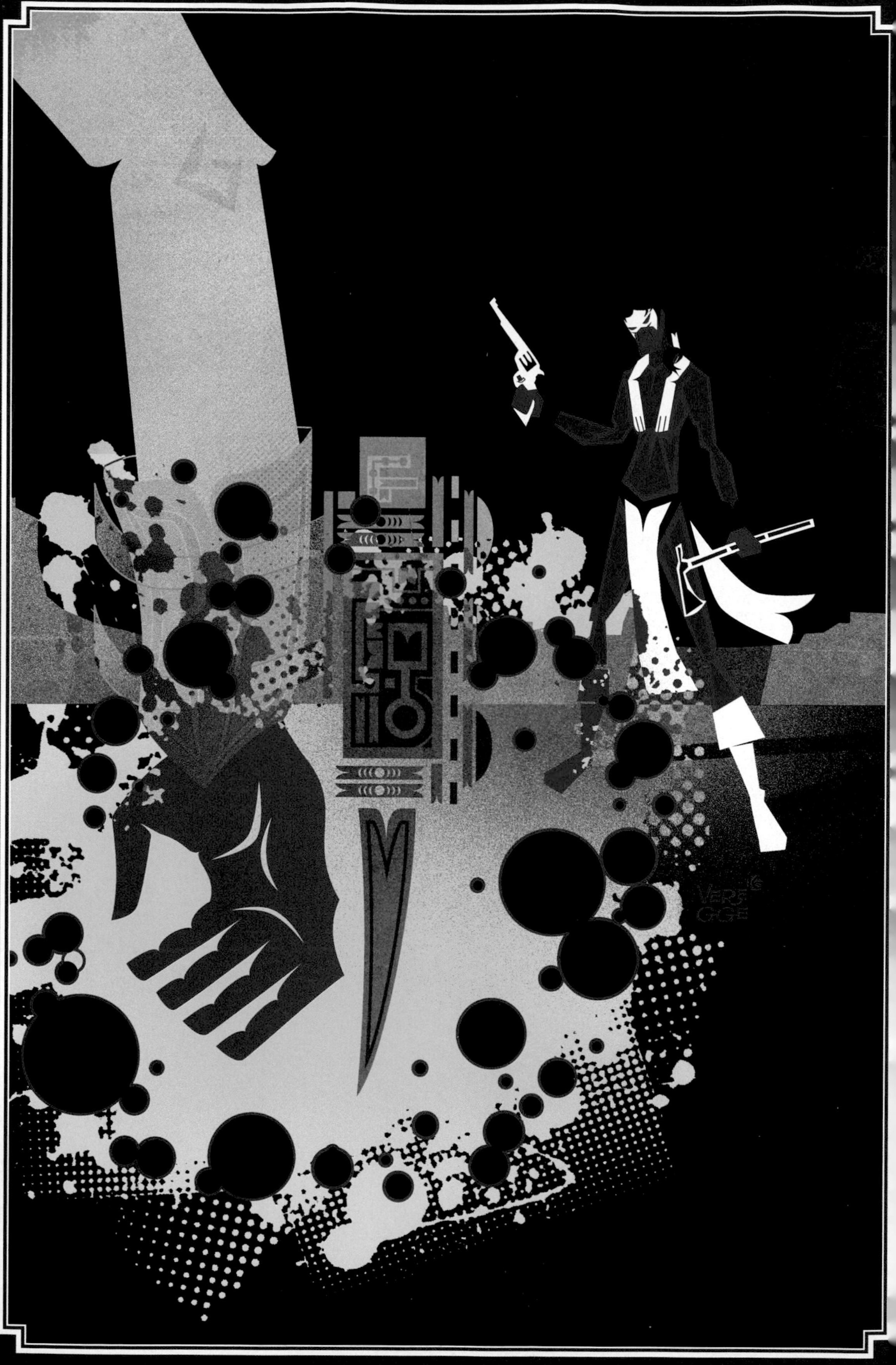

6

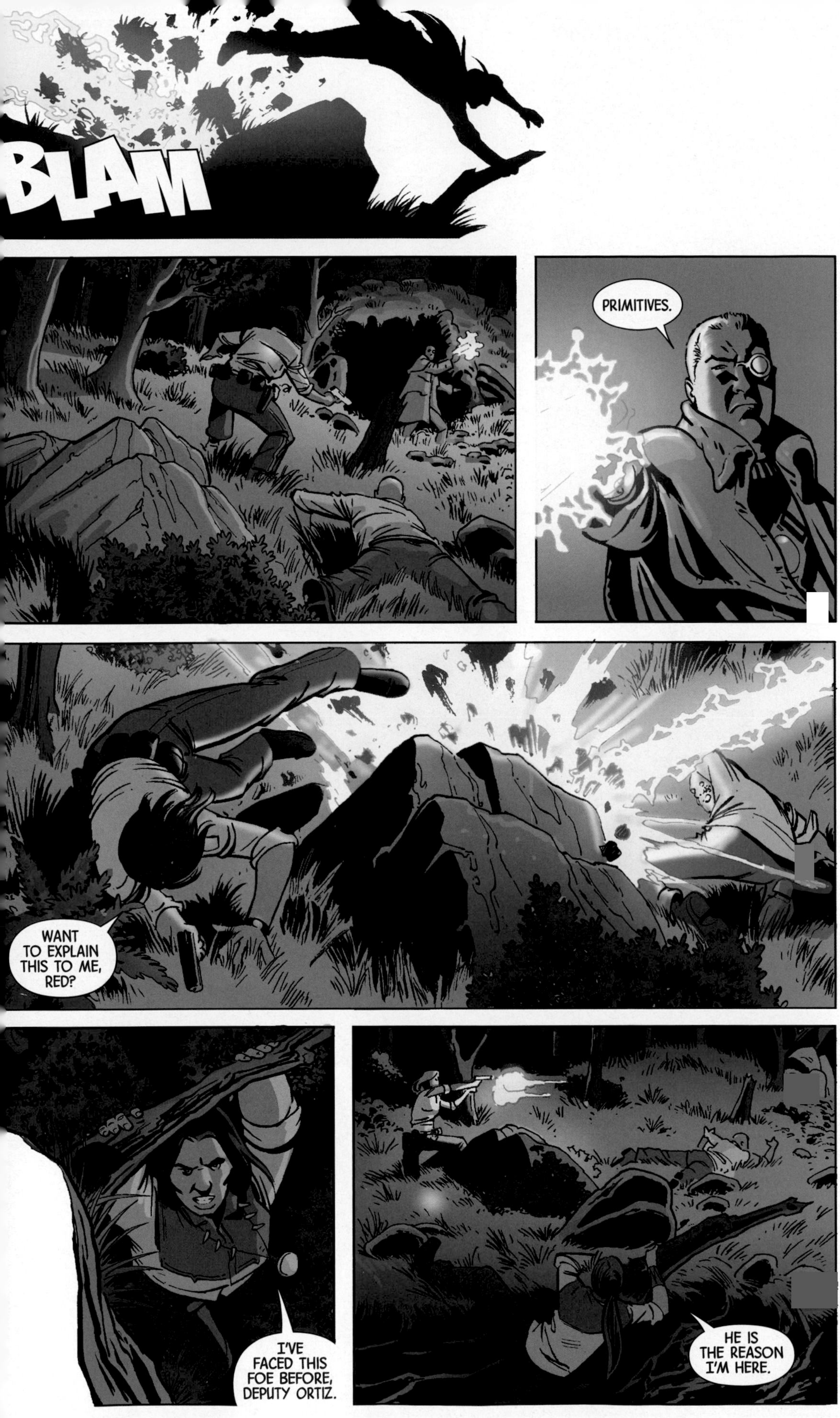
BLAM
PRIMITIVES.
WANT TO EXPLAIN THIS TO ME, RED?
I'VE FACED THIS FOE BEFORE, DEPUTY ORTIZ.
HE IS THE REASON I'M HERE.

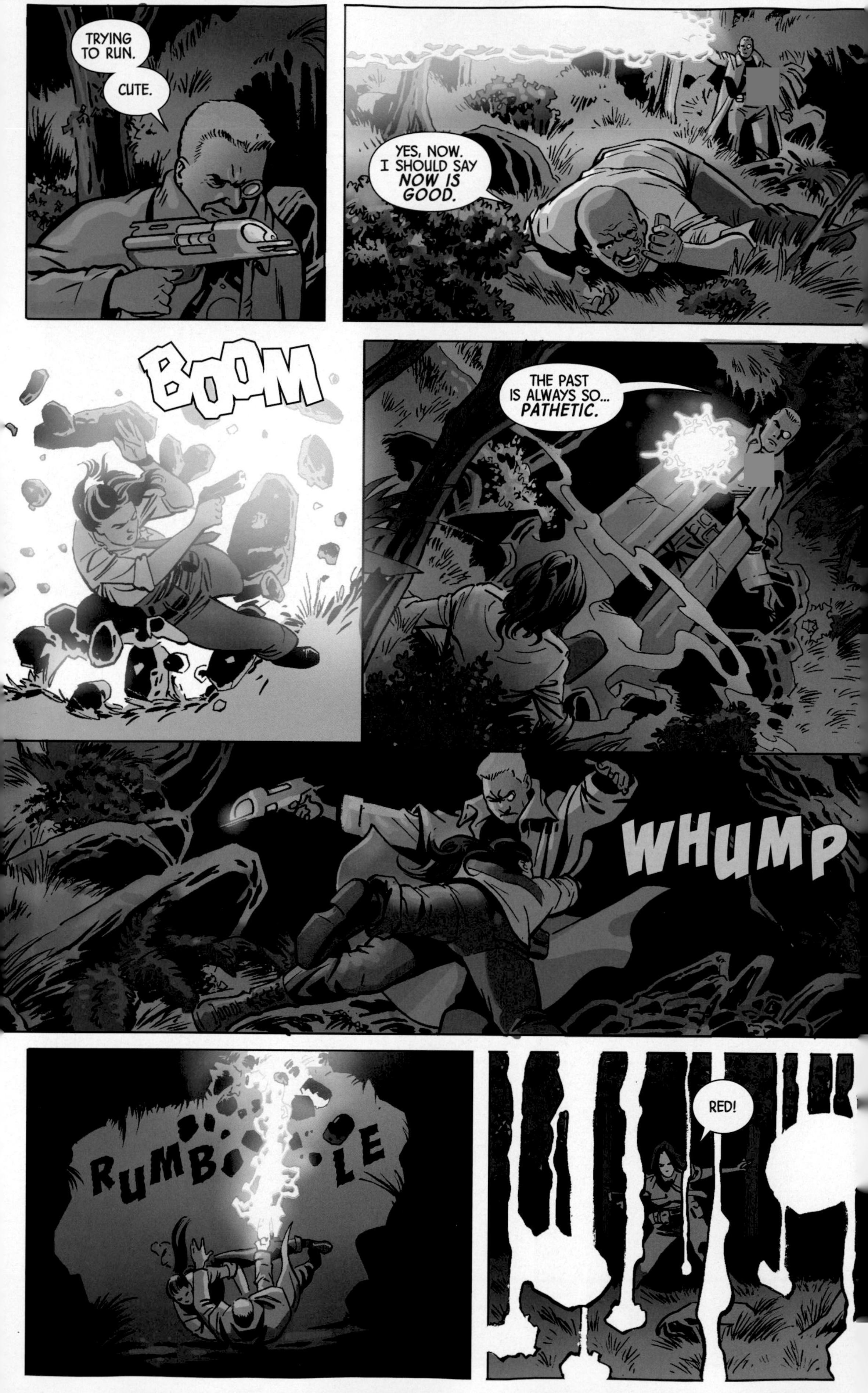
TRYING TO RUN.
CUTE.
YES, NOW. I SHOULD SAY *NOW IS GOOD.*
BOOM
THE PAST IS ALWAYS SO... *PATHETIC.*
WHUMP
RUMBLE
RED!

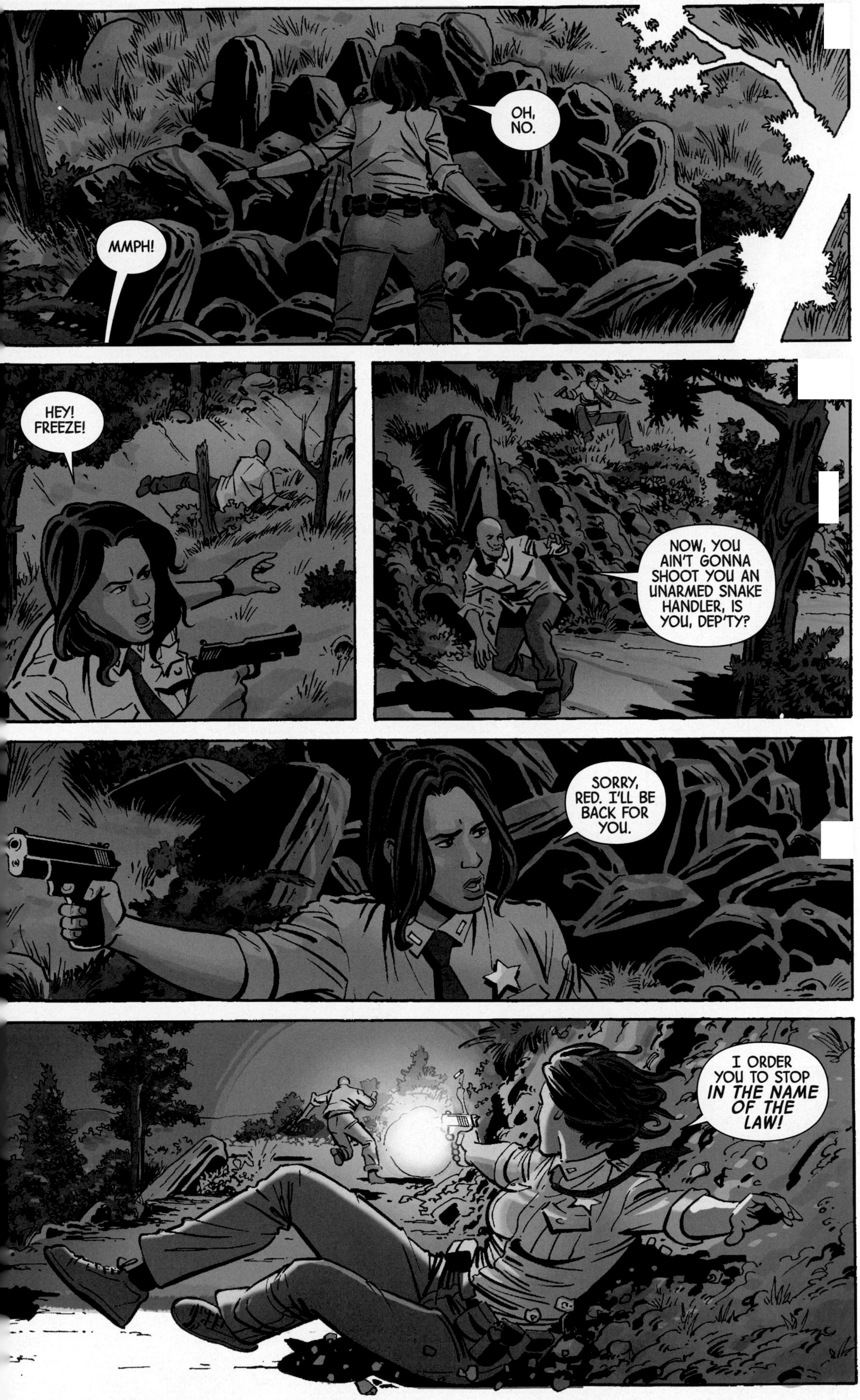
OH, NO.
MMPH!
HEY! FREEZE!
NOW, YOU AIN'T GONNA SHOOT YOU AN UNARMED SNAKE HANDLER, IS YOU, DEP'TY?
SORRY, RED. I'LL BE BACK FOR YOU.
I ORDER YOU TO STOP IN THE NAME OF THE LAW!

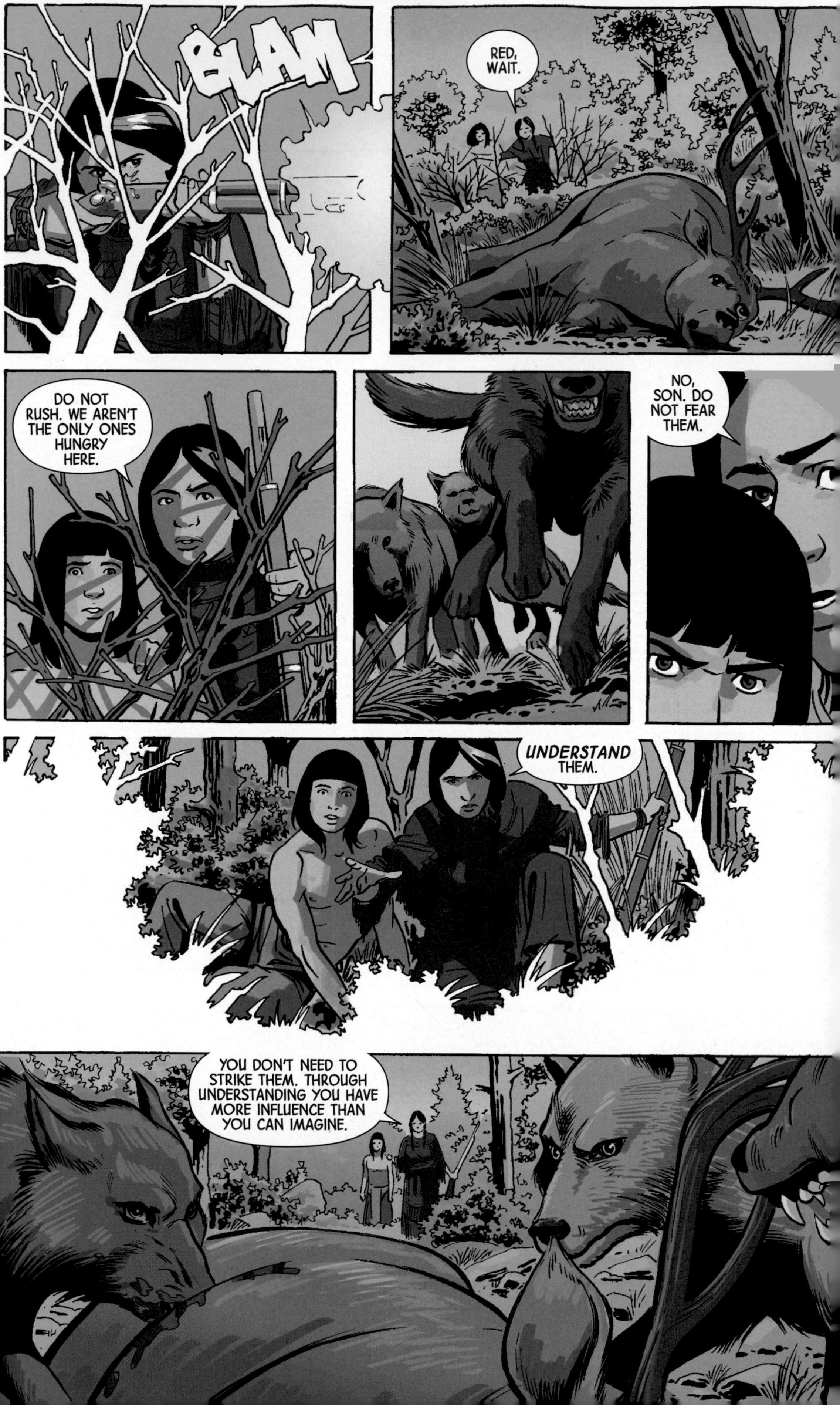
BLAM
RED, WAIT.
DO NOT RUSH. WE AREN'T THE ONLY ONES HUNGRY HERE.
NO, SON. DO NOT FEAR THEM.
UNDERSTAND THEM.
YOU DON'T NEED TO STRIKE THEM. THROUGH UNDERSTANDING YOU HAVE MORE INFLUENCE THAN YOU CAN IMAGINE.

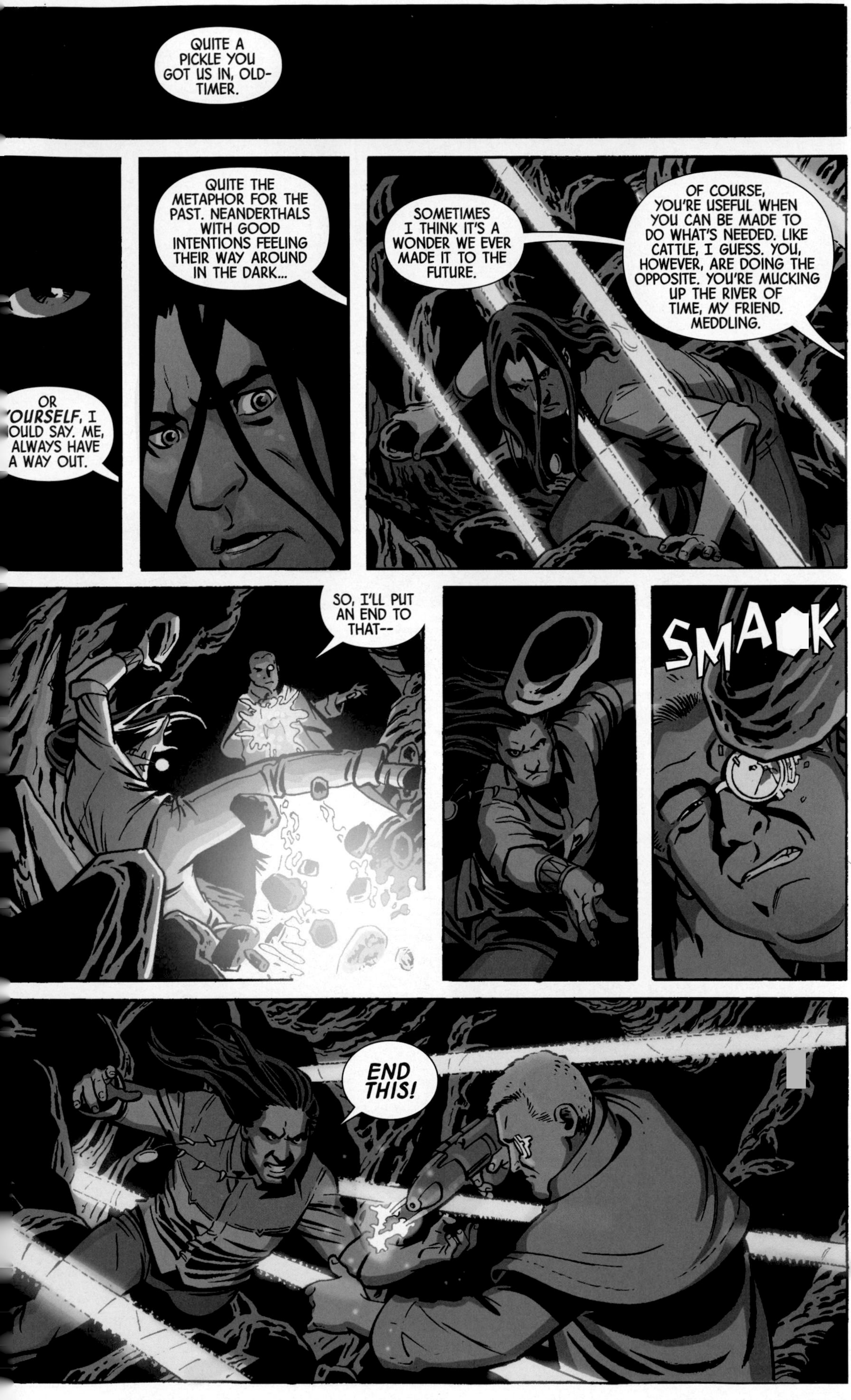
QUITE A PICKLE YOU GOT US IN, OLD-TIMER.
OR YOURSELF, I WOULD SAY. ME, I ALWAYS HAVE A WAY OUT.
QUITE THE METAPHOR FOR THE PAST. NEANDERTHALS WITH GOOD INTENTIONS FEELING THEIR WAY AROUND IN THE DARK...
SOMETIMES I THINK IT'S A WONDER WE EVER MADE IT TO THE FUTURE.
OF COURSE, YOU'RE USEFUL WHEN YOU CAN BE MADE TO DO WHAT'S NEEDED. LIKE CATTLE, I GUESS. YOU, HOWEVER, ARE DOING THE OPPOSITE. YOU'RE MUCKING UP THE RIVER OF TIME, MY FRIEND. MEDDLING.
SO, I'LL PUT AN END TO THAT--
SMACK
END THIS!

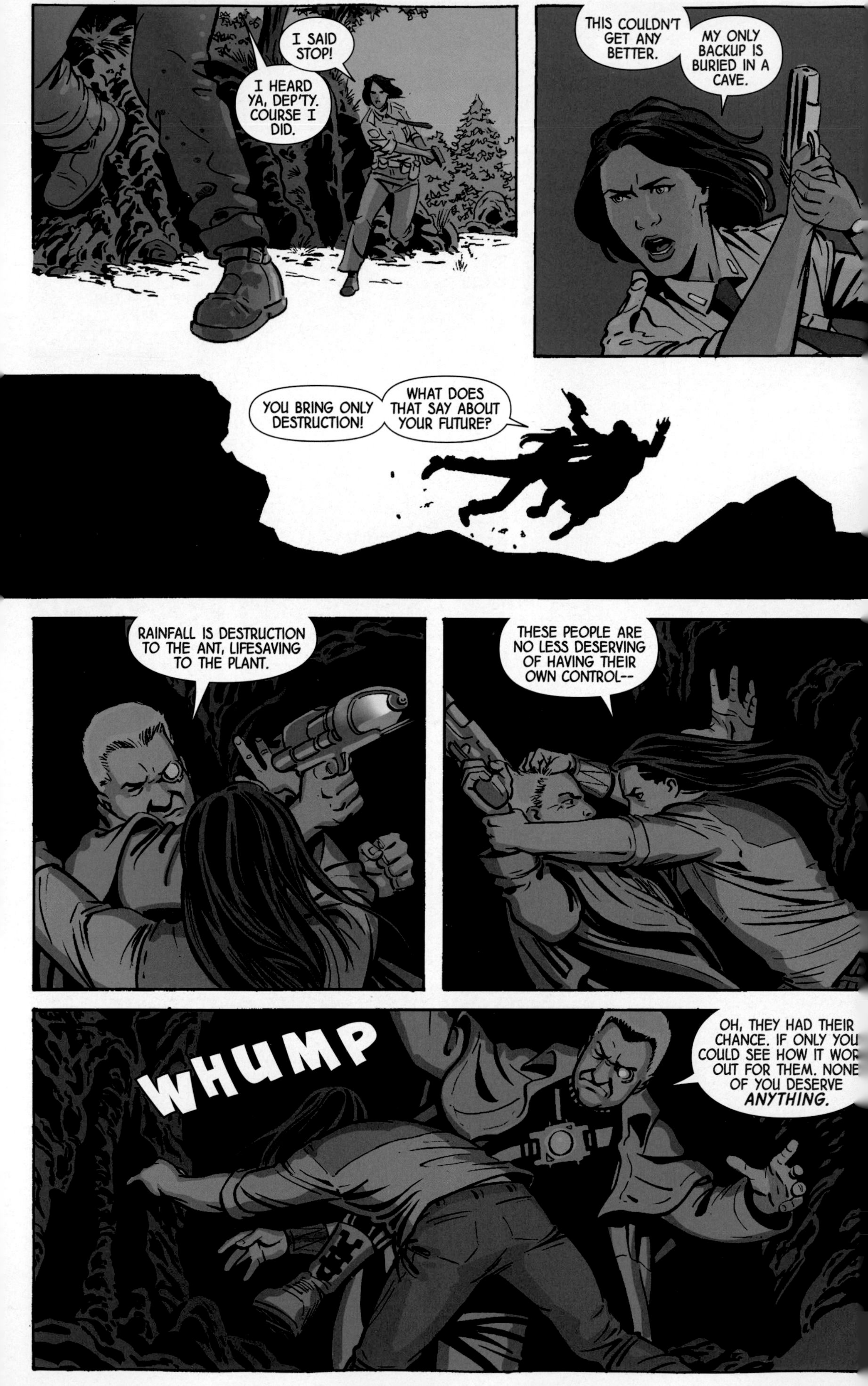
I SAID STOP!
I HEARD YA, DEP'TY. COURSE I DID.
THIS COULDN'T GET ANY BETTER.
MY ONLY BACKUP IS BURIED IN A CAVE.
YOU BRING ONLY DESTRUCTION!
WHAT DOES THAT SAY ABOUT YOUR FUTURE?
RAINFALL IS DESTRUCTION TO THE ANT, LIFESAVING TO THE PLANT.
THESE PEOPLE ARE NO LESS DESERVING OF HAVING THEIR OWN CONTROL--
WHUMP
OH, THEY HAD THEIR CHANCE. IF ONLY YOU COULD SEE HOW IT WOR OUT FOR THEM. NONE OF YOU DESERVE *ANYTHING.*

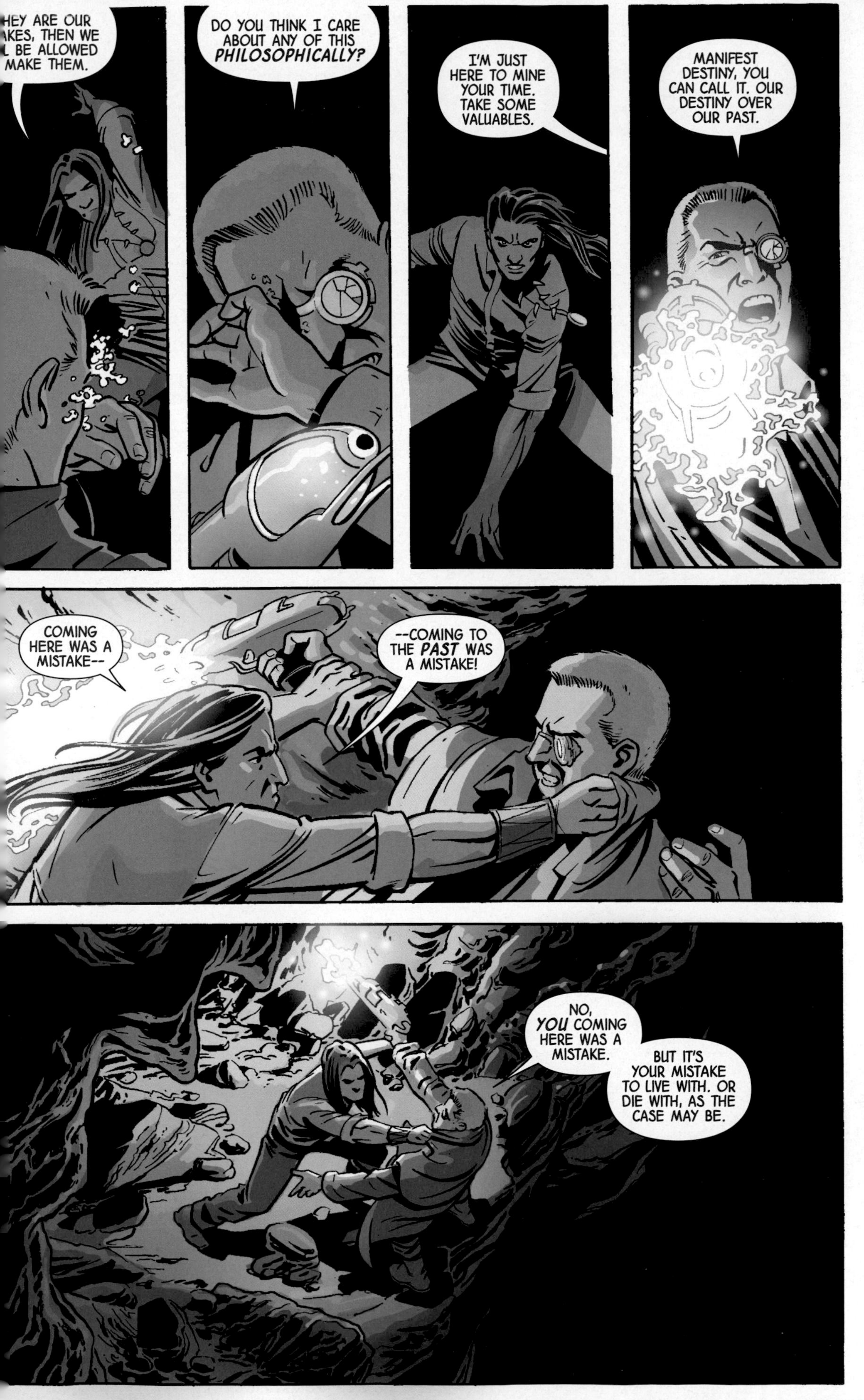

HEY ARE OUR
AKES, THEN WE
L BE ALLOWED
MAKE THEM.
DO YOU THINK I CARE ABOUT ANY OF THIS *PHILOSOPHICALLY?*
I'M JUST HERE TO MINE YOUR TIME. TAKE SOME VALUABLES.
MANIFEST DESTINY, YOU CAN CALL IT. OUR DESTINY OVER OUR PAST.
COMING HERE WAS A MISTAKE--
--COMING TO THE *PAST* WAS A MISTAKE!
NO, *YOU* COMING HERE WAS A MISTAKE.
BUT IT'S YOUR MISTAKE TO LIVE WITH. OR DIE WITH, AS THE CASE MAY BE.

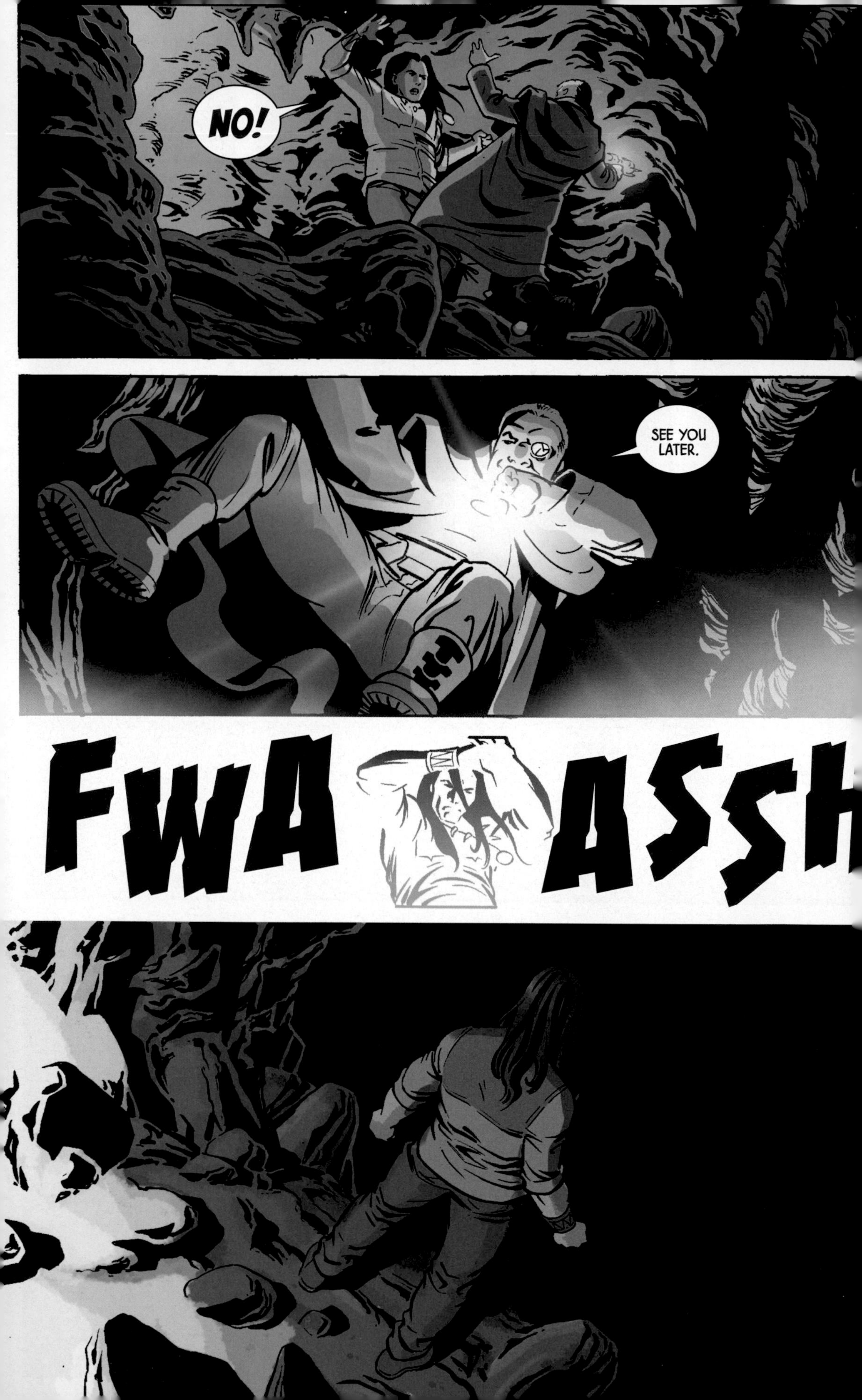
NO!
SEE YOU LATER.
FWAASSH

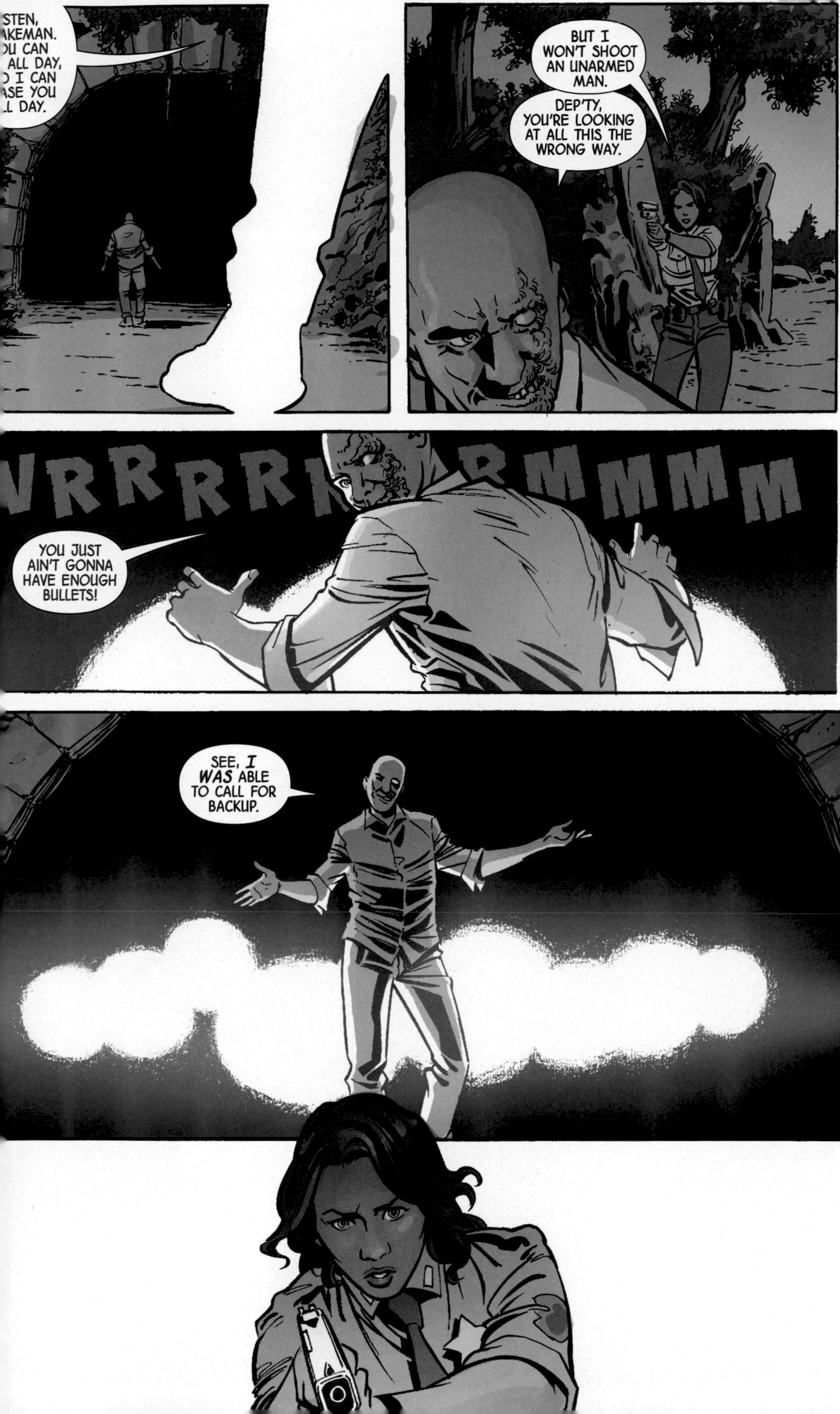
STEN,
AKEMAN.
OU CAN
ALL DAY,
I CAN
ASE YOU
L DAY.
BUT I WON'T SHOOT AN UNARMED MAN.
DEP'TY, YOU'RE LOOKING AT ALL THIS THE WRONG WAY.
VRRRRRRMMMMMM
YOU JUST AIN'T GONNA HAVE ENOUGH BULLETS!
SEE, I WAS ABLE TO CALL FOR BACKUP.

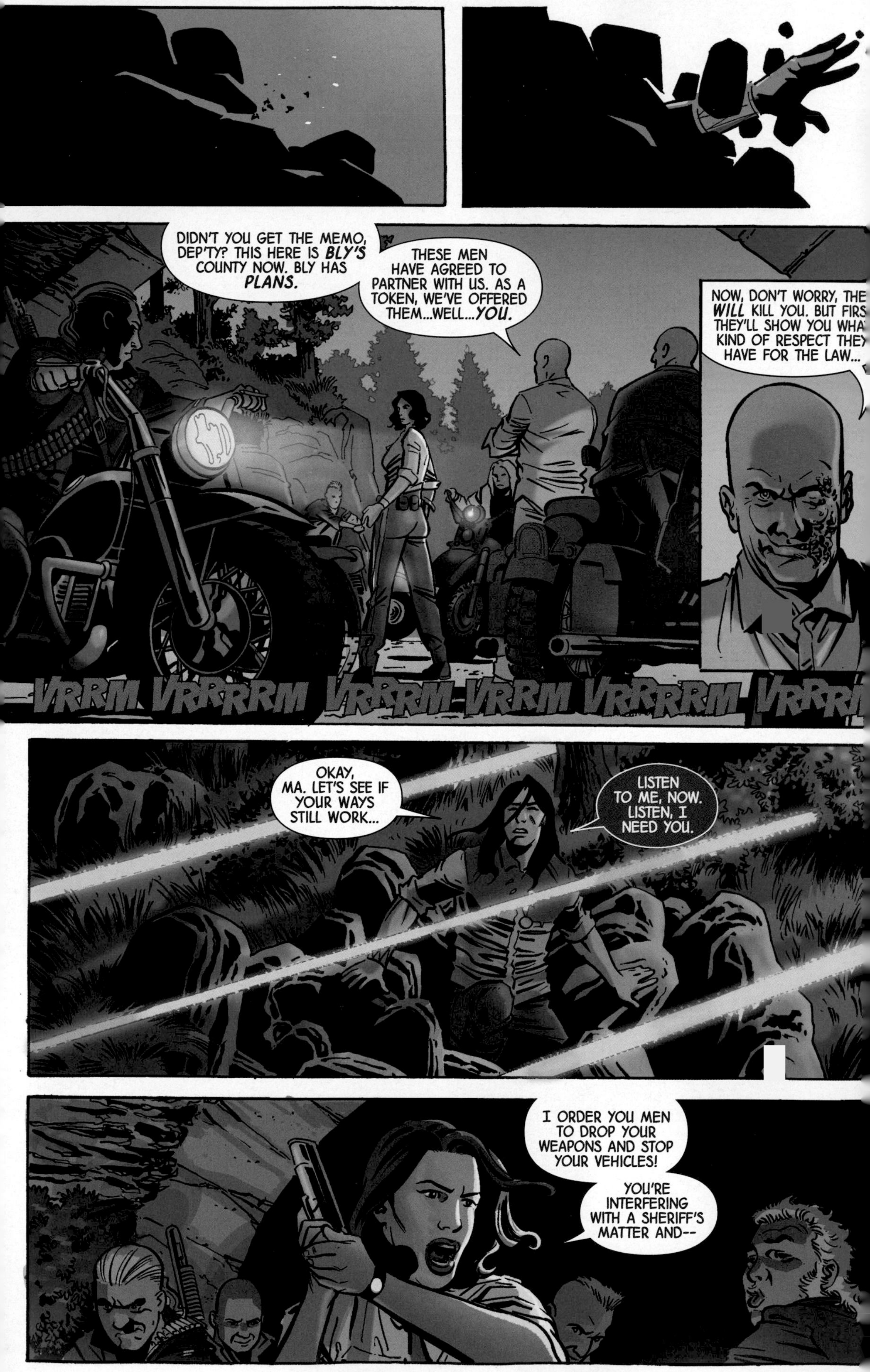
DIDN'T YOU GET THE MEMO, DEP'TY? THIS HERE IS BLY'S COUNTY NOW. BLY HAS PLANS.
THESE MEN HAVE AGREED TO PARTNER WITH US. AS A TOKEN, WE'VE OFFERED THEM...WELL...YOU.
NOW, DON'T WORRY, THE WILL KILL YOU. BUT FIRS THEY'LL SHOW YOU WHA KIND OF RESPECT THEY HAVE FOR THE LAW...
VRRM VRRRRRM VRRRRM VRRM VRRRRRM VRRRI
OKAY, MA. LET'S SEE IF YOUR WAYS STILL WORK...
LISTEN TO ME, NOW. LISTEN, I NEED YOU.
I ORDER YOU MEN TO DROP YOUR WEAPONS AND STOP YOUR VEHICLES!
YOU'RE INTERFERING WITH A SHERIFF'S MATTER AND--

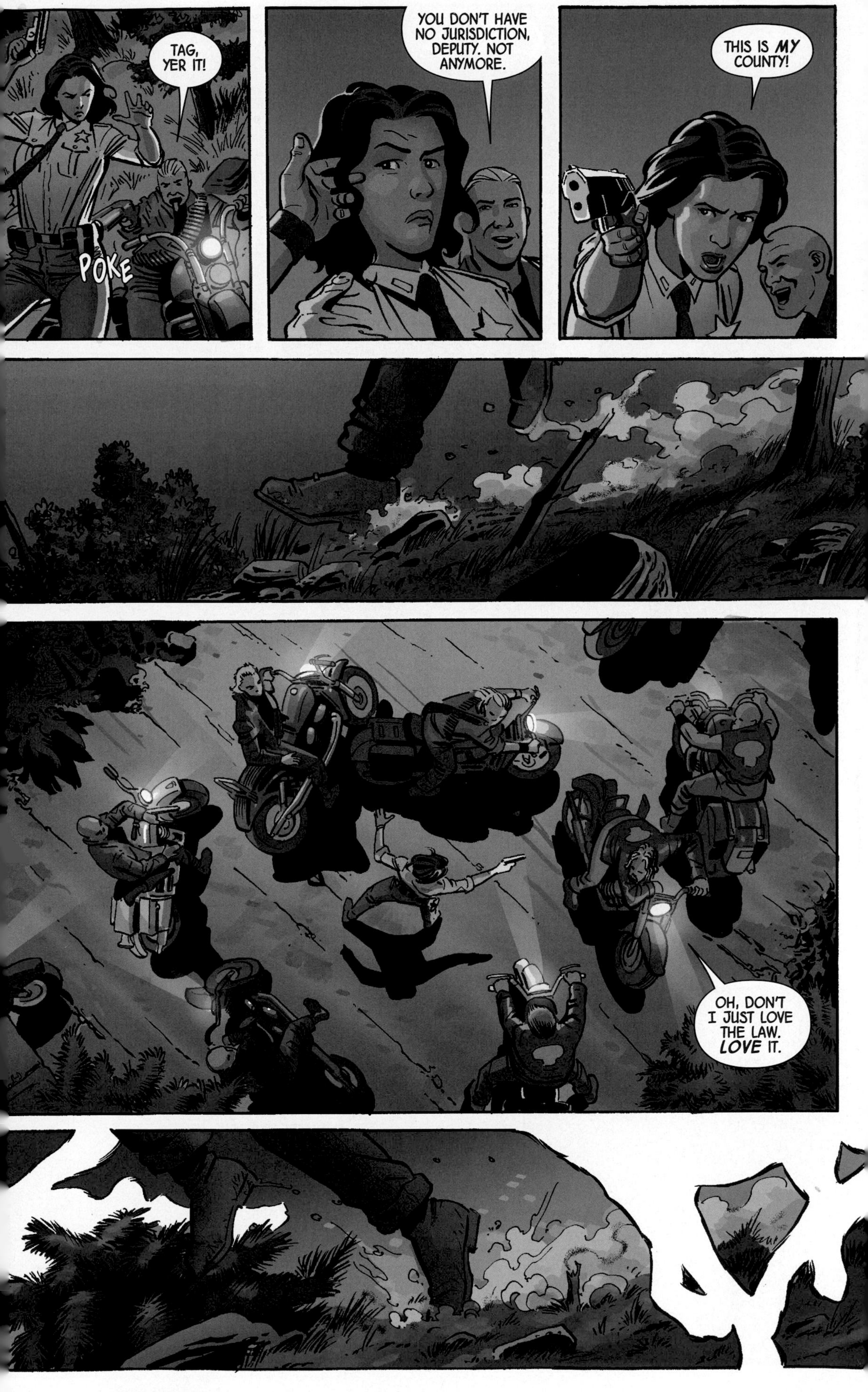
TAG, YER IT!
POKE
YOU DON'T HAVE NO JURISDICTION, DEPUTY. NOT ANYMORE.
THIS IS *MY* COUNTY!
OH, DON'T I JUST LOVE THE LAW. *LOVE* IT.

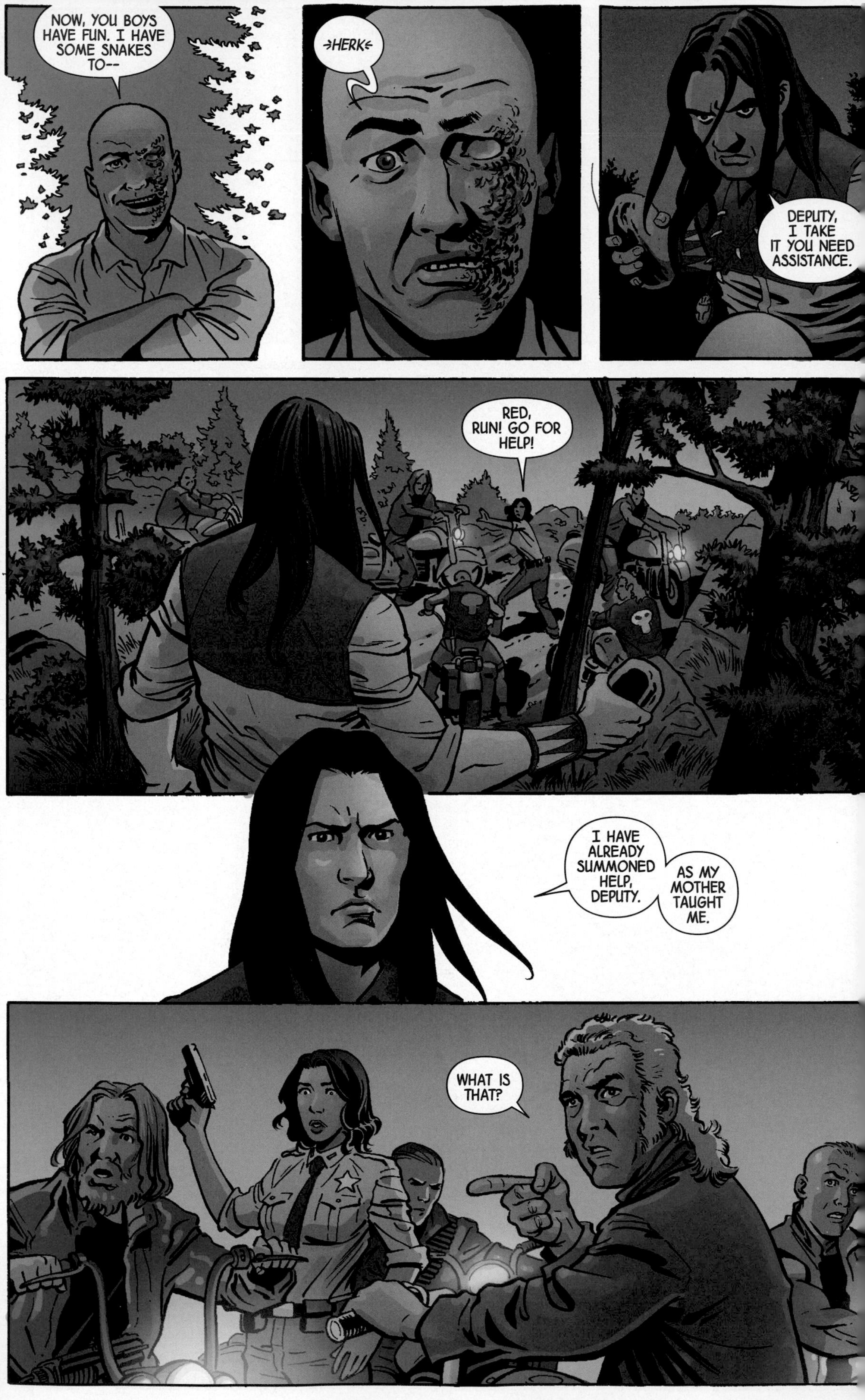
NOW, YOU BOYS HAVE FUN. I HAVE SOME SNAKES TO--
HERK
DEPUTY, I TAKE IT YOU NEED ASSISTANCE.
RED, RUN! GO FOR HELP!
I HAVE ALREADY SUMMONED HELP, DEPUTY.
AS MY MOTHER TAUGHT ME.
WHAT IS THAT?

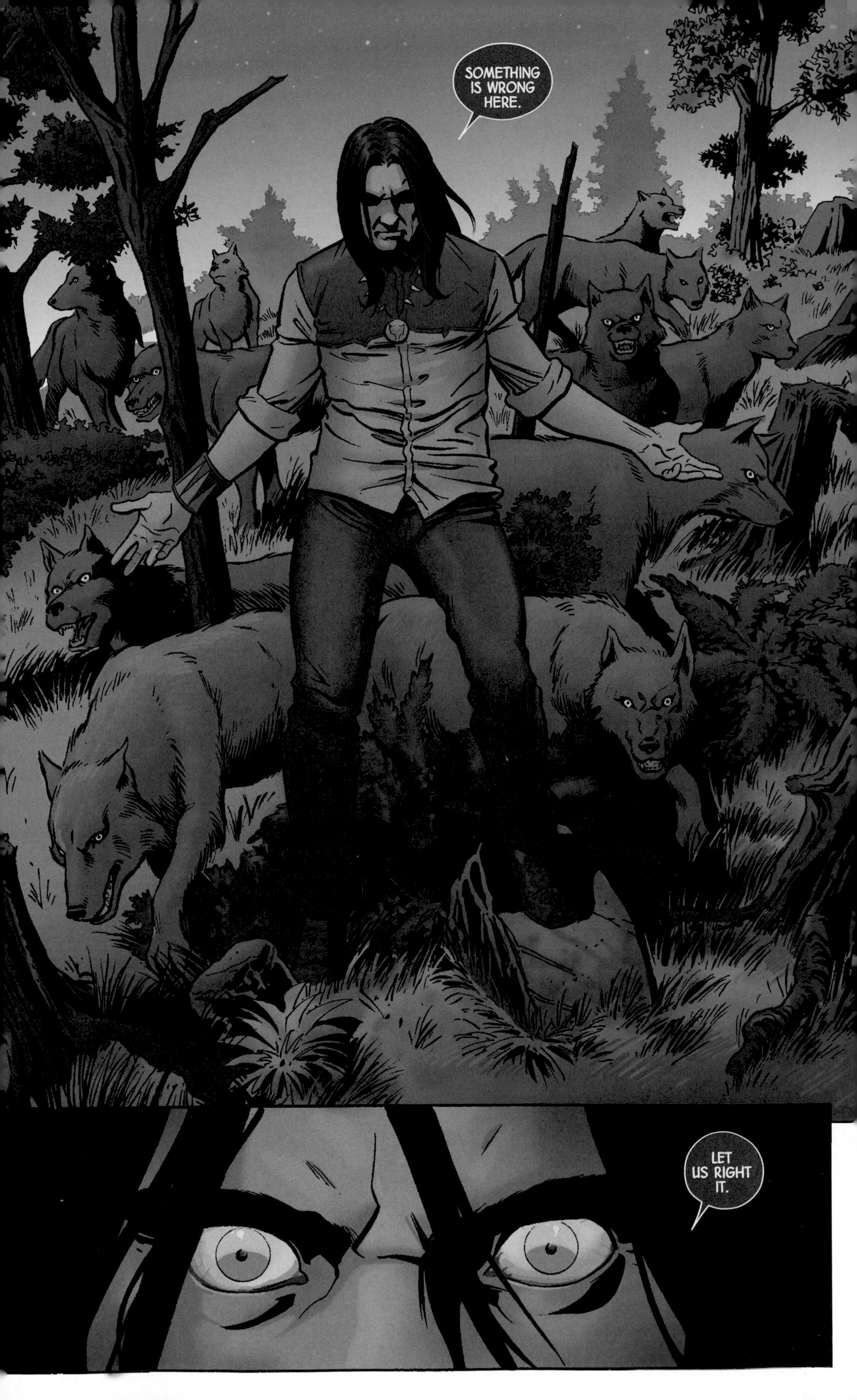
SOMETHING IS WRONG HERE.
LET US RIGHT IT.

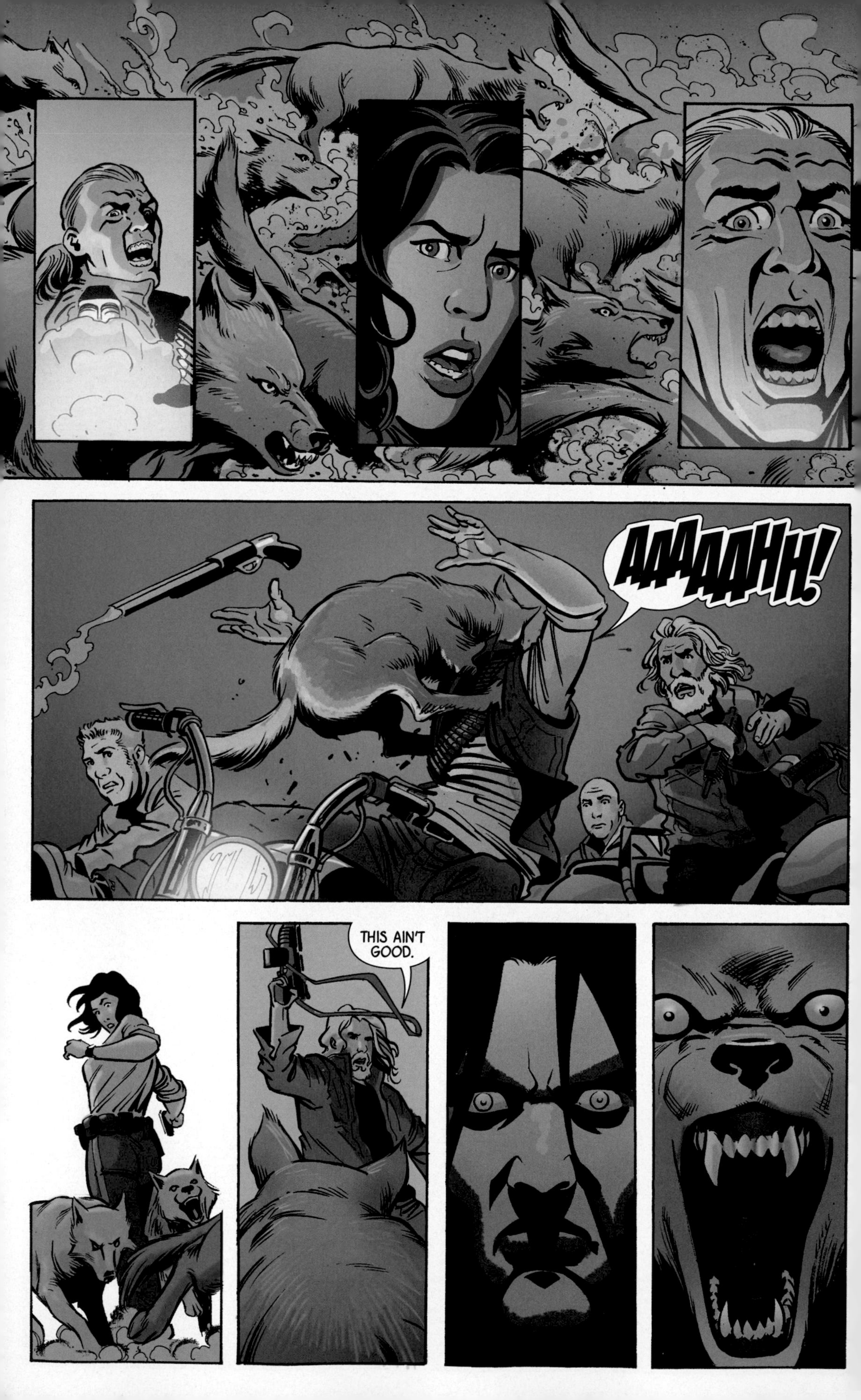
AAAAAHH!
THIS AIN'T GOOD.

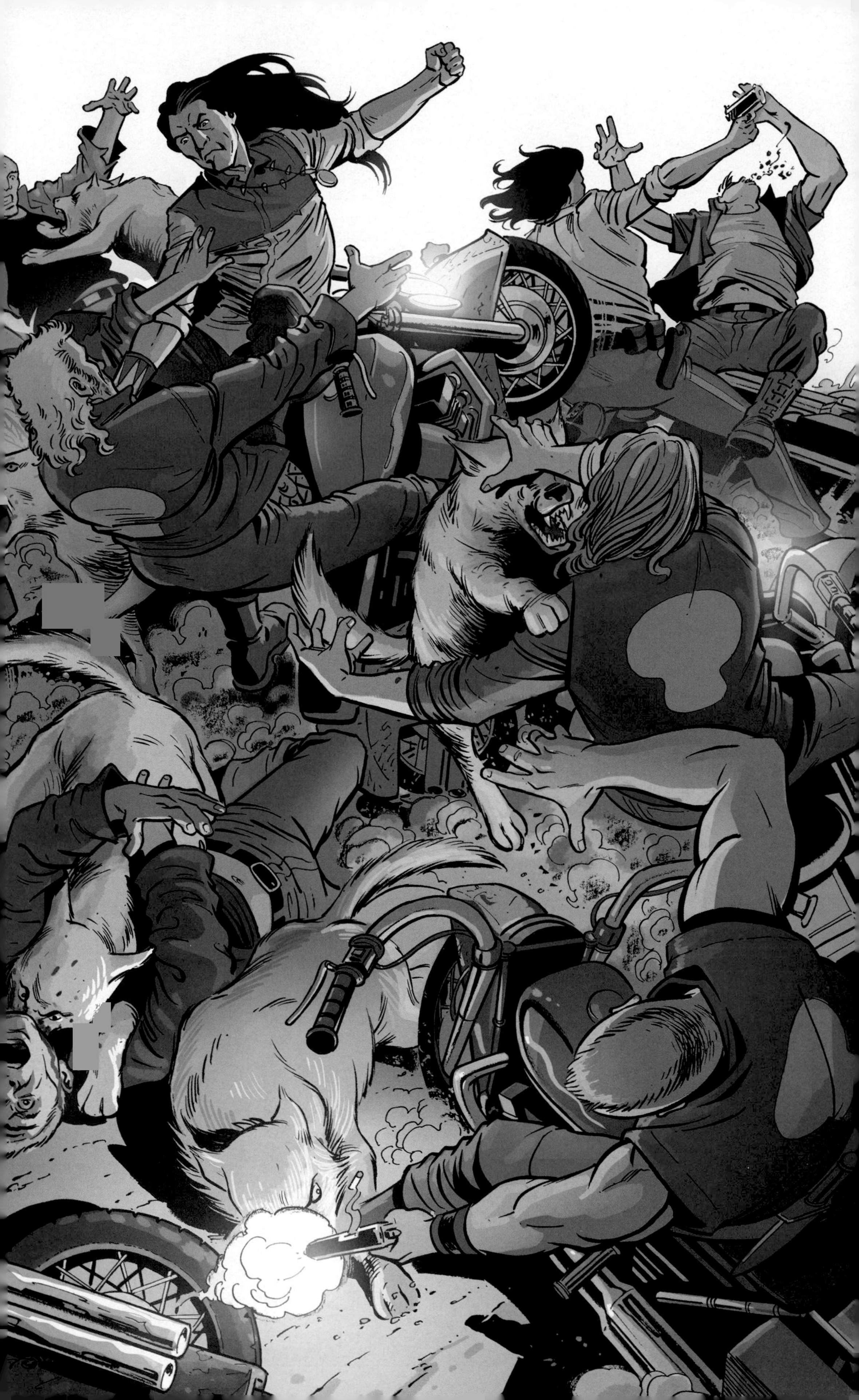

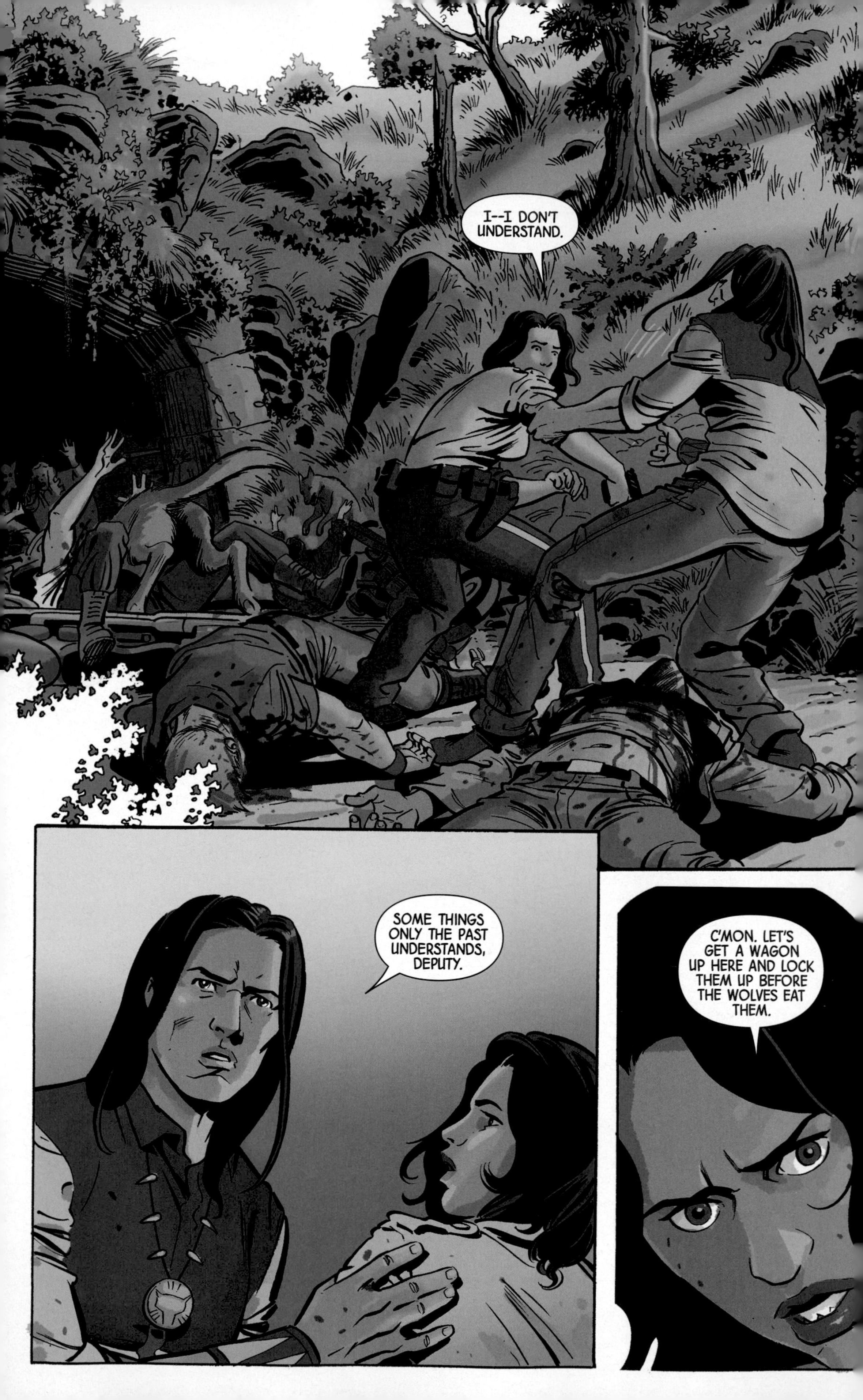
I--I DON'T UNDERSTAND.
SOME THINGS ONLY THE PAST UNDERSTANDS, DEPUTY.
C'MON. LET'S GET A WAGON UP HERE AND LOCK THEM UP BEFORE THE WOLVES EAT THEM.

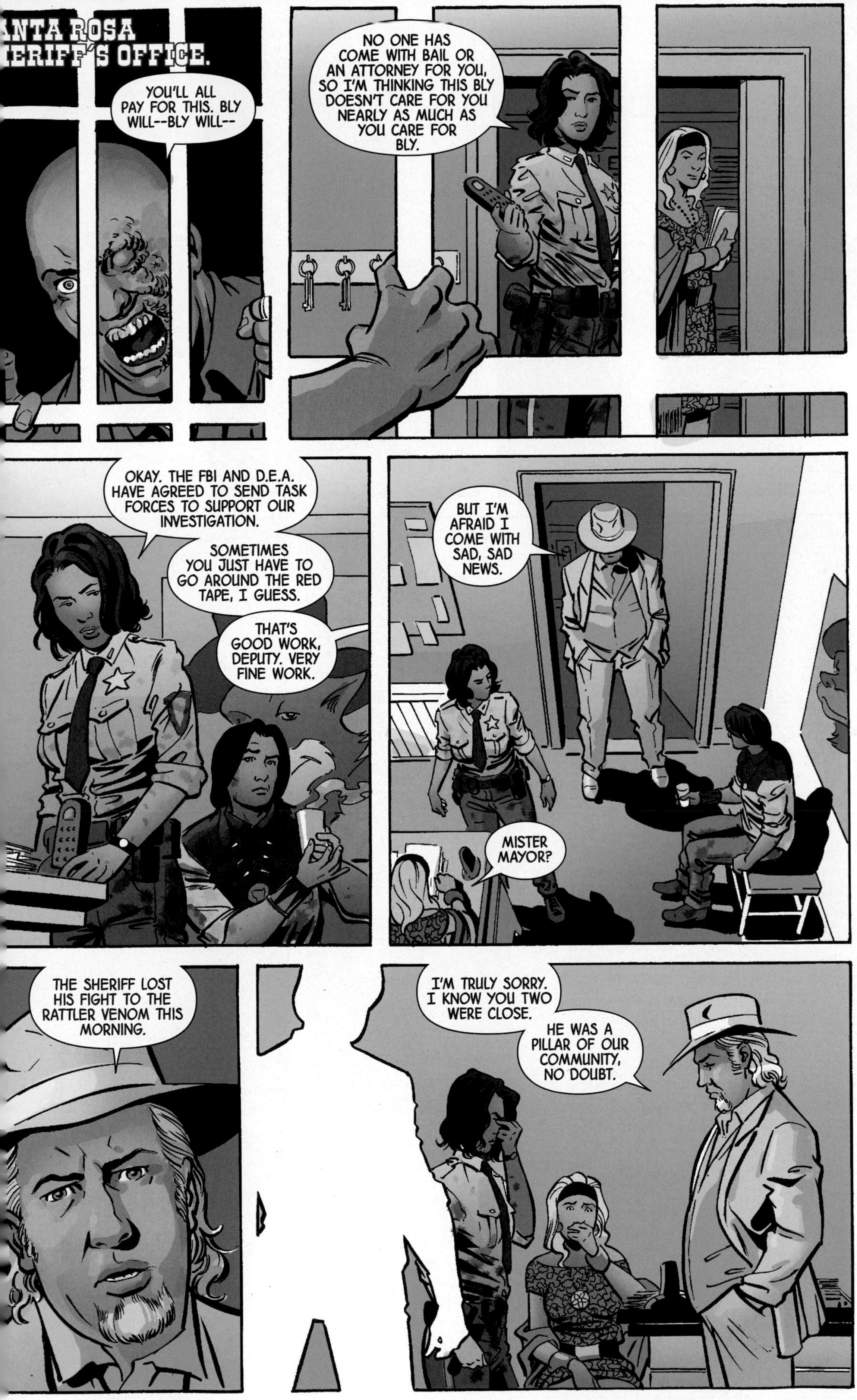

...ANTA ROSA ...ERIFF'S OFFICE.
YOU'LL ALL PAY FOR THIS. BLY WILL--BLY WILL--
NO ONE HAS COME WITH BAIL OR AN ATTORNEY FOR YOU, SO I'M THINKING THIS BLY DOESN'T CARE FOR YOU NEARLY AS MUCH AS YOU CARE FOR BLY.
OKAY. THE FBI AND D.E.A. HAVE AGREED TO SEND TASK FORCES TO SUPPORT OUR INVESTIGATION.
SOMETIMES YOU JUST HAVE TO GO AROUND THE RED TAPE, I GUESS.
THAT'S GOOD WORK, DEPUTY. VERY FINE WORK.
BUT I'M AFRAID I COME WITH SAD, SAD NEWS.
MISTER MAYOR?
THE SHERIFF LOST HIS FIGHT TO THE RATTLER VENOM THIS MORNING.
I'M TRULY SORRY. I KNOW YOU TWO WERE CLOSE.
HE WAS A PILLAR OF OUR COMMUNITY, NO DOUBT.

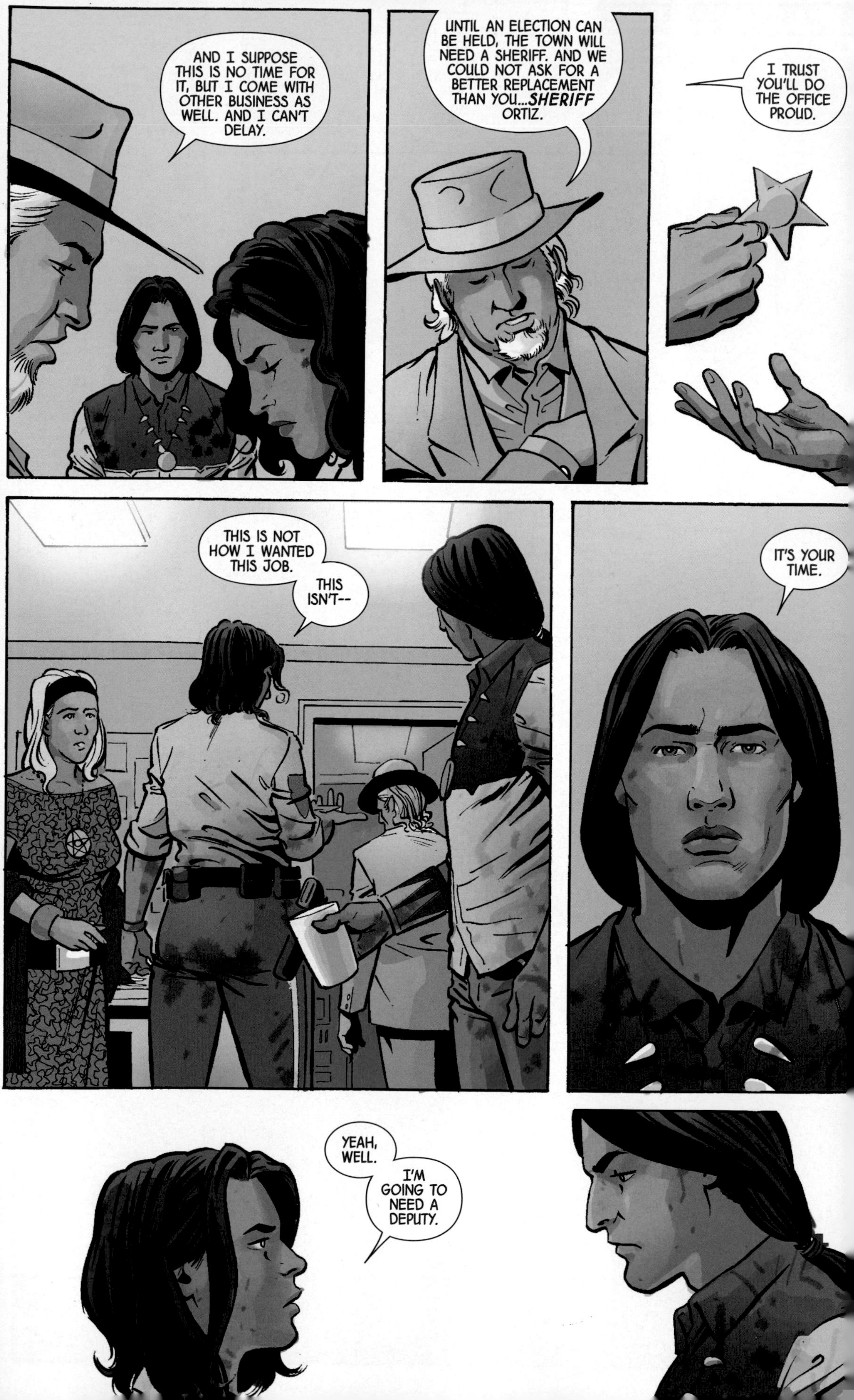
AND I SUPPOSE THIS IS NO TIME FOR IT, BUT I COME WITH OTHER BUSINESS AS WELL. AND I CAN'T DELAY.
UNTIL AN ELECTION CAN BE HELD, THE TOWN WILL NEED A SHERIFF. AND WE COULD NOT ASK FOR A BETTER REPLACEMENT THAN YOU...SHERIFF ORTIZ.
I TRUST YOU'LL DO THE OFFICE PROUD.
THIS IS NOT HOW I WANTED THIS JOB.
THIS ISN'T--
IT'S YOUR TIME.
YEAH, WELL.
I'M GOING TO NEED A DEPUTY.

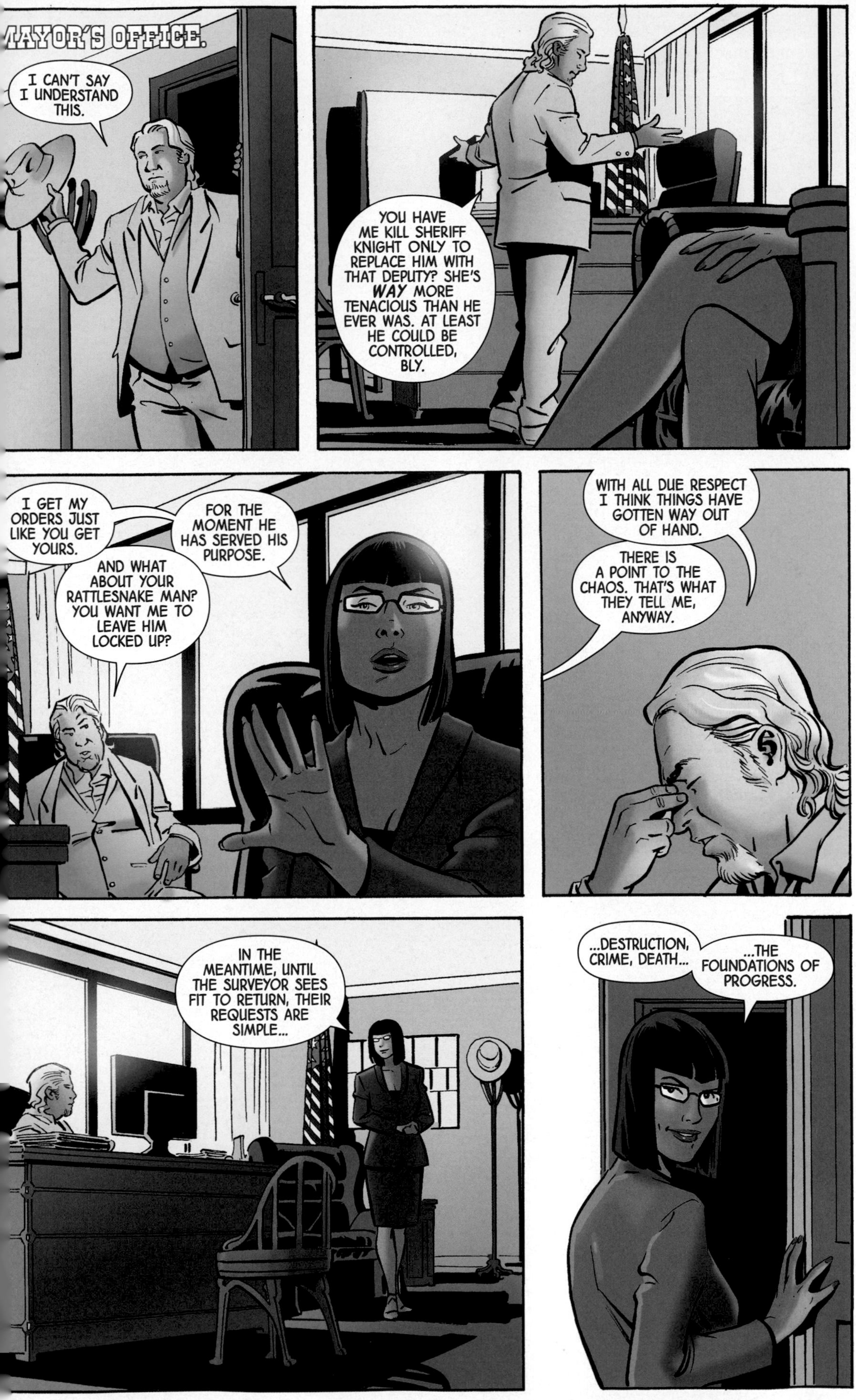
MAYOR'S OFFICE.
I CAN'T SAY I UNDERSTAND THIS.
YOU HAVE ME KILL SHERIFF KNIGHT ONLY TO REPLACE HIM WITH THAT DEPUTY? SHE'S *WAY* MORE TENACIOUS THAN HE EVER WAS. AT LEAST HE COULD BE CONTROLLED, BLY.
I GET MY ORDERS JUST LIKE YOU GET YOURS.
FOR THE MOMENT HE HAS SERVED HIS PURPOSE.
AND WHAT ABOUT YOUR RATTLESNAKE MAN? YOU WANT ME TO LEAVE HIM LOCKED UP?
WITH ALL DUE RESPECT I THINK THINGS HAVE GOTTEN WAY OUT OF HAND.
THERE IS A POINT TO THE CHAOS. THAT'S WHAT THEY TELL ME, ANYWAY.
IN THE MEANTIME, UNTIL THE SURVEYOR SEES FIT TO RETURN, THEIR REQUESTS ARE SIMPLE...
...DESTRUCTION, CRIME, DEATH...
...THE FOUNDATIONS OF PROGRESS.

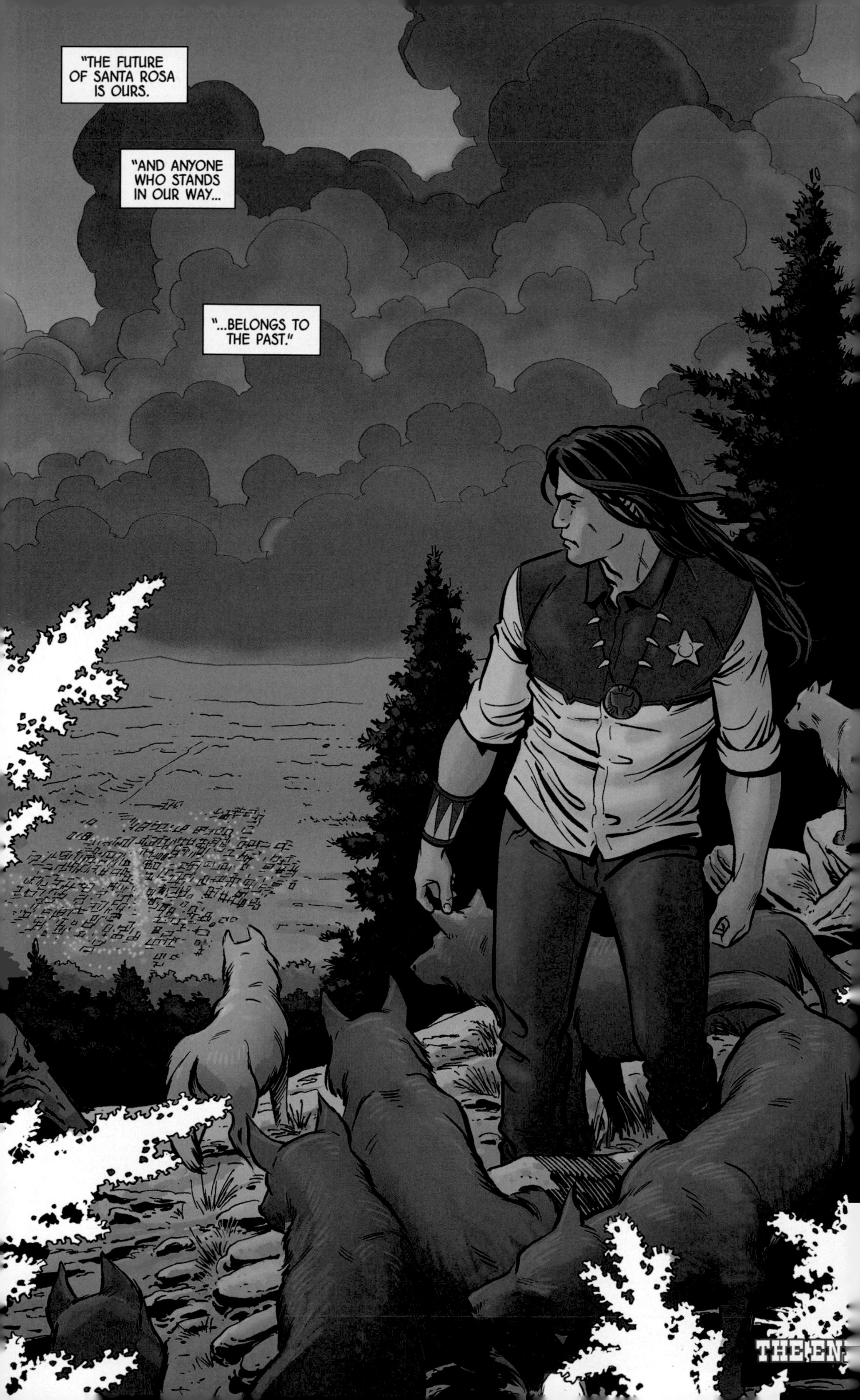
"THE FUTURE OF SANTA ROSA IS OURS.
"AND ANYONE WHO STANDS IN OUR WAY...
"...BELONGS TO THE PAST."
THE EN

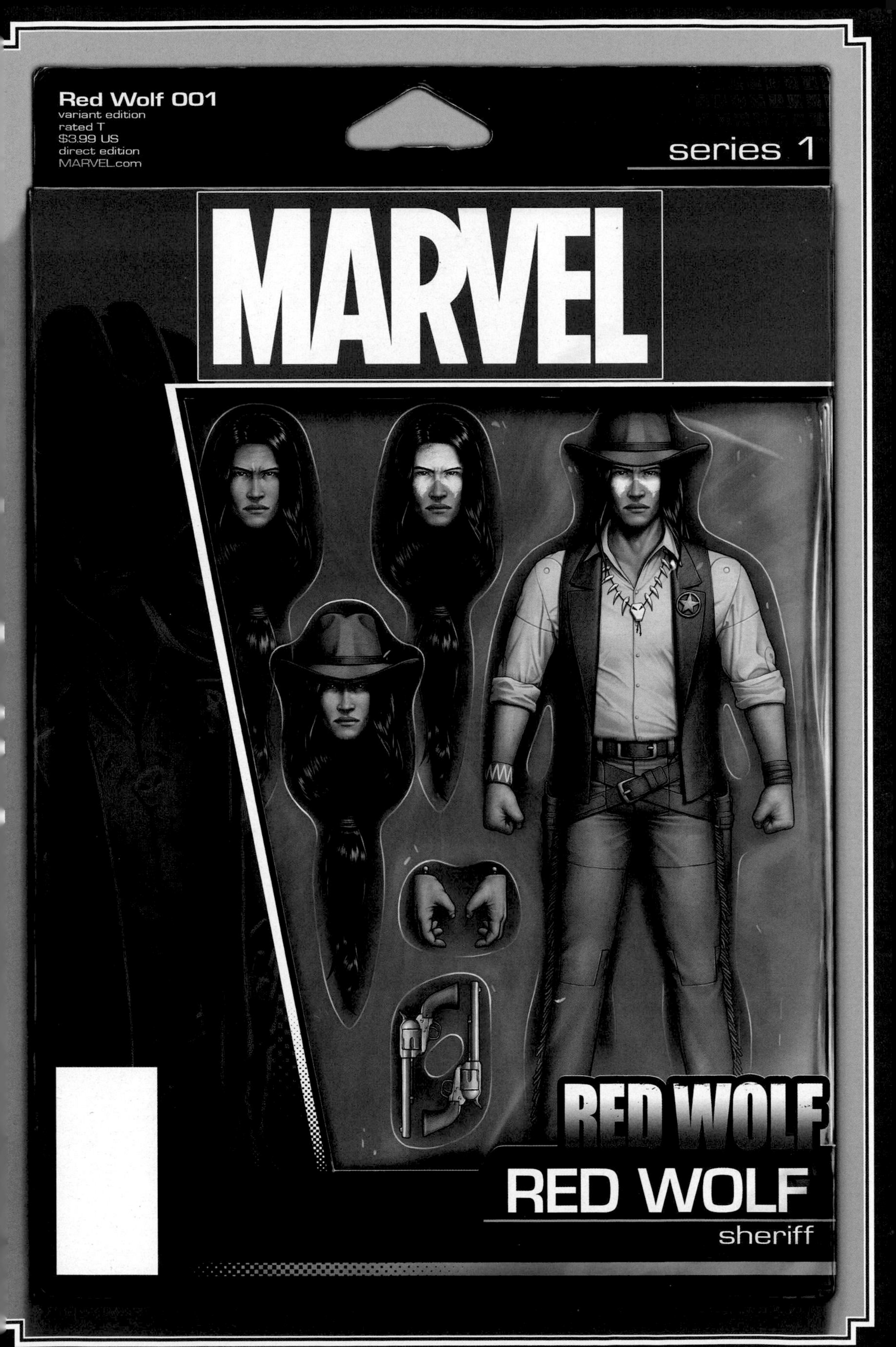
Red Wolf 001
variant edition
rated T
$3.99 US
direct edition
MARVEL.com
series 1
MARVEL
RED WOLF
RED WOLF
sheriff

No. 1 Action Figure variant by JOHN TYLER CHRISTOPHER

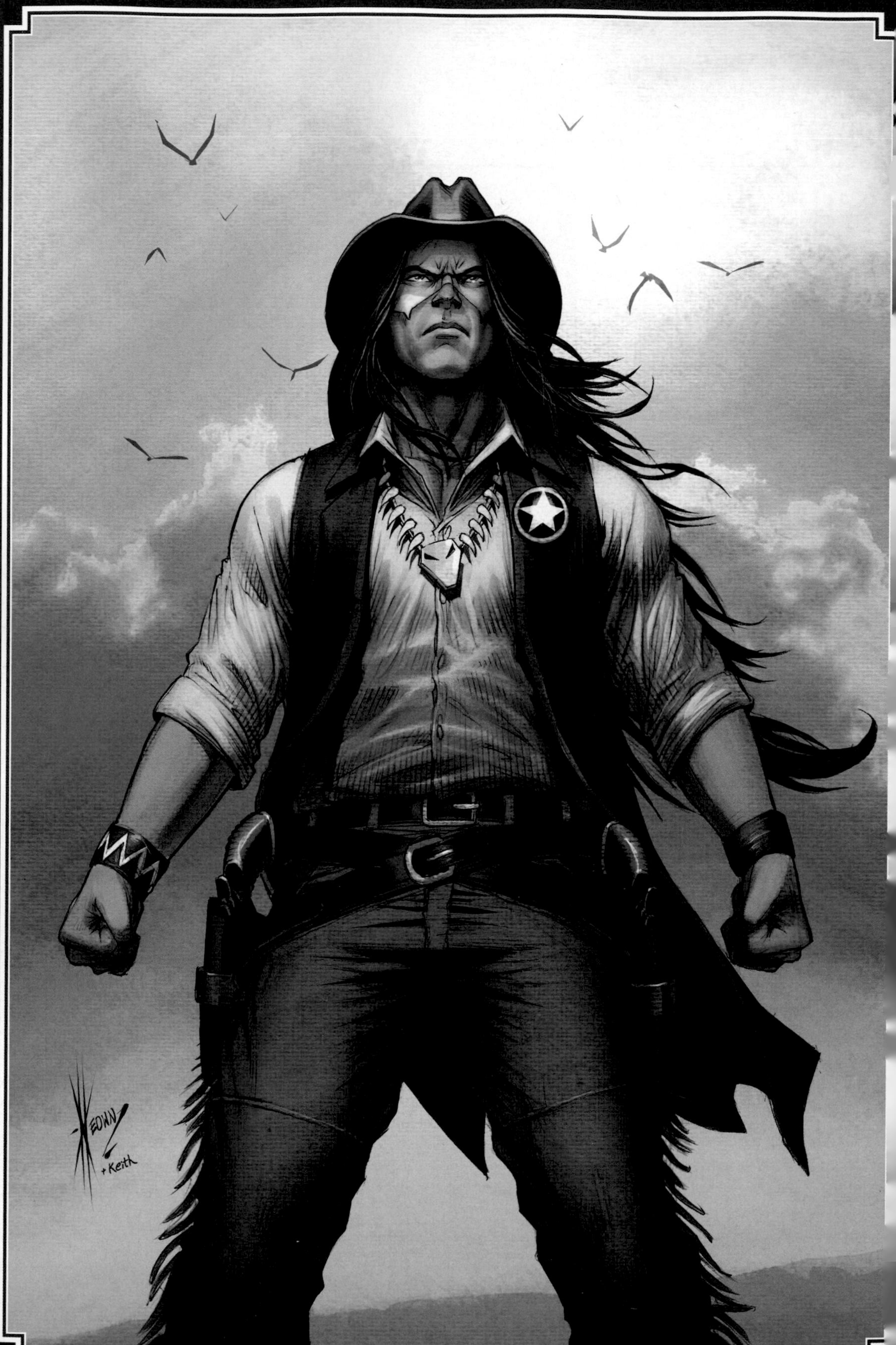

No. 1 variant by **DALE KEOWN & JASON KEITH**

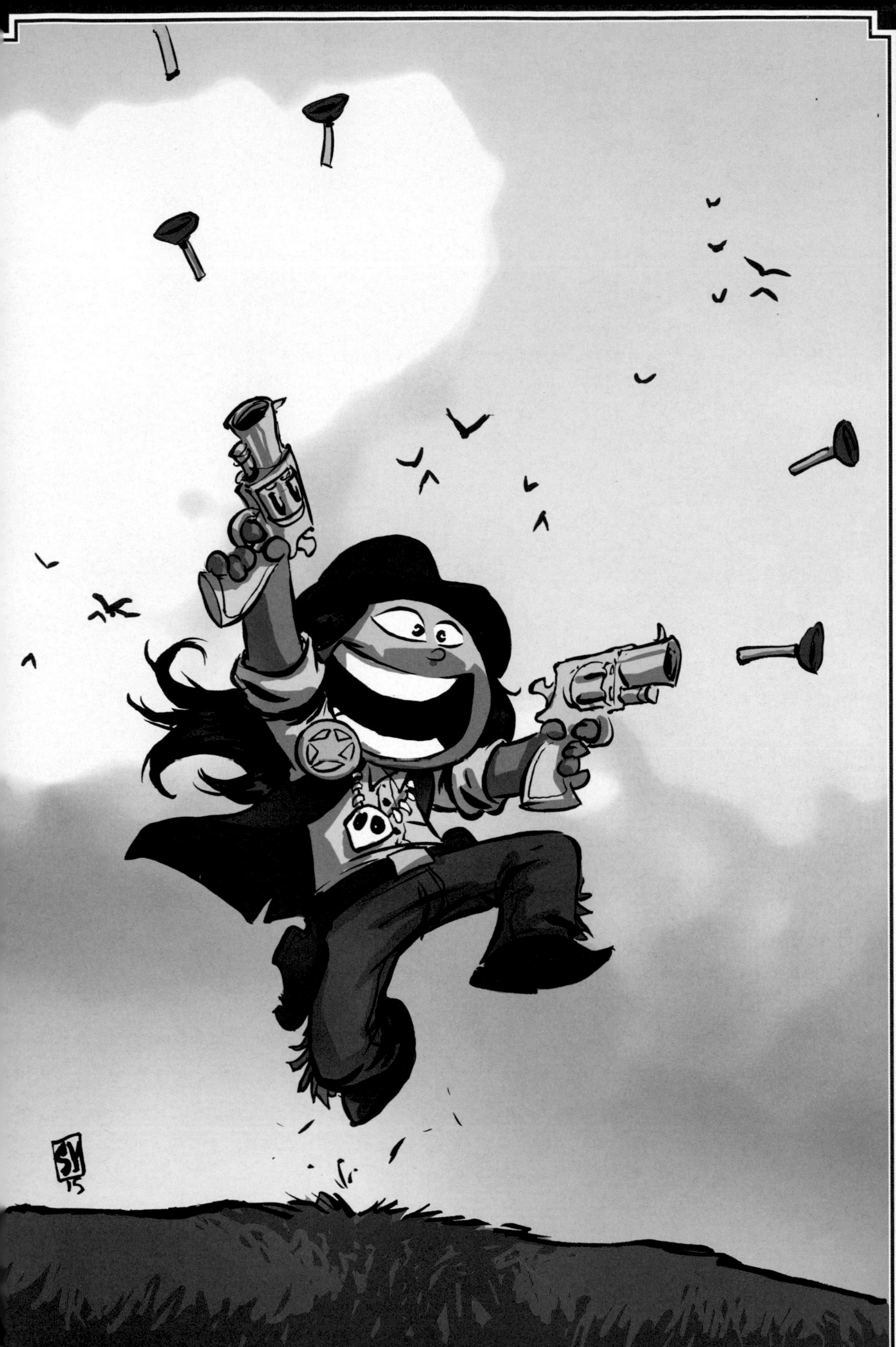

No. 1 variant by **SKOTTIE YOUNG**

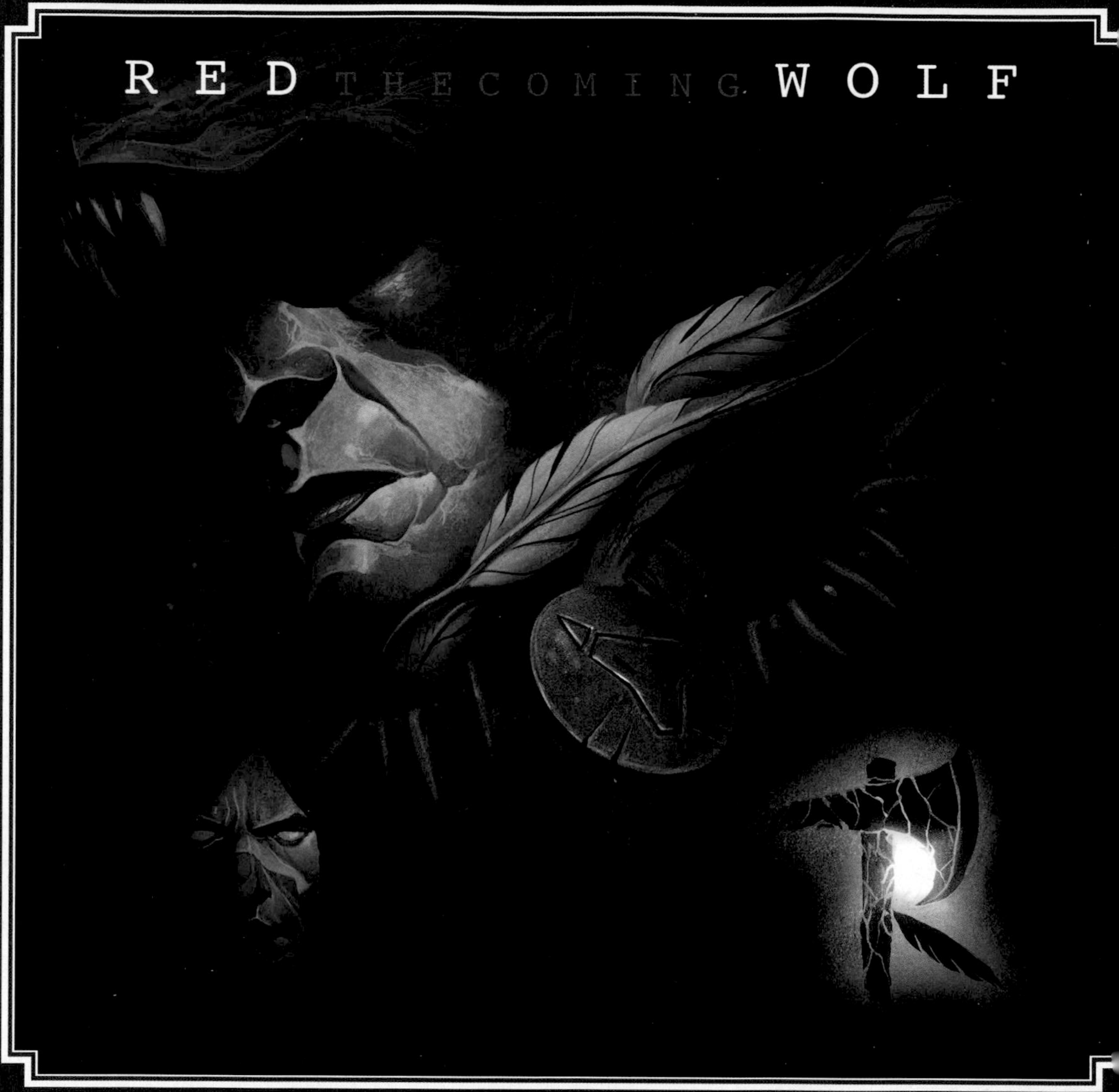
RED THE COMING WOLF

No. 1 Hip-Hop variant by **MIKE DEL MUNDO**

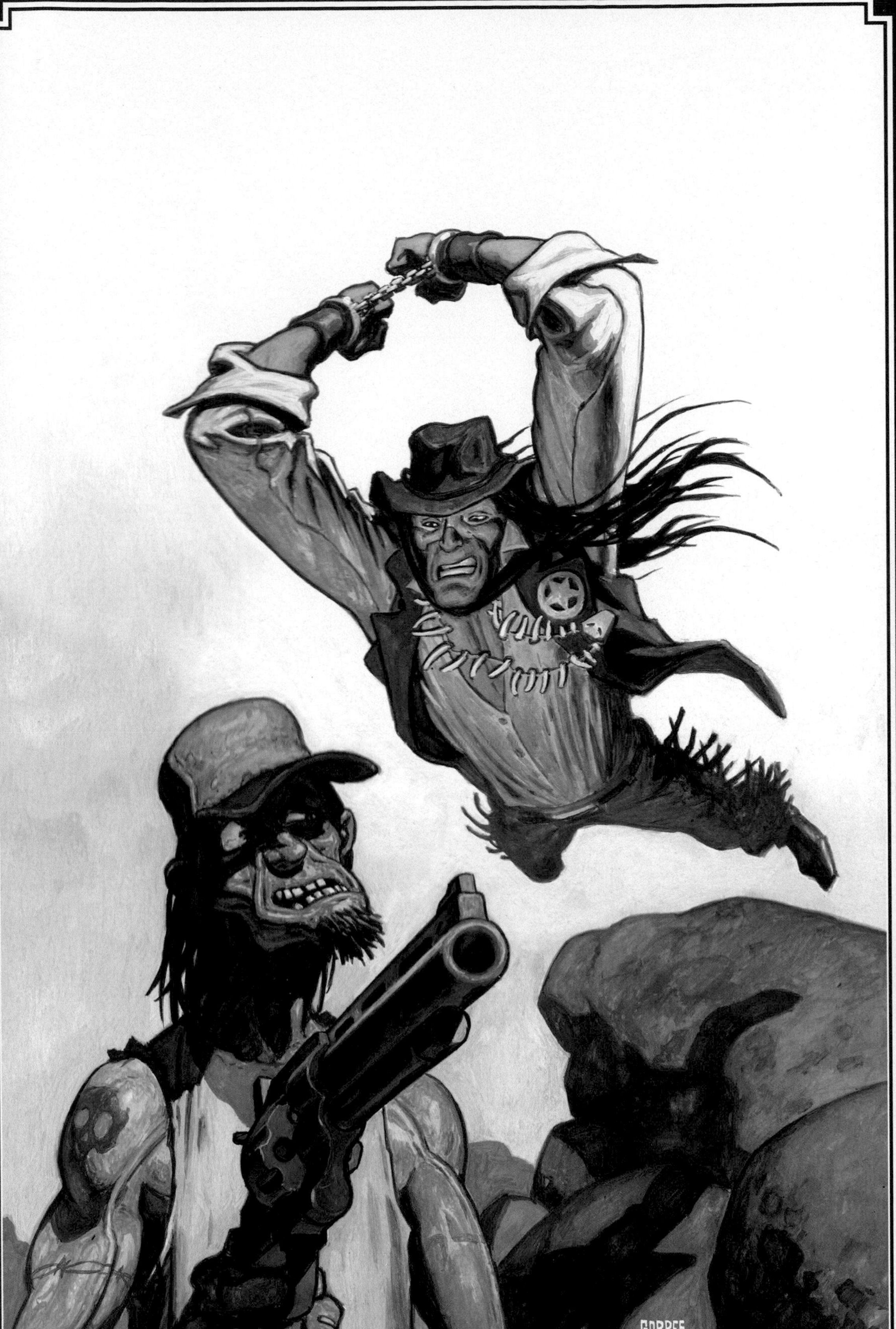
GARRES

No. 2 variant by **RAFA GARRES**

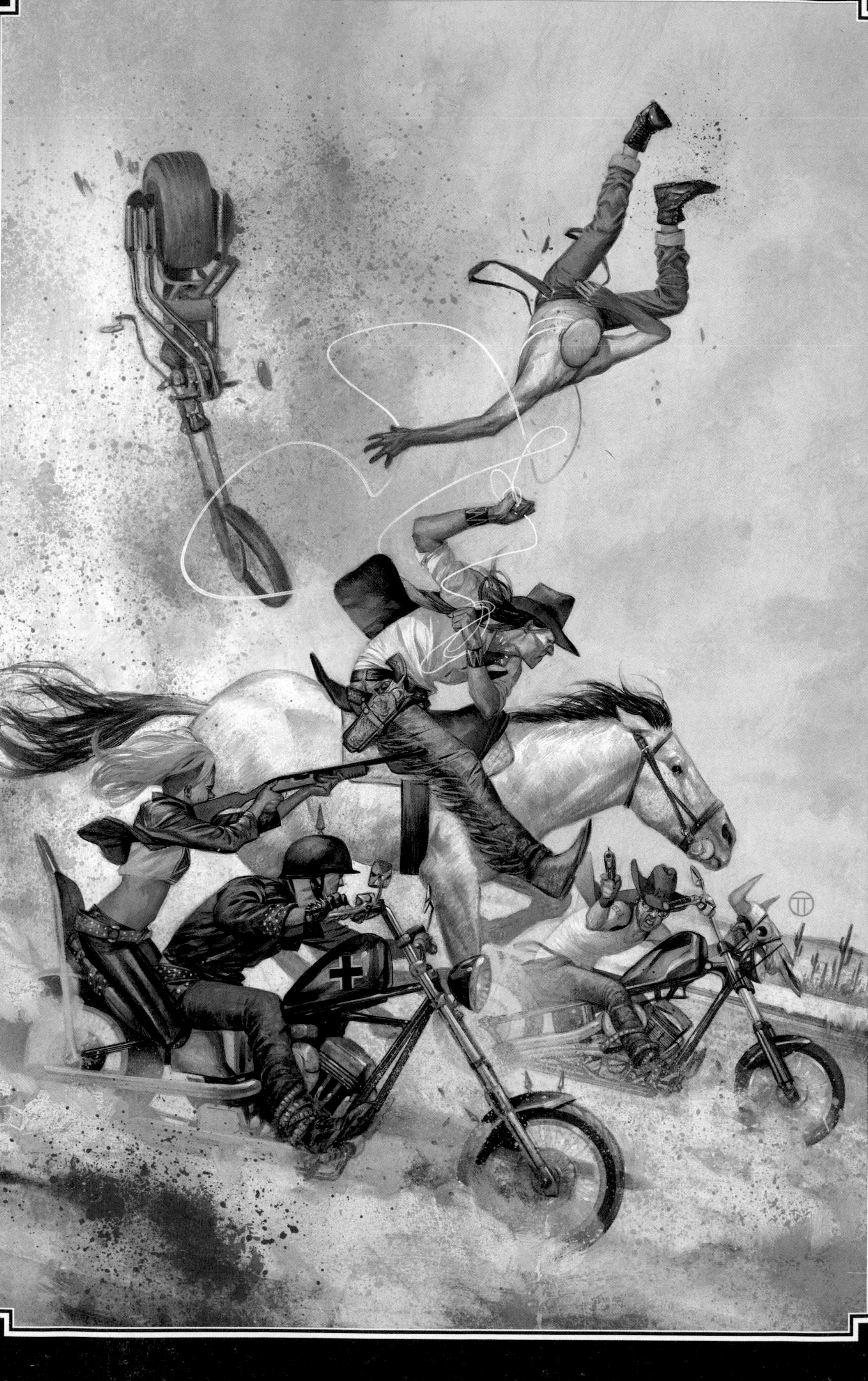

No. 3 variant by **JULIAN TOTINO TEDESCO**